Representing Rape

Language and sexual consent

Susan Ehrlich

London and New York

First published 2001 by Routledge
11 New Fetter Lane, London EC4P 4EE

Simultaneously published in the USA and Canada
by Routledge
29 West 35th Street, New York, NY 10001

Routledge is an imprint of the Taylor & Francis Group

© 2001 Susan Ehrlich

Typeset in Garamond by BC Typesetting, Bristol
Printed and bound in Great Britain by
Biddles Ltd, Guildford and King's Lynn

British Library Cataloguing in Publication Data
A catalogue record for this book is available from the British Library

Library of Congress Cataloging in Publication Data
Ehrlich, Susan (Susan Lynn)
     Representing rape: language and sexual consent/Susan Ehrlich.
       p.   cm.
     Includes bibliographical references and index.
     1. Rape.   I. Title.

   K5197.E37 2001
   345.73′02532–dc21   00-059232

ISBN 0–415–20521–2 (hbk)
ISBN 0–415–20522–0 (pbk)

To the memory of my father, Reinhart Ehrlich

Contents

Acknowledgements

A number of years ago at a Language and Social Psychology conference in Ottawa, Sally McConnell-Ginet suggested that I turn my work on the language of sexual assault trials into a book. At the time, the suggestion seemed like a polite, innocuous comment and the project seemed unimaginable. However, a seed had been planted and with the completion of this book, I have Sally to thank for her (perhaps unwitting) encouragement of this project. Many other friends and colleagues have made the writing of this book possible. I thank Debbie Cameron (a reader for Routledge), Bettina Bradbury and Lorraine Code for reading draft chapters and providing incisive and penetrating critique. For discussions that helped me clarify many of the ideas presented in this book, I am grateful to Peter Avery, Elissa Flagg, Alice Freed, Bernie Frohmann, Jila Ghomeshi, Marlene Kadar, Ruth King, Sue Levesque and Kate McPherson. In particular, Peter Avery's generosity of spirit over the last two decades has been an unfailing source of intellectual support. I thank Catherine O'Sullivan and Barbara Watson for assistance with legal-related research and Sara Mackenzie for invaluable help in preparing the final manuscript for submission to Routledge. The research upon which this book is based was funded, in part, by Regular Research Grants from the Social Sciences and Humanities Research Council of Canada (Grants #410–94–1056 and #410–2000–1330). The completion of the manuscript was made possible by a York University Faculty of Arts Leave Fellowship, which gave me time away from my teaching and administrative responsibilities during the 1999–2000 academic year. Finally, I thank Deborah Esch, for her unwavering, long-standing friendship, and Colin Campbell, for European companionship during many of the stages of this project.

Notes on transcription

Transcription conventions (adapted from Jefferson 1978) are as follows:

.	indicates sentence final falling intonation
,	indicates clause-final intonation (more to come)
?	indicates rising intonation followed by a noticeable pause
. . .	indicates pause of 1/2 second or more
=	indicates no interval between adjacent utterances (second is latched to the first)
[a lot] [I see]	brackets indicate overlapping utterances
–	indicates a halting, abrupt cutoff
o:	colon indicates an extension of the sound or syllable it follows
bold	bold indicates emphatic stress
((sniff))	double parentheses indicate details of the conversational scene or vocalizations

Introduction

Contemporary feminist critiques of the law have often cited the rape trial as embodying all that is problematic about the legal system for women. From the revictimization of rape victims to the legitimization of normative views of female and male sexuality, the discriminatory qualities of rape trials have led some feminist legal theorists to conclude that 'judicial rape' can be more damaging than an actual rape, 'masquerading' as it does 'under the name of justice' (Lees 1996: 36). For Smart (1989: 161), the rape trial is illustrative of the law's *juridogenic* potential: frequently the harms produced by the so-called remedy are as bad as the original abuse. Documenting the capacity of cross-examining lawyers to dominate and revictimize rape victims, or to perform 'rape of the second kind' (Matoesian 1995: 676), work by Conley and O'Barr (1998) and Matoesian (1993) has convincingly demonstrated the pivotal role of 'talk' in achieving such effects. Yet, this book shows that perhaps more insidious – and thus resistant to challenge – in the sexual assault adjudication proceedings analysed here was not the power of 'talk' to revictimize victims but rather its role in defining and delimiting the meanings that came to be attached to the events and subjects under scrutiny. 'Seeing' the events and participants in question was not a transparent process, but one made opaque and partial by a range of culturally- and institutionally-authorized linguistic practices. Indeed, the overarching interpretive framework that I argue structured these proceedings was so seamless in its coverage that subaltern (i.e., victims') understandings of the events were rendered unrecognizable or imperceptible. Thus, departing from previous linguistic scholarship on rape trials, this book ascribes a largely constitutive role to language. That is, in analysing the language of sexual assault adjudication processes, I attempt to give empirical substance to theoretical claims about the primacy of discourse in constructing and constituting social realities.

The 'turn to language' that has characterized much recent scholarship in the social sciences and humanities identifies 'discourse' as an important site in the construction and constitution of social relations. While this so-called 'linguistic' turn owes much to the study of linguistics, discussions of discourse in these disciplines do not typically attend to the nitty-gritty linguistic details of actual verbal interaction. Assuming language to be the most important of the practices Foucault (1972: 49) includes in his well-known definition of 'discourses' — 'practices that systematically form the objects of which they speak' — I adopt an approach to discourse that locates its constitutive power not only in socially- and historically-constructed domains of knowledge, but also in the linguistic details of socially-situated interactions. In fact, I want to suggest that analyses of discourse that are grounded in instances of socially-situated interactions can deepen our understanding of the structuring effects of language. For, it is not free-floating 'discourse' that itself constructs and defines the nature of the events under investigation in these sexual assault proceedings. What accounts for the power of these discursive practices in 'form[ing] the objects of which they speak' is their embodiment in particular institutional settings. That is, it is only to the extent that these discursive practices are embedded in institutions and subject to institutional constraints that they come to be constitutive of 'the social'.

In the chapters that follow, I delineate both the discursive constraints imposed upon speakers' rights in these institutional settings and the effects of these constraints in shaping and structuring the interpretive framework that imbued the events and participants with meaning. Chapter 1 reviews scholarly work within feminist linguistics and feminist legal studies, arguing that studies of gender performativity must be attentive to the way that institutions — specifically legal institutions — constrain and shape 'gendered' performances. Indeed, what I demonstrate in my own analysis of sexual assault adjudication processes (in Chapters 2–5) is the way that the production of gendered identities is 'filtered' through the ideological frameworks that dominated the proceedings. Chapter 2 considers what I call the accused's 'grammar of non-agency' and its legitimization in both of the institutional contexts in which his case was heard. While at times pushing the limits of contextual acceptability, the accused's testimony was intelligible and comprehensible to adjudicators, justified, in part, by appeals to hegemonic notions of male sexuality. Chapter 3 provides an analysis of question–answer sequences between the accused's representatives and the complainants. Identifying a series of propositions presupposed or (pseudo)asserted in these questions, I suggest that, taken together, they comprise an ideological perspective that deemed lack of 'utmost resistance' on the part of the complainants as tantamount to consent. Thus, while Chapter 2 shows dominant ideologies of male and female sexuality and violence against women to inform judicial reasoning, Chapter 3 shows their discursive circulation within the trial process itself. And as discursive reflexes of cultural ideologies, presupposed in questions, these propositions help to constitute the complainants' institutional identities. That is, in response to questions that presupposed their behaviour to be lacking in appropriate resistance, the complainants were produced as 'ineffectual agents' who 'consented' to sex by failing to resist. In Chapter 4, then, I document the complainants' 'grammar of ineffectual agency'.

Chapter 5 explores an explanatory model for acquaintance rape also invoked in these proceedings — male/female miscommuniciation. Here the complainants' 'lack of appropriate resistance' manifests itself in a somewhat different form. Set against an ostensibly masculine communicative code, the complainants' signals of non-consent were found deficient as signals of resistance because they lacked strength and forcefulness. Given the insidiousness with which the discursive practices of these proceedings (re)constructed the complainants' behaviour as weak and lacking in resistance, Chapter 5 begins to theorize a reconfigured discursive frame that recognizes the socially-structured inequities that can shape women's responses to men's sexual aggression. Drawing upon concepts from pragmatics, speech act theory and feminist legal theory, I propose a transformed set of propositions, which when encoded in questions, recontextualize the complainants' 'ineffectual agency' as strategic agency. In Chapter 6, I summarize my findings and consider the relationship between the discursive practices of these legal settings and their material effects.

1 The institutional coerciveness of legal discourse[1]

Introduction

Central to an investigation of language as it is embodied within institutional settings is both an understanding of the relationship between linguistic practices and speakers' social identities and an exploration of the institutional and cultural backdrop against which speakers adopt such practices. Building on scholarship in feminist linguistics, sociolinguistics and feminist legal studies, I develop in this chapter an approach to the language of sexual assault adjudication processes that brings together what has traditionally been two separate (but related) strands of research within feminist language studies: (1) the study of language use: how individuals draw upon linguistic resources to produce themselves as gendered and (2) the study of linguistic representations: how culturally-dominant notions of gender are encoded (and potentially contested) in linguistic representations. Because, as Conley and O'Barr (1998: 3) note, 'the details of everyday legal practices consist almost entirely of language', language is the primary vehicle through which cultural and institutional ideologies are transmitted in legal settings. Thus, to the extent that such ideologies are expressed linguistically in legal settings, the (gendered) linguistic practices of participants may be influenced by other kinds of linguistic practices. Put another way, my approach elucidates how the 'talk' of participants, specifically witnesses, is filtered through cultural and institutional ideologies which themselves are manifest in 'talk'.[2] Specifically, by investigating the linguistic details of a sexual assault trial and tribunal, not only do I provide a concrete demonstration of how dominant ideas about male and female sexuality and violence against women are reproduced and recirculated in the 'talk' of these institutional contexts, but also how such discursive formations shape and/or constrain the kinds of gendered identities that are produced. In developing my theoretical approach, I first draw upon the feminist linguistics literature, arguing that investigations of gendered 'talk' must be attentive to the way that institutions – specifically legal institutions – constrain and shape 'gendered' performances. I then turn to the specific ways that legal discourse can be shown to make possible or thwart certain performances of gender.

Enacting gender though 'talk'

Debates over the nature of gender identity and its social construction, origi-
nating in feminist work of the 1990s, have in recent years informed research
in sociolinguistics generally and feminist linguistics more specifically. In particular, conceptions of gender as categorical, fixed and static have increasingly
been abandoned in favour of more constructivist and dynamic ones. Cameron
(1990: 86), for example, makes the point (paraphrasing Harold Garfinkel)
that 'social actors are not sociolinguistic "dopes"', mindlessly and passively
producing linguistic forms that are definitively determined by social class
membership, ethnicity or gender. Rather, Cameron argues for an understanding of gender that reverses the relationship between linguistic practices and
social identities traditionally posited within the quantitative sociolinguistics
or variationist paradigm. Work in this tradition has typically focused on
establishing correlations between linguistic variables and social factors such
as age, race, ethnicity and sex, implicitly assuming that these aspects of
social identity exist prior to and are determinate of linguistic behaviour
(and other social behaviour). Indeed, early research in language and gender
(in the 1970s and 1980s) was largely conducted within this research paradigm, focusing specifically on the correlation of linguistic variables with
the independent variable of sex. By contrast, more recent formulations of
the relationship between language and gender, following Butler (1990),
emphasize the performative aspect of gender: linguistic practices, among
other kinds of practices, continually bring into being individuals' social
identities. Under this account, language is one important means by which
gender – an ongoing social process – is enacted or constituted; gender is something individuals *do* – in part through linguistic choices – as opposed to
something individuals *are* or *have* (West and Zimmerman 1987). Cameron's
comments are illustrative:

> Whereas sociolinguistics would say that the way I use language reflects or
> marks my identity as a particular kind of social subject – I talk like a
> white middle-class woman because I am (already) a white middle-class
> woman – the critical account suggests language is one of the things
> that *constitutes* my identity as a particular kind of subject. Sociolinguistics
> says that how you act depends on who you are; critical theory says that
> who you are (and are taken to be) depends on how you act. (emphasis
> in original)
>
> (Cameron 1995: 15–16)

The idea that an individual's linguistic behaviour does not simply arise from
a set of permanent and invariant social attributes is also suggestive of the
contextually-variable nature of social identities. If identities are not fixed
and static, then their 'performance' can vary across social, situational, and
interactional contexts. It is in this regard that Schiffrin (1996) is critical of

variationist studies within sociolinguistics, in particular, the practice of coding aspects of social identity as categorical and invariant across contexts. Schiffrin argues for a different view, one in which social identities are locally situated and constructed: 'we may act more or less middle-class, more or less female, and so on, depending on what we are doing and with whom. This view forces us to attend to speech activities, and to the interactions in which they are situated' (Schiffrin 1996: 199). Likewise, Goodwin in an ethnographic study of urban African-American children in Philadelphia suggests that stereotypes about women's speech collapse when talk in a whole range of activities is examined:

> In order to construct social personae appropriate to the events of the moment, *the same individuals articulate talk and gender differently as they move from one activity to another.* The relevant unit for the analysis of cultural phenomena, including gender, is thus not the group as a whole, or the individual, but rather situated activities. (emphasis mine)
> (Goodwin 1990: 9)

Goodwin's comments not only argue for a dynamic and variable conception of gender identity, they also point to the variable linguistic resources drawn upon in performances of gender from one activity to another.

While much language and gender research in the 1970s and 1980s took 'difference' between men and women's linguistic behaviour as axiomatic and as the starting point for empirical investigations, scholarly work in the 1990s (such as Goodwin's), attentive to the way that the linguistic production of gendered identities varies according to contextual factors, has questioned such assumptions on both empirical and political grounds. Henley and Kramarae (1991) argue, for example, that focusing on differences rather than similarities between women and men functions to exaggerate and reinforce gender polarities (arguably, a focus that does not serve the interests of feminism) and abstracts gender away from the specificities of its social context. Indeed, many of the claims about gender-differentiated language that emerged from studies in the 1970s and 1980s (the most notable being that women's speech styles are cooperative, while men's are competitive) were based on studies that did just this: they were based on limited populations – white, North American and middle class – engaged in cross-sex conversations where, as Freeman and McElhinny (1996) note, gender is probably maximally contrastive, yet their results were overgeneralized to all women and men. Newer conceptions of the relationship between language and gender, then, not only question the fixed and static quality of gender *within* individuals but also *across* individuals and social groups. Like feminist scholarship, more generally, work in feminist linguistics has attempted to challenge universalizing and essentialist descriptions of women, men and language – descriptions that are more accurately characterized as contextually, historically, or culturally specific.

One influential attempt to theorize the relationship between gender and language in terms of *local* communities and social practices is the 'communities of practice' framework developed by Eckert and McConnell-Ginet (1992a, 1992b, 1999). Advocating a shift away from overarching generalizations about women, men and 'gendered' speech styles, Eckert and McConnell-Ginet (1992a: 462) emphasize the need to 'think practically and look locally'. They recommend that the interaction between language and gender be examined in the everyday social practices of particular local communities (what they term 'communities of practice') because they claim that (1) gender is not always easily separated from other aspects of social identity and relations, (2) gender will not always have the same meaning across communities, and (3) the linguistic manifestations of gender will also vary across communities. In Eckert and McConnell-Ginet's (1992b: 95) words: 'gender is produced (and often reproduced) in differential membership in communities of practice'. For Eckert and McConnell-Ginet, then, it is not gender *per se* that interacts with linguistic practices, but rather the complex set of communities of practices in which individuals participate. That is, just as women's and men's involvements in 'gendered' communities of practice will vary, so women's and men's relations to normative constructions of gender (including linguistic ones) will vary. Although gender undoubtedly influences the kinds of communities of practice to which individuals have access and/or in which they participate, the mediating variable of 'practice' in Eckert and McConnell-Ginet's framework leaves open the possibility of linguistic practices being variable *within* an individual speaker as well as *across* individual speakers of the same sex/gender (Cameron 1996, 1997).

In a discussion of an experimental setting (Freed and Greenwood 1996) that produced similar linguistic behaviour in both female and male subjects, Freed (1996: 67) provides a more concrete description of the way in which gender is produced through involvement in certain social practices or activities. Freed and Greenwood found that women and men involved in same-sex dyadic conversations with friends, displayed strikingly similar linguistic behaviour – behaviour typically associated with the so-called cooperative speech style of women.

> First, participating in the same practice produced in the women and men the same kind of talk; second, outside of this experimental setting, it is possible that women and men would be less likely to find themselves in such similar settings, given the sex- and gender-differentiated society in which we live . . . Thus language and gender studies conducted in natural settings may often find differences not similarities in women's and men's speech simply because women and men are frequently engaged in different activities (see M. Goodwin 1990) and not because of any differences in women and men themselves. Since it is increasingly clear that speech patterns are products of the activities that people are engaged in and not inherent to the participants, we can conclude that communicative

styles are customs related to actions, activities and behaviors differentially encouraged for women and men.

(Freed 1996: 67)

That linguistic forms are not *inherent* to the gender of speakers is a point also made by Ochs (1992: 340) when she argues that 'few features of language directly and exclusively index gender'. A direct indexical relationship between linguistic forms and gender is evident in personal pronouns that denote the gender of an interlocutor. To say that most linguistic features *indirectly* index gender, then, is to say, like Freed and Eckert and McConnell-Ginet, that the connection is mediated by the social stances, acts and activities that women and men perform linguistically (e.g., display-ing uncertainty, showing force). In turn, these stances, acts and activities index or become conventionally associated with normative constructions of gendered behaviour in a particular community or culture. Tag questions, for example, may display or index a stance of uncertainty (among other kinds of stances) and, in turn, a stance of uncertainty may in some com-munities become associated with feminine identities (Duranti and Goodwin 1992: 335). Given the multifunctionality of linguistic forms, Ochs' account allows for the possibility that different hearers may assign different (gendered) meanings to utterances. If, for example, a particular hearer does not associate a stance of uncertainty with femininity, then that hearer may assign a different function to a woman's use of tag questions, for example, that of facilitating conversation. What is challenged, then, under Ochs' account of gender index-ing is the proposition that a particular linguistic style or linguistic form directly and exclusively marks gender, for both speakers and hearers. And what is left open is the possibility of individuals performing social stances, practices or activities that transgress or transform normative constructions of gendered behaviour (see Hirsch 1998). Indeed, dynamic and constructivist approaches to gender more generally allow for the possibility of individuals actively reproducing and/or resisting linguistic practices implicated in hegemonic notions of masculinity and femininity.

Institutional coerciveness

While the theorizing of gender as 'performative' has succeeded in problema-tizing mechanistic and essentialist notions of gender that underlie much variationist work in sociolinguistics, for some feminist linguists (e.g., Wodak 1997; Kotthoff and Wodak 1998) Butler's formulation ignores the power relations that impregnate most situations in which gender is 'performed' and hence affords subjects unbounded agency. For Cameron (1997), Butler's (1990) discussion of performativity does, arguably, acknowl-edge these power relations, that is, by alluding to the 'rigid regulatory frame' within which gendered identities are produced. Yet, as Cameron (1997: 31) also points out, often philosophical treatments of this 'frame' remain very abstract: 'for social researchers interested in applying the performativity thesis to concrete instances of behaviour, the specifics of this "frame" and its operation in a particular context will be far more significant considerations than they seem to be in many philosophical discussions.' The routine enactment of gender is often, perhaps always, subject to what Cameron calls the 'institutional cooerciveness' of social situations; in other words, dominant gender ideologies often mold and/or inhibit the kinds of gendered identities that women (and men) produce.

Addressing the tensions between local and more universal accounts of language and gender, Bergvall (1999) emphasizes the need to analyse dominant gender ideologies that pre-exist and structure local (linguistic) enactments of gender. That is, while more local and contextual accounts of language and gender (e.g., Eckert and McConnell-Ginet 1992a, 1992b, 1999) move us away from overarching and excessive generalizations about women, men and 'gendered' talk, Bergvall (1999: 282) suggests that we also consider the force of socially ascribed gender norms – 'the assumptions and expectations of (often binary) ascribed social roles against which any performance of gender is constructed, accommodated to, or resisted.' Likewise, Woolard and Schieffelin (1994: 72) argue that we must connect the 'microculture of communicative action' to what they call 'macrosocial constraints on language and behavior'. Certainly, the examination of language and gender within institutions elucidates some of the macro-constraints that pre-exist local performances of gender. Indeed, Gal (1991) suggests that because women and men interact primarily in institutions such as workplaces, families, schools and political forums, the investigation of language and gender in informal conversations, outside of these institutions, has severe limitations. It 'creates the illusion that gendered talk is mainly a personal characteristic' (p. 185), whereas, as much feminist research has revealed, gender is also a structuring principle of institutions.

Sexual assault adjudication processes are a rich and fertile site for the investigation of gendered ideologies that pre-exist and 'coerce' many performances of gender. Embedded within legal structures, feminist legal theorists (e.g., MacKinnon 1987, 1989, Bartlett and Kennedy 1991, Lacey 1998) have argued, are androcentric and sexist assumptions that typically masquerade as 'objective' truths. The crime of rape, in particular, has received attention from feminists critical of the law, because in Smart's (1989: 50) words 'the legal treatment of rape epitomizes the core of the problem of law for feminism.' Not only are dominant notions about male and female sexuality and violence against women implicated in legal statutes and judicial decisions surrounding sexual assault, I argue they also penetrate the discursive arena of the trial. Moreover, the material force with which the law legitimates a certain vision of the social order, through, for example, fines, imprisonment or execution, means that the discursive imposition of ideologies in legal settings will have a particular potency. Hence, by locating my analysis of gendered linguistic practices in the context of sexual assault adjudication processes, I propose to explore the 'institutional cooerciveness' of these particular institutional settings or, put differently, the way that these settings shape and constrain performances of gender. While acknowledging the dynamic and performative nature of gendered identities, I demonstrate in what follows how particular institutions make available or thwart certain definitions of masculinity or femininity, thereby homogenizing what in other contexts might be realized as variable and heterogeneous performances of masculinity or feminity. That is, outside of these institutional settings, when unaffected by the discursive and ideological constraints that permeate these contexts (i.e., when engaged in other kinds of social practices and activities), the male defendant and female complainants might recount their narratives quite differently. Concomitantly, the nature of their gendered (linguistic) identities, because they are mediated by the particular social practices and activities (e.g., communities of practice) within which the participants are engaged, might also be quite different outside of these institutions. While, as Eckert and McConnell-Ginet suggest, gendered identities, and social identities more generally, arise out of individuals' participation in a diverse set of communities of practice, institutional forces may constrain such identities, belying the complexity of their formation. And, to the extent that certain gendered identities are inhibited or facilitated by the sexual assault hearings analysed here, this kind of institutional discourse provides a window onto the 'rigid regulatory frame' (Butler 1990) within which gender is often enacted.

Gendered linguistic representations

At the outset of this chapter, I outlined my theoretical approach to the analysis of sexual assault adjudication processes, noting that it brings together two separate (but related) strands of research within feminist linguistics: how individuals produce themselves as gendered through language and how linguistic representations encode culturally-dominant notions of gender. While this distinction has served as an organizing principle for much work in the field, Cameron problematizes it, as I do, suggesting that 'in many cases it is neither possible nor useful to keep these aspects apart'.

> When a researcher studies women and men speaking she is looking, as it were, at the linguistic construction of gender in its first- and second-person forms (the construction of 'I' and 'you'); when she turns to the representation of gender in, say advertisements or literary texts, she is looking at the same thing in the third person ('she' and 'he').
>
> (Cameron 1998a: 963)

Put in Cameron's terms, this book explores the way that the linguistic representation of gender 'in the third person' shapes the enactment of gender 'in the first person'. That is, encoded in third-person forms, talk by lawyers and adjudicators *about* the accused, the complainants and violence against women more generally represents male sexual aggression in particular ways, that is, 'his' sexual prerogatives are privileged and protected at the expense of 'her' sexual autonomy. Such representations transmit androcentric values and attitudes; yet, they also have a strongly constitutive function: they shape and structure witnesses' *own* accounts of the events and concomitantly the way that gender is enacted in the first person. Having explicated the relevant aspects of the first kind of inquiry in feminist linguistics – the linguistic construction of gender 'in the first person' – I turn now to an explication of the second: what is meant by 'the linguistic construction of gender in the third person'? Moreover, how can the linguistic construction of gender in the third person shape enactments of gender in the first person?

Sexist language

Early work on gendered linguistic representations (in the 1970s and 1980s) focused on the way that language differentially represents men and women. Schulz (1975), for example, documented what she called the 'semantic derogation' of women in unequal word pairs such as *bachelor–spinster, master–mistress, governor–governess* or *warlock–witch*. Although parallel at some point in the history of English, Schulz argued that these pairs have not developed in a uniform way: systematically over time the terms designating women have taken on negative connotations in a way that the terms designating men have not. In addition to elucidating the perjorative nature of terms referring to women, early work on sexist language pointed to the way that masculine generics such as *he* and *man* render women invisible. Empirical support for such claims has been adduced by a substantial body of psycholinguistic research that shows *he/man* generics to readily evoke images of males rather than of males and females, to have detrimental effects on individuals' beliefs in women's ability to perform a job and to have a negative impact on women's own feelings of pride, importance and power. (For a review of this work see Henley 1989.) Thus, whether or not generic readings are intended by the use of *he/man* language, empirical research suggests that in many contexts interpretations do not correspond to intentions. Indeed, the documentation of the negative effects of *he/man* generics – both material and symbolic – was a major impetus behind nonsexist language reform efforts of the 1970s and 1980s. Attempting to challenge the androcentric and sexist values encoded in language, advocates of nonsexist language reform introduced alternative linguistic forms into languages, with the intention of supplanting male-defined meanings and grammar. For example, by replacing masculine generics (e.g., *he, man*) with neutral generics (e.g., singular *they, he/she*, generic *she*) language reformers challenged the claim implicit in the use of masculine generics, that is, that men are the typical case of humanity, with women constituting a deviation from this norm. While most attempts at linguistic reform have focused on codified instances of sexist language, that is, on those aspects of languages that are in some sense intrinsic to its grammatical and lexical structure, feminist linguistic resistance has also involved the coining of new terms to express women's perceptions and experiences, phenomena previously unexpressed in a language encoding a male worldview. The claim made by Spender (1980: 164) is that lexical gaps are not innocent; rather, 'when one groups holds a monopoly on naming, its bias is embedded in the names it supplies' and the names it does not supply. Thus, innovative terms such as *sexism*, *sexual harassment* and *date rape* are said to be significant in that they give a name to the experiences of women. As Gloria Steinem (1983: 149) says of these terms: 'a few years ago, they were just called life.'

In arguing for the necessity of gender-based language reform, feminist linguists have generally assumed that language is not a neutral and transparent means of designating social realities. Rather, a particular vision of social reality is assumed to be inscribed in language – a vision of reality that does not serve all of its speakers equally. The idea that language does not merely reflect but also creates and maintains unequal social relations is one that underlies the efforts of nonsexist language reformers and has its origins in the work of two American anthropological linguists, Edward Sapir and Benjamin Whorf. The Sapir–Whorf hypothesis, as it is known within the disciplines of linguistics and anthropology, holds that the grammatical and lexical structure of a given language has a powerful mediating influence on the ways that speakers of that language come to view the world. Whorf's comments are illustrative:

> We dissect nature along lines laid down by our native languages. The categories and types that we isolate from the world of phenomena we do not find there because they stare every observer in the face; on the contrary, the world is presented in a kaleidoscopic flux of impressions which has to be organized by our minds – and this means largely by the linguistic systems in our minds. We cut nature up, organize it into concepts, and ascribe significances as we do, largely because we are parties to an agreement to organize it in this way – an agreement that holds throughout our speech community and is codified in the patterns of our language. The agreement is, of course, an implicit and unstated one, BUT ITS TERMS ARE ABSOLUTELY OBLIGATORY; we cannot talk at all except by subscribing to the organization and classification of data which the agreement decrees. (emphasis in original)
>
> (Whorf 1956: 213–14)

For Whorf, speakers of radically different languages are led by the structure of their language to develop radically different ways of categorizing and viewing the world. Indeed, in describing Hopi, an Amerindian language, Whorf's goal was to establish the worldview he believed to be embedded in the grammatical and lexical patterns of the language. The strongest articulation of the Sapir–Whorf hypothesis within language and gender studies appears in the work of Dale Spender (1980), who argued that because men have had a 'monopoly on naming', it is their view of the world that is encoded in language.

While the Sapir–Whorf hypothesis is an appealing one and still influential in 'weaker' forms (e.g., Gumperz and Levinson 1996), the 'strong' version of the hypothesis as articulated above has few adherents today. The fact that speakers of a particular language can make conceptual distinctions that their language appears not to allow constitutes a powerful argument against the 'strong' version of the hypothesis. Crystal (1987) cites some Australian aboriginal languages, for instance, that have few words for numbers: the number lexicon may be restricted to general words such as *all, many, few* and then words for *one* and *two*. Yet it is not the case that speakers of such languages cannot count beyond two nor perform complex numerical operations. Indeed, subsequent scholarship on Hopi has shown that Whorf's claims about the 'worldview' possessed by Hopi speakers – claims upon which much of his theoretical work was based – are themselves questionable (Duranti 1997). A weaker version of the Sapir–Whorf hypothesis (which has generally come to replace the 'strong' version popular in the mid-part of the twentieth century) suggests that recurrent patterns of language use may predispose speakers to view the world in particular ways, but that such a worldview is not all-determining. Clearly, a feminist or antiracist critique of the sexist and racist assumptions embodied in language (such as Spender's) would be impossible if the grammatical and lexical structures of languages were so powerful as to prevent thought or a worldview outside of those structures. Speakers 'can see through and around the settings' (Halliday 1971: 332) of their language, but to do so may require interrogating some of the most basic 'common-sense' assumptions encoded in familiar and recurring uses of language. This is not to say that sexist and androcentric language is of no significance. On the contrary, foregrounding the ideological perspectives that languages encode can be difficult precisely because of their insidious and commonsensical quality. As Cameron (1998b: 11) says, whether or not one subscribes to a 'strong' version of Sapir–Whorf hypothesis, the sexism of language matters: 'to the extent that our lives are carried on in language (which is to a considerable extent, for most of us), the sexism of language must constantly re-enact and reinforce the commonsense "normality" of sexist assumptions.'

Gendered discursive representations

Beginning in the 1980s, feminist linguistics witnessed a broadening in its conception of sexist linguistic representations, shifting the focus of inquiry beyond single words and expressions to larger units of language and to the way that meanings are negotiated and modified in actual social interactions. That is, early reformers' (e.g., Spender 1980, Miller and Swift 1976) attention to sexist language at the level of the individual word (e.g., *he/man* language, non-parallelism of terms such as *poet/poetess*) has given way to an emphasis on the gendered nature of linguistic representations in *discourse*. This shift in focus has been motivated by a number of considerations. First, restricting one's attention to codified instances of sexist language misses many instances of discriminatory linguistic practices. Cameron (1998b), for example, considers stylistic conventions in the print media's coverage of rape, demonstrating how a range of linguistic features, none of which would be deemed problematic by a word-based critique of sexist language, can together function to construct rape in sexist and androcentric ways, that is, as a crime against men. Comparable examples dealing with sexual harassment are presented below; they are taken from the mainstream print media and describe a case in which a provincial member of parliament in British Columbia (Canada) – Robin Blencoe – was fired from his minister's post and finally ousted from his party's caucus because a number of women alleged that he sexually harassed them. What is noteworthy in these examples is that the women who claim to have been sexually harassed – the victims of sexual harassment – are effectively erased from the description of the events. That is, sexual harassment is represented here as victimizing the perpetrator, not the victim. (For an extended analysis of these and related data see Ehrlich and Levesque (1996).)

1   *BC minister fired over allegations of sex harassment*
Government Services Minister Robin Blencoc has been fired from the cabinet and kicked out of the NDP caucus after two more allegations of sexual harassment were levelled against him.
(*Globe and Mail*, 5 April 1995)

2   *Blencoe takes medical leave*
A week after he was fired from cabinet over sexual harassment allegations, Robin Blencoe announced Tuesday he is taking a medical leave of absence.
(*Vancouver Sun*, 12 April 1995)

3   *After harassment claims, MLA says career to end*
Ex-cabinet minister Robin Blencoe says he's decided it's time to move on. Blencoe, ousted from cabinet and the New Democractic party caucus this spring over sexual harassment allegations, announced Friday he will not seek re-election.
(*Vancouver Sun*, 22 July 1995)

4   *Fired minister still in limbo after 113 days*
The former government services minister took a medical leave after being fired from the NDP cabinet and ejected from caucus amid allegations of sexual harassment.
(*Vancouver Sun*, 12 July 1995)

In examples 1–4, a causal relationship is established between Robin Blencoe's being fired and allegations of sexual harassment. In 1, we have the headline

BC minister fired over allegations of sex harassment. In the body of the article, we see that *Robin Blencoe has been fired after two more allegations of sexual harassment.* In examples 2 and 3 he is fired and ousted from cabinet *over sexual harassment allegations*, in 4 he is fired *amid allegations of sexual harassment*, and so on. That is, Blencoe's misfortunes in these examples are depicted as the result of seemingly agentless allegations of sexual harassment. Indeed, the use of the nominalization *allegations* allows the women's role in the events to be eliminated which, in turn, functions to obscure the behaviour (i.e., sexual harassment) that resulted in the women's allegations. Even when the women's acts of reporting or laying charges is represented, it is without mention of the women. In example 1, for instance, *allegations* is the subject of the agentless passive, *two more allegations of sexual harassment were levelled against him*, allowing deletion of the woman who levelled the charges against Blencoe. Without any of the word-based instances of sexist language discussed above (e.g., no masculine generics, no derogatory noun phrases designating women), then, what emerges here is a representation of sexual harassment as a harm inflicted upon the perpetrator (and not the victims). Allegations of harassment seem to have acted independently of the women who laid the charges (and who were perhaps sexually harassed) and led to the demise of Blencoe's political career. Like Cameron's illustration of the print media's discursive practices surrounding rape, these examples (and the analysis from which they are drawn) point to the limitations of word-based critiques of sexist language in identifying many cases of gendered linguistic practices.

The sexism of these institutionalized linguistic conventions notwithstanding, early nonsexist reform efforts also failed to consider the social process by which linguistic forms, including nonsexist linguistic innovations, are endowed with meaning. That is, simply introducing nonsexist terms (e.g., singular *they*, *he/she*, generic *she*) or terms with feminist-influenced meanings (e.g., *sexual harassment, date rape*) into a language says nothing about how such terms will be used once they circulate within the wider speech community, especially given the sexist and androcentric values that pervade this larger community. In work that considered the fate of nonsexist and feminist linguistic innovations as they travel within the mainstream print media, Ehrlich and King (1992, 1994) identified a number of discursive strategies by which the expressions' intended meanings were routinely modified and reconstructed. While such terms supposedly encode feminist and nonsexist meanings and thus signify success for nonsexist language reformers, these meanings are often lost, depoliticized or reversed as the terms become invested with dominant (sexist) values and attitudes. As Eckert and McConnell-Ginet (1992a: 42) remark, 'linguistic forms do not come permanently glued to meanings but are endowed with meanings in the course of social practice'.

Identifying the problems associated with word-based or 'naming' accounts of sexist language, as I have done above, leads naturally to an investigation of sexism and androcentrism as they are manifest in *discourse*. In other words, the kind of linguistic analysis required to capture the instances of problematic language evident in the Robin Blencoe examples (a range of linguistic features which construct sexual harassment as a harm inflicted on the perpetrator) and in the meaning appropriations documented by Ehrlich and King falls within the purview of discourse analysis, as this term is understood within the discipline of linguistics. Attending to larger, socially-contextualized units of language, as discourse analysis does, is, arguably, part of a larger trend within linguistics to move beyond, or to supplement, the formal study of decontextualized units of language. Generative linguistics, for example, the dominant linguistics paradigm associated most notably with Noam Chomsky, has purposively ignored the social dimensions of language use, investigating the formal properties of language at a level of abstraction where the effects of social variation are insignificant. By contrast, Jaworski and Coupland (1999: 5) remark that 'language studied as discourse opens up countless new areas for the critical investigation of social and cultural life – the composition of cultural groups, the management of social relations, the constitution of social institutions, the perpetuation of social prejudices, and so on.' Perhaps indicative of this broadening trend is Schiffrin's (1994) characterization of discourse analysis as one of the most vast and least-defined areas of linguistics. Nonetheless, in her attempt to impose some order and coherence on the field, she identifies two prevalent definitions of discourse – (1) discourse as a unit of language larger than the sentence and (2) discourse as language embedded in social interaction – and suggests that they have their origins in formalist and functional theories of language, respectively. Returning to the limitations of word-based critiques of sexist language described above, we can see that each of these approaches to discourse is useful in identifying gendered linguistic practices that are not encoded in single words or expressions. First, by considering units of language larger than the sentence (i.e., discourse in Schiffrin's first sense), it is possible to identify a constellation of linguistic forms within a given text, as opposed to a single sentence, that all function in gendered ways (as in the Blencoe examples). (Moreover, the *inter-sentential* relations of the question–answer sequences I analyse throughout this book require attending to units of language larger than the sentence.) Second, by considering language as it is embedded within social interaction (i.e., discourse in Schiffrin's second sense), it is possible to account for the way that linguistic forms – nonsexist and feminist linguistic innovations, for example – are socially constructed and constituted, that is, endowed with meaning in the course of actual social interactions.

Influenced by the work of Michel Foucault, scholars outside of linguistics have further proliferated definitions and understandings of the term discourse. For Foucault, power is exercised through discourses of knowledge (e.g., social sciences, medical sciences) which define and categorize and concomitantly regulate and control the objects of their expertise. That is, social identities and social practices are brought into being as a result of the conventions of socially- and historically-constituted domains of knowledge,

what Foucault terms *discourses*. A primary division, then, exists between
linguists, who engage in close analysis of discourses or texts under the
assumption that their formal and functional regularities can be of interest
in their own right, as opposed to scholars in the humanities and social
sciences, influenced by the work of Foucault, whose use of the term is
much more general and indeed at times does not even refer to language
(i.e., it can refer to the design of prisons, for example). As Fairclough and
Wodak (1997: 261) comment, 'Foucault's work has generated immense
interest in discourse analysis amongst social scientists, but analysis of a
rather abstract sort that is not anchored in close analysis of texts.'

That the nitty-gritty details of socially-situated verbal interactions may be
connected to discourse in this more abstract sense is a position articulated by a
number of critical discourse analysts and anthropological linguists (e.g., Kress
1985, Fairclough 1992, 1995, Goodwin and Goodwin 1997, Conley and
O'Barr 1998). For example, in an article intended to explicate the tradition
of 'critical discourse analysis', Fairclough and Wodak define discourse in
the following way:

> Like other approaches to discourse analysis, critical discourse analysis
> (henceforth CDA) analyses real and often extended instances of social
> interaction which take a linguistic form, or a partially linguistic
> form. . . . CDA sees discourse – language use in speech and writing –
> as a form of 'social practice'. Describing discourse as social practice
> implies a dialectical relationship between a particular discursive event
> and the situation(s), institution(s) and social structure(s) which frame
> it. A dialectical relationship is a two-way relationship: the discursive
> event is shaped by situations, institutions and social structures, but it
> also shapes them. To put the same point in a different way, discourse
> is socially constitutive as well as socially shaped: it constitutes situations,
> objects of knowledge, and the social identities of and relationships
> between people and groups of people. It is constitutive both in the
> sense that it helps to sustain and reproduce the social status quo, and
> in the sense that it contributes to transforming it.
>
> (Fairclough and Wodak 1997: 258)

Of interest here is the constitutive function Fairclough and Wodak ascribe to
particular discursive events: particular discursive events, while shaped by the
social context in which they are produced, can also 'constitute objects of
knowledge' and 'the social identities of and relationships between people
and groups of people'. Influenced by Foucault, it would seem, Fairclough
and Wodak are suggesting that discourse at the micro-level of social interaction (i.e., 'real and . . . extended instances of social interaction which
take a linguistic form') can contribute to discourses and their effects at the
macro-level of social and political interaction.

Like Fairclough and Wodak, I adopt an approach to discourse that locates its constitutive force not only in socially- and historically-constructed domains of knowledge, but also in the linguistic details of socially-situated interactions. Grounding my analysis in the concrete verbal interactions of sexual assault adjudication processes, I elucidate the way that such inter-actions encode culturally-dominant discourses (and potentially counter-hegemonic ones) about violence against women. As language that embodies sexist and androcentric assumptions, these particular representations comprise a part of the 'rigid regulatory frame' or the 'macro-social constraints' that make available certain gendered subject positions and thwart others. Thus, to the extent that these linguistic practices, informed by dominant gender ideologies, shape or constitute the social identities and relationships of the participants involved – also expressed, in part, through linguistic prac-tices – we see the way that the linguistic construction of gender in the third person cooerces enactments of gender in the first person. I now turn to the specific ways that legal discourse, and specifically the legal discourse of rape, can been shown to exhibit 'institutional cooerciveness'. That is, like other kinds of discourse, legal discourse embodies sexist and androcentric assumptions; hence to what extent do these assumptions structure social identities and social relations within legal settings – and beyond?

The gendered nature of legal discourse

For many feminist legal theorists (e.g., Smart 1989, Lees 1997, Lacey 1998) and legal anthropologists (e.g., Merry 1990, Lazarus-Black and Hirsch 1994, Mertz 1994), the law does not only exert its power through the enactment of rules and the imposition of punishments; it also has the capacity to impose and affirm culturally powerful definitions of social reality. Indeed, Smart (1989) argues that law manifests 'disciplinary' power in Foucault's sense, that is, it does not only exercise power through 'its material effects (judge-ments)' (p. 11) but also functions as a discourse 'which is able to refute and disregard alternative discourses and to claim a special place in the definition of events' (p. 162). While relying on Foucauldian notions of power and dis-course, Smart departs from Foucault in suggesting that the law and legal institutions display characteristics he associates primarily with domains of knowledge in the natural and social sciences. That is, for Smart, the law can exercise its power in subtle, dispersed and intangible ways (i.e., as disci-plinary power), thereby functioning as a mechanism of social normalization and control. In fact, Lacey (1998: 10) argues that it is precisely the 'normal-izing' effects of the law that are strongly indicative of its 'disciplinary' power. Laws, for example, that do not extend to gay and lesbian couples the same rights and privileges afforded to heterosexual couples express cultural assumptions about what constitutes 'normal' sexualities. That is, the law generates definitions and categories that discursively regulate and control social life in addition to imposing sanctions (e.g., fines, imprisonment, executions) to ensure compliance with certain social norms (Merry 1990).

In expanding our conception of the law (and its power) to include legal discourse as well as legal doctrine, Lacey argues that we also expand our understanding of what constitutes relevant objects of inquiry within the law:

> Feminist (like other critical) analyses are interested here not just in legal doctrine but also in legal discourse, i.e., how differently sexed legal subjects are constituted by and inserted within legal categories via the mediations of judicial, police or lawyers' discourse. The feminist approach therefore mounts a fundamental challenge to the standard ways of conceptualising law and the legal, and moves to a broader understanding of legally relevant spheres of practice.
>
> (Lacey 1989: 10)

While Lacey is writing in the 1990s, earlier feminist work on the law of rape and sexual assault also included within its domain of critique, not only statutes surrounding rape (i.e., legal doctrine), but also 'the mediations of judicial, police or lawyers' discourse'. Although not articulated in terms of the 'disciplinary' power of law's 'discourses', a work like Susan Estrich's *Real Rape* (1987) is suggestive of the social control and regulation exercised by the criminal justice system in its treatment of what Estrich calls 'simple rape' as opposed to 'real rape'. The question Estrich explores is why many cases of rape that meet the statutory definition are not considered as such by police, prosecutors, judges and juries. That is, Estrich argues that the law differentially prosecutes perpetrators and differentially protects the interests of victims. And, paradoxically, it is the cases of rape that are least frequent that the law treats most aggressively. (Research by Russell (1982, 1984) has shown that women are much more likely to be raped by husbands, lovers and dates than by strangers.) In cases of 'stranger rape' (what Estrich terms 'real rape'), when the perpetrator is an armed stranger 'jumping from the bushes', and, in particular a black stranger attacking a white woman, Estrich argues, the law is likely to arrest, prosecute and convict the perpetrator. By contrast, in cases of what Estrich calls 'simple rape', that is, when a woman is forced to engage in sex with a date, an acquaintance, her boss or a man she met at a bar, when no weapon is involved and when there is no overt evidence of physical injury, rapes are much less likely to be treated as criminal by the criminal justice system. Marcus (1992) provides support for Estrich's claims, elaborating on the intersection of racism and sexism in the criminal justice system's prosecution of rapists. While inter-racial rape cases make up a minority of rapes committed and brought to trial, when white women are raped by black men (especially strangers) they are much more likely to obtain convictions than in cases where the perpetrator is white. Clearly, racist ideologies inform judges' and juries' decisions in rape cases, demonizing black men and protecting white women; that is, the law's abhorrence of the rapist in stranger cases is exacerbated when the rapist is a man of colour.[3]

To the extent that stranger rape is considered to be 'real rape' by the criminal justice system, the magnitude of the problem of rape diminishes (at least, from the system's point of view). First, stranger rape is a relatively infrequent event and second, when it does occur, it tends to be prosecuted more successfully and more frequently than many other violent crimes (Estrich 1987: 4). Estrich comments:

> The dimensions of the problem of rape in the United States depend on whether you count the simple, 'technical' rapes. If only the aggravated cases are considered rape – if we limit our practical definition to cases involving more than one man, or strangers, or weapons and beatings – then 'rape' is a relatively rare event, is reported to the police more often than most crimes and is addressed aggressively by the system. If the simple cases are considered – the cases where a woman is forced to have sex without consent by only one man, whom she knows, who does not beat her or attack her with a gun – then rape emerges as a far more common, vastly underreported, and dramatically ignored problem.
> (Estrich 1987: 10)

Put in slightly different terms, the 'discourses' that surround the prosecution of real rape vs. simple rape cases in the criminal justice system (i.e., Lacey's 'mediations of judicial, police or lawyers' discourse') bring into being definitions and categories of what constitutes a 'legitimate' or believable victim and a 'legitimate' perpetrator. 'Legitimate' perpetrators, for example, are strangers to their victims, carry a weapon, and inflict physical injury upon their victim, beyond the sexual violence; 'legitimate' or believable victims are women raped by precisely these kinds of perpetrators. The discourses of rape that surround the criminal justice system's treatment of rape, then, construct stranger rape as 'real rape' and render the vast majority of rapes invisible. Consider the relationship between the differential treatment of real rape and simple rape (i.e., real rape is 'addressed aggressively by the system' whereas simple rape is not) and their disclosure and reporting rates. In a well-cited survey of approximately 1,000 adult women in 1978, Russell found that 56 per cent of her respondents said that at some point in their life they had been a victim of 'forced intercourse' or 'intercourse obtained by threat'. Of this group, 82 per cent of the rapes involved non-strangers, yet less than 10 per cent of these were reported to the police. On the basis of a number of other studies investigating rape reporting rates, Estrich draws the generalization that women are less likely to report rape 'the closer the relationship between victim and assailant' (1987: 11). That is, while rape generally is a vastly under-reported crime, 'real rapes' are much more likely to be reported than 'simple rapes'. MacKinnon (1987: 81) speculates as to the conditions under which women will report rape: 'the rapes that have been reported . . . are *the kinds of rape women think will be believed* when we report them. They have two qualities: they are by a stranger and they are by a Black man' (emphasis mine). In a similar way, Estrich suggests that victims who do not disclose and report rape are those who are not deemed 'legitimate victims by the police and criminal justice system' (1987: 15). In other words, definitions and categories of 'real rapes' and 'legitimate' or believable victims are socially controlling in the sense that they determine the likelihood of women disclosing and reporting rape. (Arguably, the reporting of rape is a necessary step in the law's (ostensible) attempts to deter rape.) It is not only through coercive legal measures, then, that (some) men's sexual interests and prerogatives are protected by the criminal justice system at the expense of women's sexual autonomy; it is also through culturally-powerful legal discourses that achieve their force through self-regulation and self-surveillance.

The translation of Estrich's insights into a language of 'discourses' and 'disciplinary power' is consistent with and runs parallel to work by Lees (1996, 1997), who conceptualizes the rape trial as means of controlling female sexuality. According to Lees (1997: 86) 'insufficient attention has been paid to the function of the [rape] trial process in policing women's sexuality.' Analysing British rape trials that occurred over a four month period in 1993, Lees concentrates on the trials' (i.e., cross-examining lawyers') preoccupation with victims' intimate bodily functions. Constantly focusing on bodily fluids such as menstruation in their questioning, Lees argues that cross-examining lawyers cast doubt on the 'rationality' of victims, given the control that bodies and particularly menstruation are said to exert on women's abilities to 'reason'. Of relevance here are MacKinnon's (1987) remarks about the 'pornographic' nature of rape trials. It is perhaps only in pornography that the intimate details of a man removing a tampon from a woman's vagina – the topic of questioning in one of Lees' examples – would be expressed in a public forum. Hence not only does the public spectacle of sexualizing victims' bodies call into question their ability to reason, it also casts aspersions on their 'respectability'. Indeed, in Smart's (1989: 39) terms they are obliged to participate in a 'pornographic vignette'. Lees' argument ultimately associates this 'defilement of the complainant through language' with social control and regulation:

> Rape trials today can be seen both as operating as a warning, and a way of restricting the activities of women through inciting fear of the public sphere, but also through punishing a victim for breaking the silence enforced by the emphasis on female respectability and chastity.
>
> (Lees 1997: 73)

In the same way that the discourses of 'simple rape' and 'real rape' engender self-regulation and self-surveillance with respect to victims' disclosure and reporting of rape, so the rape trial, according to Lees, functions as a mechanism of 'disciplinary' power. But, not only do the rape trial's degrading and humiliating qualities discourage victims from engaging with the criminal justice system, Lees suggests that, as a form of social control, the rape trial may extend its reach beyond victims of rape. That is, the activities of women more generally may be curtailed by a mechanism that 'incite[s] fear of the public sphere'.

Statutes and other discourses

Broadening the scholarly focus of feminist legal studies to include what Lacey calls 'the mediations of judicial, police or lawyers discourse' has not been motivated solely by the turn to Foucauldian notions of discourse that has characterized social sciences and humanities scholarship more generally. It has also received its impetus from the often large discrepancy that exists between 'law-as-legislation' and 'law-as-practice' (Smart 1986). For example, in spite of sweeping legislative reform to sexual assault and rape statutes in the 1970s, 1980s and 1990s in Canada and the United States,[4] other aspects of sexual assault legal processes (e.g., judicial decisions) continue to be informed by culturally-powerful interpretive frameworks that legitimate male violence and reproduce gendered inequalities. As Comack (1999: 235) says of the progressive reforms to Canadian sexual assault law in the 1980s and 1990s, 'while Parliament may be amenable to implementing reforms in sexual-violence laws through statute ("law-as-legislation"), it is still the case that the decisions of judges will have a determining effect on legal outcomes ("law-as-practice").' Given that the law's failure to conform to its statutory objectives undoubtedly lies in other kinds of legal practices (e.g., police interrogations, trials, judge's decisions), an understanding of this failure requires moving beyond legal doctrine to legal discourse more generally.

Statutory discourse

In Canada, revisions to criminal laws governing acts of sexual aggression were legislated by Parliament in 1983, 1985, 1992 and 1995, largely in response to concerted feminist lobbying (Comack 1999). The major changes in 1983 involved replacing the offences of rape (and indecent assault) with the more general offences of *sexual assault*. Such changes functioned to expand the narrow view of sexual aggression denoted by rape, making criminally punishable sexual acts of aggression that did not necessarily involve penetration. More significantly perhaps these changes marked a shift in the way the Canadian Criminal Code conceptualized rape – as a crime of violence rather than a crime of sex. Designating rape as a kind of assault emphasized the affinity between unwanted sexual aggression and other forms of assault and battery.[5] The 1983 legislation also abolished the marital exemption rule which had made it impossible for husbands to rape their wives; the corroboration rule which required that a complainant's testimony be supported by independent evidence; and the recent complaint rule which obligated the complainant to make a prompt complaint in order that her testimony be deemed reliable. While the 1983 legislation introduced fairly strict conditions under which complainants' sexual history could be admissible as evidence, this so-called rape shield provision was struck down by the Supreme Court of Canada in 1991. Responding to the strong lobbying efforts of Canadian feminists, legislation in 1992 reintroduced rape shield amendments setting out a new test for determining the admissibility of a complainant's past sexual history as evidence in sexual assault trials (Mohr and Roberts 1994). In addition, the 1992 amendments provided a definition of 'consent' with respect to sexual offences and restricted the defence of mistaken belief in consent 'to situations in which the defendant actually took "reasonable steps" to ascertain that the complainant was consenting' (Busby 1999: 271). Of significance in the 1992 redefinition of consent is its focus on what the complainant said or otherwise communicated at the time of the (alleged) sexual assault, rather than on what the defendant thought she communicated or on what she might have communicated at some other point in time. According to Busby:

> By this law, initiators of sexual activity should no longer be able to rely upon stereotypes or fantasies about women or even their knowledge of specific complainants' sexual lives to assume consent, but rather have the positive obligation of determining whether the real, present woman is agreeing on the particular occasion to sexual activity.
>
> (Busby 1999: 270)

Moreover, the 1992 redefinition asserts that consent is not obtained under certain conditions including: if a third party consents on behalf of the complainant; if the complainant is incapable of consenting; if the accused induces the complainant to consent by abusing a position of trust, power or authority. What these provisions make criminally punishable are instances of coerced sex that don't necessarily involve physical violence or the threat of physical violence.

Statutory reform in the United States has had a different history, as feminist reformers in the 1970s believed that introducing a formal requirement of consent for sexual acts of aggression would focus undue attention on complainants in trials, for example, on the extent to which they resisted, on their 'provocative' clothing and behaviour and/or on their 'promiscuous' sexual history. Interestingly, what has been heralded as a progressive reform by Canadian feminists in the 1990s (see Busby above) – focusing on the complainants' behaviour and whether or not she communicated consent – was deemed as strategically problematic by American feminists in the 1970s. Thus, emerging in the legislative reform of the 1970s was a focus on the defendant's conduct rather than the complainant's, which brought with it a renewed emphasis on 'forcible compulsion' as the core of sexual assault offences, of which physical force and violence was one form (Schulhofer 1998: 31). Arguably, this focus on 'forcible compulsion' leaves open the possibility of physical violence or the threat of physical violence becoming a necessary criterion for the crime of sexual assault, thereby perpetuating the criminal justice system's preoccupation with cases of what Estrich calls 'real rape' in which the armed stranger 'jumps from the bushes' to attack his victim. Nonetheless, state legislative change in the 1970s instituted a number of progressive reforms: corroboration rules were abolished in virtually every state; resistance requirements were abolished or softened; marital exemption rules were eliminated or weakened; and rape shield provisions were introduced in every state to restrict conditions under which evidence pertaining to complainants' sexual history was admissible (Schulhofer 1998: 33). Post-1970 reform, not surprisingly, has had to grapple with the issue of 'forcible compulsion', specifically, how to extend legal concepts of force and coercion so that they include more than just physical violence or the threat of physical violence. Representative of the most progressive changes in this regard is a 1992 New Jersey Supreme Court decision, which in essence redefined 'physical force' – a requirement for a sexual assault conviction by New Jersey law – to mean non-consent:

> Physical force in excess of that inherent in the act of sexual penetration is not required for such penetration to be unlawful. The definition of 'physical force' is satisfied . . . if the defendant applies any amount of force against another person in the absence of what a reasonable person would believe to be affirmatively and freely-given permission.
>
>   (*M.T.S.*, 609 A.2d 1266 (N.J. 1992) cited in Schulhofer 1998: 96)

Of particular interest here is the focus on the complainant's behaviour, specifically, on her 'affirmatively and freely-given permission'. Returning to issues of consent and non-consent, Schulhofer (1998: 96) notes that states like New Jersey 'bring the tactics of rape reform full circle'. While New Jersey was among many states in the 1970s that eliminated any reference to the consent of the complainant and instead defined sexual assault in terms of the 'forcible compulsion' of the defendant, the M.T.S. decision removes any requirement of force and coercion. An illustration of the changing tactics of rape-law reformers, Sanday (1996: 285) argues that deeming sexual aggression unlawful in the absence of what she calls the 'affirmative consent' of complainants – as the New Jersey decision and recent statutes in Illinois, Washington and Wisconsin do – affords women sexual autonomy and agency and 'more than any other development in the twentieth century . . . promises to end unquestioned male dominance'. If Sanday's comments seem overly optimistic, they are tempered by other comments throughout her book-length study of celebrated American acquaintance rape trials about the failure of statutory reform in the context of sexist and misogynist cultural stereotypes: 'although our rape laws define the line [between sex and rape] and the punishment, these laws are useless if juror attitudes are affected by ancient sexual stereotypes. We must see these stereotypes for what they are – attitudes that encourage male violence' (p. 293). Indeed, what Sanday is optimistic about is the possibility of women's affirmative consent becoming a *cultural norm*, recognizing that the interpretation of progressive statutory laws is impossible to separate from the cultural backdrop against which it is interpreted.

Judges' discourse

The discrepancy between 'law as legislation' and 'law as practice' is probably most explicit in judicial decision-making. Within the Canadian context, Comack (1999: 234) remarks that despite the widespread reform to Canadian sexual assault law in the 1980s and 1990s (of the type discussed above), 'judicial decisions continue to reflect traditional cultural mythologies about rape'. For example, although 1983 reforms replaced the offence of rape with the offence of sexual assault (attempting, among other things, to include under its rubric acts of sexual aggression that did not only involve penetration), a year later, a New Brunswick Court of Appeal judge held that grabbing a woman's breasts did not constitute sexual assault because women's breasts, 'like a man's beard', were only secondary sexual characteristics (*R. v. Chase* 1984). According to Mohr and Roberts (1994: 5), because the drafters of the 1983 legislation did not define sexual assault, 'it is judges who, by default, become the law-makers as far as the definition of the offence is concerned.'[6] In a more recent Canadian judicial decision (*R. v. Ewanchuk* 1998), an Alberta Court of Appeal judge upheld the acquittal of a defendant on the basis of the complainant's 'implied' consent. While the complainant testified that she feared resistance would cause the accused to become violent, the judge determined that 'her suppressed concerns about the possibility of force from Ewanchuk' were tantamount to (implied) consent. His comments also included reference to her dress: 'it must be pointed out that the complainant did not present herself to Ewanchuk [the defendant] or enter his trailer *in a bonnet and crinolines*' (emphasis mine) and to more 'appropriate' ways that she might have resisted the accused: 'the sum of the evidence indicates that Ewanchuk's advances to the complainant were far less criminal than hormonal. In a less litigious age going too far in the boyfriend's car was better dealt with on site – a well-chosen expletive, a slap in the face or, if necessary, a well-directed knee.'[7] In sum, without indicators of resistance, whether that took the form of wearing 'a bonnet and crinolines' or slapping the accused in the face, the judge determined that the complainant had implied consent. Defining consent as the absence of resistance departs dramatically from the 1992 statutory provision, which defines consent as 'the voluntary agreement of the complainant to engage in the sexual activity in question'; moreover, such a definition suggests that it is women who are responsible for controlling men's sexual urges.

More systematic investigation of Canadian judicial decisions has been conducted by Coates *et al.* (1994). Analysing the language of twelve sexual assault trial judgements written between 1986 and 1992, Coates *et al.* determined that judges were limited in the 'interpretative repertoires' (Wetherell and Potter 1988) they deployed in describing sexual assaults. That is, in describing 'stranger' rapes, judges employed a language of assault and violence; however, in describing acquaintance rapes, Coates *et al.* (p. 191) demonstrate that 'the vocabulary . . . used was often more suitable to consensual acts than to assault'. For example, the unwanted touching of a young girl's vagina was described as 'fondling' in one trial judgement; in another, a judge described a defendant acquitted of rape and forced fellatio as 'offering' his penis to his victim's mouth. Expressions such as 'fondling' and 'offering a penis' conjure up an image of affectionate, consensual sex, thereby situating 'the violent acts that were at issue into a framework of normal sexual activity' (p. 193). Thus, in spite of the fact that 1983 statutory reforms explicitly reconceptualized sexual assault as a crime of violence rather than a crime of sex, most of these decisions (even in cases where the accused was convicted) adopted a language of erotic, affectionate and consensual sex in depicting sexual assault. And, consistent with Estrich's claims about the criminal justice system's difficulty in treating non-stranger rape or acquaintance rape as criminal, it was in the non-stranger cases that this 'anomalous' language, inconsistent with Canadian law, was used.

Trial discourse

In her book-length study of acquaintance rape trials, Sanday (1996) elucidates some of the failures of American sexual assault legal reforms, as evidenced within the context of trials. Describing the notorious William Kennedy Smith trial that took place in Florida in the fall of 1991, Sanday remarks: 'the trial was an example of how a woman's reputation can be dragged through the mud even in the face of the legal reform that explicitly forbids such information into court' (p. 217). Of relevance here is the fact that Florida was in the forefront of rape law reforms in the 1970s and instituted, among other progressive provisions, a rape shield provision which held that a complainant's past sexual history was only admissible as evidence under very restricted circumstances. Indeed, under this law the judge prohibited the defence attorneys from asking any questions about the complainant's, Patricia Bowman's, past sexual history. According to Sanday, however, the defence lawyer (Roy Black) was nonetheless able to introduce such evidence 'through the back door':

> Questions about her bar-going habits painted a certain picture, as did her underwear, which Black asked the jurors to examine for tears to show that Smith had not forced her. As the black Victoria's Secret panties and sheer black bra with blue satin trim were passed from hand to hand to be

checked for tears or stains, along with the newly bought Ann Taylor dress, it was obvious that another, more important message was attached to the show. . . . Roy Black left the indelible impression that this un-attached young woman, who had left her illegitimate child at her mother's for the night, was out for a night on a town famous for its bars frequented by rich men and fortune-seeking women. All of this without explicitly getting into Bowman's past sexual history.

(Sanday 1996: 219)

By contrast, the prosecuting lawyer was unable to introduce 'one iota' of William Kennedy Smith's past sexual history into the trial in spite of three other women coming forward to say that they had been sexually assaulted by the accused during the period from 1983 to 1988 (p. 219). The judge dis-allowed this evidence and for many legal experts this particular ruling 'won the case for the defense'. Without the testimony of these other women, the picture that emerged in the courtroom was of an unstable, sexually provoca-tive, fortune-seeking woman picked up in a bar by a seemingly respectable (white) doctor from a prominent American family (Sanday 1996: 220). Significant for my purposes about the trial (and Sanday's analysis) is the fact that Bowman's sexual reputation was so thoroughly tarnished in spite of Florida's progressive rape shield provisions that severely restrict the conditions under which a complainant's sexual history is admissible in court.[8]

Unpacking the discourse of law

That judicial decisions and trials often contravene the hard-won statutory reforms of feminists is a dilemma Smart (1989: 164) sees as primary to any feminist engagement with the law. Because 'legislation is in the hands of individuals and agencies far removed from the values and politics of the women's movement', she suggests that the outcome of statutory reform is always unpredictable. In a discussion of sexual harassment cases, Chamallas elaborates upon the variable and unpredictable nature of the legal interpreta-tion of statutes:

The law as it stands, the governing legal standards, are capable of being interpreted in either a victim-oriented or perpetrator-oriented fashion. The basic legal concepts are contested, such that the outcome in sexual harassment cases may ultimately turn on the orientation of the particular judge or the political views of the members of the jury. To be sure, the language of the law is the language of objectivity and there is the back-ground assumption that legal proceedings are fair. But there is also remarkable variation in the meanings ascribed to core legal concepts.

(Chamallas 1995: 3)

While legal categories and concepts may be encoded in statutes, such encodings do not 'fix' and 'cement' their meanings; indeed, as we have seen, they can be interpreted and implemented in ways that are far removed from their intended, feminist-influenced meanings. Of central importance to feminist critiques of the law, then, are the actual practices whereby legal concepts (e.g., 'consent' and 'sexual assault') give rise to, often variable and contested, meanings and interpretations. That is, if legal concepts are endowed with meaning during the course of socially-situated legal practices (e.g., judicial decision-making, trials), then understanding and deconstructing this meaning-making process requires an investigation of such legal practices in relation to the social context in which they are embedded. Indeed, Smart goes even further in her problematizing of legislation, arguing that engaging with law at the level of statutory or policy reform 'only legitimate[s] the legal forum and the form of law' (p. 165). Rather than focusing on law as legislation, Smart suggests that

> It is law's power to define and disqualify which should become the focus of feminist strategy rather than law reform as such. It is in its ability to redefine the truth of events that feminism offers political gains.
>
> (Smart 1989: 164)

For Smart, then, it is the law's power to impose and affirm culturally-powerful visions of social reality that should be the object of feminist critique. As Comack (1999: 65) says of Smart's project, 'the task becomes one of unpacking the discourse of law to reveal the context in which it has been constituted and the biases it contains.'

'Unpacking the discourse of law' to elucidate its sexist and androcentric biases is an endeavour that resonates with feminist linguists' efforts to analyse sexist language in the 1970s and 1980s and more recently to understand the way that gendered meanings are constructed and reproduced in discourse (Cameron 1998a). Indeed, to the extent that legal discourse embodies gendered assumptions, it comprises part of the 'rigid regulatory frame' that shapes and constrains performances of gender – a primary focus of this book. That the legal discourse of sexual assault constructs and produces certain kinds of (gendered) sexual subjects is evident from the preceding discussion. Women are legitimate victims of rape when they are subject to violent attacks from strangers (Estrich 1987); otherwise, they are held responsible for men's sexual aggression. For example, the complainant in the *R.* v. *Ewanchuk* case was chastised for not wearing 'a bonnet and crinolines' that would presumably have controlled the accused's sexual advances; and, Patricia Bowman was represented as a gold-digging seductress out to entrap an eligible and wealthy bachelor. Constructed both as victims (when the perpetrator is heinous) and agents (when the perpetrator is respectable), the complainants occupy contradictory subject positions in line with the contradictions that imbue dominant notions of female and male sexuality and sexual violence. Crenshaw elaborates on the restricted, but contradictory, subject positions women come to occupy in the discourse of rape law:

> Part of the regulation of sexuality through rape law occurs in the perception of the complaining witness at the rape trial . . . Feminist legal work has emphasized the ways that perceptions of the credibility of witnesses, for example, are mediated by dominant narratives about the ways that men and women 'are' . . . The routine focus on the victim's sexual history functions to cast the complainant in one of several roles, including the whore, the tease, the vengeful liar, the mentally or emotionally unstable, or, in a few instances the madonna. Once these ideologically informed character assignments are made, 'the story' tells itself, usually supplanting the woman's account of what transpired between the complainant and the accused with a fiction of villainous female intentionality that misleads and entraps the 'innocent' or unsuspecting male.
>
> (Crenshaw 1992: 408)

As we have seen previously, justifying the acquittal of certain kinds of defendants involved in certain kinds of rapes ('simple' rapes) can involve the deployment of 'dominant narratives' that cast women as 'the whore' or 'the tease' and men as 'entrapped by women' (as in the William Kennedy Smith case) or 'driven by hormones' (as in *R. v. Ewanchuk*). The madonna role, in line with Estrich's claims, is undoubtedly reserved for victims of 'real rape'.

Rape myths embedded in the legal discourse of sexual assault not only reflect powerful social discourses about sexual violence, but also about normative heterosexuality (Gavey 1999). That is, a woman will say 'no' with sincerity to a man's sexual advances but the 'no' gets filtered through a series of dominant discourses about what constitutes 'normal' sex and the woman's 'direct negative' is transformed into an 'indirect affirmative': 'she is playing hard to get, but of course she really means yes' (McConnell-Ginet 1989: 47). Because women are supposed to be the passive recipients of male sexual desire, or at least must not express their own desire until overcome by the seductive power of men, women's protests are an expected part of 'normal' heterosexual sex. Moreover, that men disregard women's signals of resistance and transform their 'direct negatives' into 'indirect affirmatives' is sanctioned by 'traditional ideals of heterosexual romance' that 'suggest a woman's quiet desire' is 'waiting to be awakened by a man's expert seduction' (Gavey 1999: 60). Representations of 'normal' heterosexual sex, then, include within their domain sexual interactions where there are no positive responses, or worse, overt expressions of resistance, on the part of women. As Gavey (p. 61) concludes, 'male seduction can be enacted on a woman whose willingness is always in question'.

The dominant notions about normative heterosexuality that transform a woman's 'no' into 'yes' not only give meaning to the sexual interactions of women and men, but also animate the legal discourse of rape and sexual assault. Lees (1996: 260), for example, argues that the primary reason rape law is so unsatisfactory 'in all advanced countries' is because judges fail 'to adopt a modern communicative model of sexuality which implies that there must be positive responses by both parties'. As discussed earlier, Coates *et al.* (1994) found Canadian judges to be extremely limited in the language they deployed in describing sexual assaults. Either they adopted a language of assault and violence, when describing stranger rapes, or a language of affectionate, consensual sex, when describing acquaintance rapes. Since normative sex, according to dominant views of heterosexuality, can involve women expressing resistance, the distinction between it and acquaintance rape (where women may also express resistance) is likely to become blurred, leading to the 'anomalous' descriptions of acquaintance rape that Coates *et al.* (1984) document. What Coates *et al.* (p. 204) recommend is the development of language that can accurately represent instances of unwanted sex in familiar surroundings perpetrated by someone the victim knows – 'vocabulary for fitting words to these deeds'.

The discourse of acquaintance rape hearings

Given my emphasis on the way that discourse, as it is manifest in the nitty-gritty details of actual linguistic interactions, is constitutive (and potentially transformative) of dominant gendered social relations and identities, I have chosen to ground my investigation in the language of acquaintance rape hearings. This choice reflects a number of considerations, related to both the particular legal practice – the trial – and to the particular offence – acquaintance rape. First, the legal and extralegal hearings I analyse occur in the Canadian context, where sweeping statutory reform surrounding sexual assault is considered exemplary by feminists around the world (e.g., Lees 1997, Lacey 1998).[9] Thus, this investigation is potentially revealing of the discrepancy between law at the level of rules and sanctions and law as it is manifest in socially-situated practice. Specifically, by 'unpacking' the micro-discourse of acquaintance rape hearings, I elucidate some of the processes whereby legal concepts, such as 'consent', 'non-consent' and 'sexual assault', are endowed with meanings in the course of everyday legal practices – meanings that often depart dramatically from Canadian statutory definitions of these terms.

Second, the interactive, dialogical nature of trial discourse provides a unique setting for investigating the way that legal discourse produces 'differently-sexed legal subjects' (Lacey 1998: 10). Work by Estrich has shown legal discourse to construct 'legitimate' and 'illegitimate' victims of rape; moreover, such constructions are sites of social control to the extent that they discourage the disclosing and reporting of rape among certain kinds of rape victims (i.e., victims of 'simple' rape). While trial discourse, like statutory and judicial discourse, produces certain kinds of gendered subjects, which have 'considerable reach in terms of their effects on women's [and men's] lives and identities' (Comack 1999: 65), its dialogic quality (absent in statutory and judicial discourse) also has the effect of shaping and constituting the (gendered) identities of participants within a particular trial. The question–answer sequences of trial discourse are illustrative of what proponents of conversational analysis label the *doubly contextual* nature of utterances (e.g., Drew and Heritage 1992). Not only does a question in a question–answer sequence depend upon previous utterances for its production and interpretation (i.e., it is *context-shaped*), it also is *context-renewing* to the extent that it shapes and constrains the form of the utterance that will follow, i.e., the answer. Questions in acquaintance rape trials, then, that potentially encode powerful social discourses about female and male sexuality and violence against women, create the context for witnesses' answers. It is in this sense that the linguistic practices of trials may 'institutionally coerce' the participants' (linguistic) performances of gender. Put differently, witnesses within trials become constituted as certain kinds of gendered subjects, in large part, through their contextually-constrained responses to lawyers' (and judges') questions.

A further and third characteristic of trial settings that has motivated this particular investigation is their adversarial nature. Trials typically involve the prosecution and the defence putting forth different understandings of the events under investigation; indeed, competing and contradictory versions of the 'facts' often emerge in these contexts. Thus, to the extent that trials are adversarial, to what extent will competing and contradictory versions of events emerge in acquaintance rape hearings? Given that acquaintance rapes are 'ambiguous' cases of rape because of their similarity to so-called instances of normal, consensual heterosexual sex, the language typically adopted in describing acquaintance rapes is indeed the language of consensual sex. Thus, if the language of consensual sex is the dominant one in describing instances of acquaintance rape, and undoubtedly the one to be adopted by the defence, what competing language might be mobilized by the prosecution in describing these kinds of sexual assaults? More generally, then, the adversarial, dynamic nature of the courtroom situation provides a window onto ways that dominant notions about male and female sexuality and sexual violence are reproduced discursively but also ways they might be resisted and challenged. Likewise, if the (linguistic) gendered performances of the participants are shaped and constrained, i.e., constituted, by a legal discourse that embodies powerful social discourses about violence against women, how might counter-hegemonic discourses shape their identities differently? I now turn to the specific details of the case study that forms the basis of my analysis.

Data

The data presented here come from two sources: they were transcribed from audiotaped recordings of a York University (Toronto, Canada) disciplinary tribunal dealing with sexual harassment.[10] In addition they come from transcripts of a Canadian criminal trial in which the same defendant was charged with two counts of sexual assault.[11] Both adjudication processes dealt with the same events – two alleged instances of acquaintance rape with two different women. The complainants were casual acquaintances prior to the alleged instances of sexual assault. They met coincidentally a short time after the incidents, discovered each other's experience with the accused, and together launched complaints against him in the context of York University and later in the context of the Canadian criminal justice system. Within the context of York University, the accused was alleged to have violated York University's Standards of Student Conduct, specifically the provisions of its sexual harassment policy. Within the context of the criminal justice system, the accused was charged on two separate counts of sexual assault on two separate complainants.

The accused and the complainants were all white undergraduate students at York University. Each of the women, on two separate nights three days apart, had been socializing with the defendant and had invited him to her dormitory room on the university campus. Thus, in Estrich's terms, these are cases of 'simple rape' as the complainants were (allegedly) assaulted by an acquaintance and not an armed stranger. Moreover, that the complainants and accused were both white meant that the legal system's demonization of men of colour in attacks against white women (MacKinnon 1987, Marcus 1992) did not enter into these cases. The first complainant, whose pseudonym is Connie, was a casual acquaintance of the accused. Both were volunteers at a centre for autistic children. Prior to the night of the alleged sexual assault, Matt, the pseudonym I use to refer to the accused, had occasion to help Connie with some personal problems relating to an abusive ex-boyfriend. On the night of the alleged assault, Connie and Matt met for dinner at approximately 10.30 in the evening. After an enjoyable dinner, according to the complainant's testimony, Connie invited Matt back to her room in university residence. At that point, he briefly massaged her and they then engaged in some consensual kissing. From that point on, Connie reported in her testimony that she objected to his further sexual advances; in spite of her objections, Matt allegedly persisted in unwanted sexual aggression. His acts of unwanted sexual aggression, according to Connie's testimony, included: removing her clothes, putting his fingers inside her vagina, putting his penis between her legs and rubbing it against her, and pushing her face onto his lap so that she was forced to perform fellatio on him until orgasm. In both the university tribunal and the criminal trial, these facts were not at issue. What was at issue was whether or not the sexual acts were consensual.

The second case involved the complainant whose pseudonym is Marg. Matt and Marg had met for the first time the night before the alleged sexual assault. On the night of the sexual assault, Marg was socializing with her friend Melinda (a pseudonym) at a downtown Toronto club. Marg's car was towed away during the period of time Marg and Melinda were at the club and, as a result, they sought help from Matt and his friend, Bob (a pseudonym for Melinda's boyfriend). Given the lateness of the hour (3 or 4 o'clock in the morning), it was decided that the four would spend the night in Marg's university residence room and that Matt would help Marg retrieve her car the next morning. After deciding that the men would massage the women (and vice versa), Marg agreed that Matt could sleep in her bed, but warned him on a number of occasions that if he crossed the line 'he was dead'. That is, in this case, the complainant did not admit to any consensual sexual activity as the first complainant did. Once in bed, according to the complainant's testimony, Matt initiated a number of unwanted sexual advances: he began to go under her clothes and touched her breasts and vagina. On a number of occasions, as a result of the unwanted sexual aggression, Marg asked Melinda, who was in the other bed with Bob, to join her in the washroom. In attempts to solicit help from Melinda, Marg recounted the details of Matt's sexual aggression on a number of occasions. On one of Marg's and Melinda's visits to the washroom, Melinda overheard Matt telling Bob that Marg was the third woman in three nights that he had been with. In spite of Marg's attempts to solicit help from Melinda, and by association, Bob, Matt continued to initiate unwanted acts of aggression, according to Marg's testimony. These included: putting his foot between her legs and inserting his toe in her vagina, unbuttoning her shirt, sucking on her breasts and putting his fingers in her vagina. As in the first case, in both the tribunal and the criminal trial, the occurrence of these particular sexual acts was not at issue; what was at issue was whether or not they were consensual.

In both the university tribunal members' decision and the judge's decision, mention was made of the similarity in the accused's behaviour with respect to the two complainants: 'in each instance, he showed a remarkable similarity of approach, in suggesting massage and progressing from there to kissing and fondling and indicating to the complainants that they owed him satisfaction to the point of one way or the other emission of semen . . . because he had done them favours. In the one instance, for being taken out to dinner, and in the other instance, for efforts to locate a car' (*Reasons for Judgement in Her Majesty the Queen and M.A.*).

The York University disciplinary tribunal

York University disciplinary tribunals operate outside of the provincial or federal legal system. Members of the university community can be tried for various kinds of misconduct, including unauthorized entry or access, theft or destruction of property, assault or threat of assault and harassment, and discrimination that contravenes the provincial Human Rights Code or the Canadian Charter of Rights and Freedoms. Each case is heard by three tribunal members who are drawn from a larger pool consisting of university faculty members and students. The tribunal members decide upon the guilt or innocence of defendants and on penalties. Penalties range from public admonition to expulsion from the university. Normally, these tribunals are open to the public and are audio-taped. The tribunal members hearing this particular case consisted of a man who was a faculty member in the Law Faculty (the tribunal's chair), a woman who was a faculty member in the Faculty of Arts, and a woman graduate student in the Faculty of Arts. The case against the accused was presented by the university's legal counsel. The accused was at times represented by a family friend, at times by his mother, and at times represented himself.

While not technically a criminal court of law, the York University disciplinary tribunals function like one to the extent that each side, the prosecution and the defence, presents its version of the events at issue to the members of the disciplinary tribunal. In the case described here, the complainants, the accused and their witnesses testified under questioning by their own representatives and by the tribunal members. All participants were also cross-examined by representatives from the other side. Thus, unlike jury trials, the 'talk' of this disciplinary tribunal was not designed for an overhearing, *nonspeaking* audience – the jury (Atkinson and Drew 1979), but rather for members of the discipinary tribunal who themselves had the right to ask questions of the accused, complainants and witnesses. The testimonies of witnesses seemed to follow no strict order in this particular tribunal. For example, both complainants testified under questioning from the university lawyer, the tribunal members and the accused's representative(s) at the beginning of the hearing and then again at the end of the hearing.

As stated previously, within the context of the university tribunal the accused was alleged to have violated York University's Standards of Student Conduct, specifically the provisions of its sexual harassment policy. According to the regulations of York University, *sexual harassment* is defined as 'the unwanted attention of a sexually oriented nature made by a person who knows or ought reasonably to know that such attention is unwanted'. In determining whether the accused had violated the standards of student conduct deemed appropriate by the university, I am assuming that the university tribunal members were employing the standard of proof that other administrative tribunals in Canada (i.e., the normal standard in civil law) employ – that of 'balance of probabilities'. That is, according to a 'balance of probabilities', the tribunal members were to decide which of the parties was to be believed more.

The criminal trial

The accused was charged by the same plaintiffs under the Criminal Code of Canada on two counts of sexual assault. (The details of sexual assault law in Canada are described in a previous section of this chapter.) In this particular criminal trial, a judge determined the guilt or innocence of the accused and the accused's sentence. The complainants were witnesses for the province (i.e., the state), which is represented by a Crown attorney; the accused was represented by a defence lawyer. In the criminal trial, then, it was the prosecuting and defence lawyers who asked questions of the defendant, the complainants and witnesses in direct and cross-examination. Unlike the university tribunal, testimony and question-asking in criminal trials follow a prescribed order: the Crown first presents its case whereby its witnesses provide testimony under questioning (from the Crown) in direct examination and (from the defence lawyer) in cross-examination; the defence then presents its case whereby its witnesses provide testimony under questioning (from the defence lawyer) in direct examination and (from the Crown) in cross-examination. All criminal trials are conducted according to three foundational principles: (1) the accused is presumed innocent until proven guilty, (2) the Crown must prove 'beyond a reasonable doubt' that the accused committed the offence and (3) the accused has the right to silence. In this particular case, the accused testified. Moreover, both the Crown and the defence agreed that the sexual acts in question had occurred. Thus, the onus was on the Crown to prove 'beyond a reasonable doubt' that the complainants had not consented to the sexual acts in question.

Critical discourse analysis

In analysing the data described above, I have adopted an approach that falls within the domain of *critical discourse analysis*, as this term is broadly understood (e.g., Fairclough 1995, Fairclough and Wodak 1997, van Dijk 1993, 1997). Like feminist linguistic studies, particularly the type that unpacks and deconstructs the sexist and androcentric assumptions encoded in linguistic representations, work in critical discourse analysis does not merely describe language in a dispassionate and disinterested way. As Harvey and Shalom (1997: 6) remark, 'its advocates are often committed to exposing the [linguistic] mechanisms of hegemony in order to facilitate the access to a language of empowerment by marginalized groups.' That is, proponents of critical discourse analysis assume that dominant social structures and processes are partly discursive in their nature and aim to expose how such discursive practices contribute to the production and reproduction of unequal social relations. Indeed, this type of discourse analysis, some would argue, is a necessary prerequisite to social change, as the ideological perspectives that linguistic practices encode and support often go unnoticed and are not easily foregrounded by speakers predisposed to think about the world in particular ways. For example, Fairclough and Wodak (1997: 258) argue that 'the ideological loading of particular ways of using language and the relations of power which underlie them are often unclear to people.' By highlighting what Fairclough and Wodak term 'opaque aspects of discourse', work in critical discourse analysis has as its goal the demystification of dominant social practices and structures. Likewise, the feminist strategy I adopt in this book attempts to make transparent 'the opaque aspects' of a particular kind of institutional discourse. And, in exposing the gendered assumptions encoded in these kinds of discursive practices, my analysis disrupts their commonsensical and naturalized quality.

2 'My shirt came off . . . I gather that I took it off'
The accused's grammar of non-agency[1]

Introduction

Of increasing interest in sociolinguistics, linguistic anthropology and socially-oriented studies of discourse is the role of language in constructing and constituting social realities. Beginning from the assumption that language is not a neutral and transparent reflection of the world, work within a variety of traditions (e.g., ethnography of communication, interactional sociolinguistics, critical discourse analysis, discursive psychology) has delineated the constitutive effects of linguistic forms. Duranti (1997: 214), for example, asserts that when speakers use language, they help constitute the reality they are trying to represent: 'not only do certain expressions require an understanding of the surrounding world for their interpretation, they also actively shape the surrounding world.' Likewise, Hutchby and Wooffitt remark that in the very process of using language to designate and describe states of affairs in the world, speakers are actively 'building the character' of those states (Hutchby and Wooffitt 1998: 228). To say that linguistic forms are constitutive elements of social realities is not to say that there is no reality beyond language; rather, the claim is that our experience of reality is *mediated* by language and the particular perspectives that it entails. Cameron (1992), for example, points to the androcentric nature of terms such as *penetration*, *fuck*, *screw*, *lay*, all of which turn heterosexual sex into something men do to women. Indeed, from a female perspective, penetration would be more appropriately encoded as *enclosure, surrounding*, or *engulfing*. What becomes clear from 'names' such as these is the extent to which language functions as an ideological filter on the world: language shapes or constructs our notions of reality rather than labelling that reality in any transparent and straightforward way.

Within the context of adjudication processes, language is the primary means by which witnesses (and lawyers and adjudicators) convey information about the events that are the subject of a court's or tribunal's deliberations. Hale and Gibbons (1999: 203) distinguish between 'two intersecting planes of reality' in the courtroom: the reality of the courtroom itself – what they call the 'courtroom reality' – and the reality that comprises the events under investigation in the courtroom – what they call 'the external reality'. In the court's representation of this 'external reality', visual images (e.g., photographs, diagrams) and physical entities (e.g., weapons, clothing) are often introduced as evidence, but Hale and Gibbons (1999: 203) remark that 'by far the most common representation of this other reality [the external reality] is . . . through testimonial evidence which consists of descriptions of the events by witnesses – *versions of the second reality presented through language*' (emphasis mine). With respect to legal cases involving sexual abuse, sexual harassment and/or sexual assault, linguistic descriptions are often the *only* basis upon which juries, judges or adjudicators determine a verdict (Capps and Ochs 1995), as the events under examination are typically without corroboration and/or physical evidence. Dramatically different accounts of what happened can emerge in the talk of sexual assault trials, for example, and on the basis of such potentially contradictory narratives, judges and juries must determine what Capps and Ochs (1995: 21) call an official story: 'on the basis of divergent versions of events, jury members [and adjudicators] construct a narrative that is plausible and coherent in their eyes, but the truth is beyond their reach. In this sense rendering a verdict is analogous not to ascertaining the facts of a case but to determining an official story.' Given the centrality of language in adjudication processes generally, and sexual assault and harassment cases specifically, the testimonies of witnesses in these contexts do not simply reflect a defence of innocence or an accusation of guilt. Rather, through their linguistic descriptions, witnesses (and lawyers) are actively involved in constructing and constituting the 'facts' of cases. Duranti eloquently articulates this position:

> Reality is routinely negotiated by participants in an interaction and 'facts' are constituted differently according to the points of view of the actors involved, the norms evoked, and the processes activated within specific institutional settings (e.g., legal, medical, educational). This view does not imply that there is no reality outside of talk or that all interpretations are equally acceptable, but rather it holds that in institutional as well as in mundane settings various versions of reality are proposed, sustained or challenged precisely by the language that describes or sustains them and that such negotiations are not irrelevant linguistic games but potentially important social acts.
>
> (Duranti 1994: 4–5)

That the lexical items designating objects and events in a trial can constitute 'potentially important social acts' is convincingly demonstrated by Danet (1980) in her analysis of a Massachusetts trial in which a Boston obstetrician-gynaecologist was charged with manslaughter for performing a late abortion. Focusing on the ways that the prosecution and the defence named and categorized the aborted entity, Danet illuminates the ideological and strategic significance of such choices: the prosecution consistently used terms such as 'baby', 'child' and 'little baby boy' whereas the defence used terms such as 'fetus' and 'products of conception'. In other words, the 'war of words' waged in this trial invoked and reproduced more general cultural debates about the 'living' status of aborted entities. After all, intrinsic to legal definitions of manslaughter, and arguably a conviction, is the concept of 'killing' which presupposes the prior existence of a 'life'. Danet comments on the significance of linguistic choices in light of the ambiguous status of the objects and acts (e.g., aborted entity, late abortion) under scrutiny in the manslaughter trial:

> One *cannot* separate what happened from the language that is used to describe or explain what happened. When the meaning of an act is ambiguous, the words we choose to talk about it become critical. (emphasis in original)
>
> (Danet 1980: 189)

The ambiguity that Danet associates with a late abortion within the context of a manslaughter trial, I would suggest, also characterizes the instances of acquaintance rape that are the subject of deliberations in the university tribunal and criminal trial analysed here. Neither conforms to Estrich's category of 'real rape': neither was performed by a stranger; neither involved a weapon; neither exhibited evidence of physical violence; and in one of the cases the complainant acknowledged that there was a certain amount of consensual intimate contact. As argued in Chapter 1, instances of 'simple rape' are, at worst, discounted and rendered invisible by the criminal justice system and the mainstream culture more generally, and, at best, display an equivocal and borderline status as rape. For Danet, the ambiguous nature of acts invests the language used to describe them with 'critical' import. Even more than in cases of 'real rape', then, the language denoting the 'simple rapes' in the sexual assault adjudication processes analysed here will, in Hutchby and Wooffitt's terms, 'build their character'.

In this chapter, I focus on the way the defendant constitutes and constructs the events under investigation through what I am calling a grammar of non-agency (cf. O'Connor 1995). Put somewhat differently, I am interested in how the defendant draws upon a variety of linguistic resources that all work to represent him as innocent of unlawful sexual acts of aggression. Given the potential importance of language in shaping social realities – especially in this type of case where linguistic descriptions are the *only* form of evidence – this chapter also considers the extent to which the defendant's linguistic construction of the 'facts' is afforded legitimacy and authority in the contexts where this case is tried. That is, in Capps' and Ochs' terms, to what extent does this particular characterization of events become the 'official story'?

Grammatical choices as social acts

Following Duranti (1994), I assume that the grammatical choices social actors make in these kinds of settings, like the lexical choices, not only construct a particular perspective on events, but are 'potentially important social acts'. In order to understand the social significance of such choices, it is important to recognize the range of linguistic alternatives available to speakers in describing a particular event. Consider the following four sentences. Each of them presents a somewhat different perspective on the same series of events – a difference that is related to the events' participant structure.

1   In the U.S. a man rapes a woman every 6 minutes.
2   In the U.S. a woman is raped by a man every 6 minutes.
3   In the U.S. a woman is raped every 6 minutes.
4   In the U.S. a woman's rape occurs every 6 minutes.

                                          (adapted from Henley *et al.* (1995))

Example 1 presents *a man* as directly involved and initiating the event; example 2 (relative to 1) shifts attention away from *a man* and onto *a woman*; and examples 3 and 4 eliminate *a man* from the representation of the event altogether. Put another way, these sentences ascribe different degrees of agency to the noun phrase, *a man*. Adopting a definition of *agent* from Duranti (1994: 125) as in 5 (below), we can say that sentence 1 (in active voice) attributes a highly agentive positioning to *a man*, as this noun phrase is the grammatical subject of the transitive verb *rape*, indicating that a man's performing of this act has consequences for the animate patient, *a woman*. Sentence 2, encoded in passive as opposed to active voice, diminishes the agentive positioning of a *man* somewhat, given its reordering of agent (i.e., *a man*) and patient (i.e., *a woman*) and the concomitant result that the agent is no longer the grammatical subject of the transitive verb, *rape*. Sentence 3 is an *agentless* passive and thus removes the agent from the representation of the event. In sentence 4 the verb *rape* is nominalized (i.e., transformed into a noun), also allowing for deletion of the agent.

5   Agent: Wilful initiator of an event that is depicted as having consequences for either an object or animate patient.

In sum, quite different depictions of men's and women's involvement in rape emerge in examples 1–4 as a result of the different syntactic encodings of the event – from representations where a man performs a purposeful act of sexual aggression that has direct consequences for a woman (as in example 1) to those that transform the action into a static occurrence with no overt cause (as in example 4). Indeed, critical discourse analysts interested in the relationship between language and ideology have often pointed to the variation in agentive positionings created by different syntactic forms as ideologically significant.

(See, for example, Sykes 1988, van Dijk 1988). Representative of this work is Trew's (1979) analysis of two British newspapers' reporting of police violence in the former Rhodesia. Arguing that the political ideologies of news media have linguistic reflexes, Trew identified a number of linguistic differences between the *Guardian*'s and *The Times'* coverage of the event, one of which involved the obscuring and elimination of agency. While the *Guardian* began its report with two active sentences – '*Police Shoot 11 Dead in Salisbury Riot; Riot police shot and killed 11 African demonstrators and wounded 15 others here today*', *The Times* began with two passive sentences, the second of which was agentless –'*Rioting Blacks Shot Dead By Police as ANC Leaders Meet; Eleven Africans were shot dead and 15 wounded when Rhodesian police opened fire on a rioting crowd of 2,000.*' According to Trew, the use of passive voice in this context shifted attention away from the agent of the killings, *the police*, and onto the patients or affected participants, *the rioting blacks* and *eleven blacks*. This is one of several linguistic moves that characterized *The Times'* reporting over the course of several days and ultimately functioned to obscure the police's role in the killings, substituting *the rioting blacks* and the *factionalism of the ANC* as the responsible parties. And, attributing violence to the factionalism and tribalism of blacks, Trew argued, was part of a more widespread ideological perspective used by the dominant white elite in Rhodesia to justify white rule in Africa.

While analysts such as Trew do not provide empirical support for the interpretations they ascribe to particular linguistic forms, there is psycholinguistic research that does. LaFrance and Hahn (1994), for example, found that active and passive voice affected the interpretation of statements; specifically, they found that their subjects tended to attribute greater *causality* to patients, as opposed to agents, when interpreting sentences represented in passive voice.[2] Likewise, Henley *et al.* (1995) found that when reports of violence against women were represented in passive voice as opposed to active voice, male subjects imputed less harm to the victim (i.e., the patient) and less responsibility to the perpetrator (i.e., the agent).[3] That is, the diminished linguistic agency associated with agents in the passive voice relative to the active voice seems to have consequences for the way subjects understand their responsibility – it is diminished. Moreover, patients are imputed with greater agent-like characteristics (e.g., have more responsibility for events) when they appear as the grammatical subjects of passive sentences. The psycholinguistic evidence, then, while not robust, supports the claims of critical discourse analysts such as Trew (among others) regarding the effects of passive vs. active sentences on interpretations of agency and responsibility. Trew's claim, for example, that *The Times'* reporting of police violence in the passive voice functioned to diminish the agency of the police is borne out by the studies conducted by LaFrance and Hahn (1994) and Henley *et al.* (1995). More generally, such evidence is further suggestive of the significance of linguistic forms in constructing and constituting social realities.

A grammar of non-agency

Previous work on the linguistic reflexes of agency and responsibility in English oral discourse (for example, O'Connor 1995, Rymes 1995) has not generally explored the phenomena within legal (and extra-legal) adjudication processes where ascriptions of responsibility and agency are, arguably, of greater consequence.[4] Like this chapter, however, Rymes' and O'Connor's work has investigated the linguistic diminishing of personal agency in speakers' accounts of their violent and/or criminal acts. Rymes (1995: 511), for example, focuses on the grammatical and prosodic mitigation of personal agency in the narratives of high school drop-outs, arguing that such mitigation functions to lessen the moral reprehensibility of the speakers' violent acts and 'displays their orientation to the good'. O'Connor (1995) also investigates the way linguistic forms can reduce personal agency. Highlighting the rehabilitative potential of discourse analysis, O'Connor focuses on epistemic statements such as 'I don't know why I shot him' or 'I don't know what made me do it' in prisoners' autobiographical narratives of their criminal acts. These statements 'problematize' the prisoners' agency in relation to these criminal acts and, according to O'Connor, provide an opening for rehabilitative thinking and talk. One of the features differentiating Rymes' and O'Connor's research from my own is the discourse genre analysed: Rymes and O'Connor draw their data from oral narratives of personal experience elicited by open-ended interview questions. By contrast, the discourse of adjudication processes is characterized by a strict, institutionally-sanctioned question–answer format in which witnesses' responses are controlled in a variety of ways by questioners. The two kinds of discourse genres do not only differ in terms of their formal properties, however; the function of adjudication processes in determining the guilt or innocence of accuseds and in assigning sanctions for guilty verdicts may produce in defendants more extreme expressions of non-agency than was evident in the narratives of Rymes' and O'Connor's speakers. Thus, both the formal properties of this discourse along with its functional character have implications for the particular kinds of linguistic expressions of agency and responsibility that emerge in these contexts.

At stake in the legal adjudication processes analysed here was the responsibility or agency of the defendant in performing *non-consensual* acts of sexual aggression. Thus, the strategy of the defendant and his representatives was not to deny the occurrence of consensual 'sexual activity', but rather to mitigate, diffuse, obscure, and/or eliminate Matt's agency in the initiation of sexual acts of aggression that could be construed as non-consensual. By contrast, when recounting the events that precipitated their charges of sexual assault, Marg and Connie (the pseudonyms I use to designate the two complainants) designated Matt (the pseudonym I use to designate the defendant) as the agent of non-consensual sexually violent acts. In examples 6–10, which come from Marg and Connie's direct testimonies in both the university tribunal (UT) and the criminal trial (CT), Matt is accorded a highly agentive positioning with respect to sexual acts of aggression: he is the grammatical subject of transitive verbs that designate acts that are wilful and intentional (e.g., *pin down*, *take off*, *roll over*) and that have consequences for their grammatical objects – usually the complainants, their body parts, or Matt's body parts, which, in turn, have consequences for the complainants.

6 MB: And *he took my shoulder and rolled me back over* and then *he started kissing me* . . . and then at the same time *he started to go down my pants* . . . and then *he started putting his fingers inside of my vagina.* (CT)

7 CD: I mean, I can tell you that early on *he took my shirt off* and I can tell you when *he unclasped my bra* and I can tell you that *he pulled my pants down* right after I tried to explain to him why I didn't want him to do that, and *he eased me back down on the bed* and *he pinned my arms against the bed* and that's when *he pulled my pants down.* (CT)

8 CD: He grabbed my hair from the back of my neck and sort of wrapped it around his hand and pushed me down in between his legs and told me that I could put it in my mouth or he would put it in. (CT)

9 MB: And while he was talking to me eh . . . *he pushed my one leg down off the window sill* and *he put* . . . *his foot in between my legs* and *he kept trying to put his toes through my track pants* . . . *into my vagina.* (UT)

10 CD: And uhm (long pause) then he (long pause) hc *he put his* . . . *his* . . . *penis between my legs* and *he was rubbing it there* and saying 'well this is what teasing is.' *He took my head and* . . . *he put it between his legs* . . . and uhm (long pause) *he was holding my hair.* Uhm and then (long pause) then I stopped and *he pulled me back up and kissed me again* a::nd then he he made me do it again . . . and then I stopped again . . . and *he pulled my head back up and kissed me again* and then *put me back and told me not to stop this time.* (long pause) I didn't. (UT)

When confronted by the university lawyer (in the tribunal) with the complainants' version of events – formulations much like those illustrated in 6 to 10 – Matt sometimes overtly denied the truth of such propositions, as in 11 to 13.

11 HL: Now then she says . . . then he grabbed my arm and squeezed it really tight and he made me promise not to tell anyone.
    MA: That is totally utterly false. (UT)

12 HL: Okay. Now . . . she says that you grabbed her wrists and pinned her down on the bed. I gather =
    MA: = That is totally false. (UT)

13 HL: Now . . . she says he kept me pinned down on the bed. I kept struggling to get up and he kept laughing at me.
    MA: Yeah that is totally false. (UT)

Far more frequent in Matt's testimony, however, were subtle and insidious linguistic expressions of mitigated and obscured agency – linguistic expressions that together comprise what I am calling Matt's grammar of non-agency. Indeed, in contrast to the representations of Matt in 6 to 10, in Matt's own version of these events he rarely cast himself in a highly agentive role. Rather, he consistently de-emphasized his agentive role by (1) mitigating his agency when casting himself as the subject of transitive verbs designating acts of aggression, (2) diffusing his agency by referring to the complainants as the agents of sexually-initiating events or referring to himself as a co-agent along with one of the complainants and (3) obscuring and eliminating his agency through grammatical constructions that concealed his responsibility in sexually-initiating sexual acts.[5]

Mitigating agency

While Matt did not generally narrate himself as the subject of transitive verbs designating sexual acts of aggression (i.e., positioning himself in a highly agentive role), when he did, as in the italicized sentences of 14 and 15 (both from cross-examination), the expressions he used either mitigated the force of his agency or the negative nature of his agentive acts.[6] In example 14, for instance, Matt employs adverbials (e.g., *perhaps*) and modal verbs (e.g., *might*) which together cast doubt on the cross-examining lawyer's implicit assertion – that Matt set the stage for the sexual acts of aggression with both complainants by saying he was hot and removing his shirt. Moreover, the sequence ends with Matt asserting that he cannot remember. According to Drew (1992: 481), in the context of courtroom discourse, a sequential object such as *I can't remember* 'not only avoids confirming what is proposed in the question, but also avoids disconfirming it: that is, the witness thereby avoids directly challenging or disputing a version proposed by the attorney, but nevertheless neutralizes that version.' Hence, the highlighted linguistic expressions of 14 'neutralize' OD's version of the events, thereby mitigating the force of Matt's agency in setting the stage for non-consensual acts of sexual aggression.

14 OD: Did you make some exclamation basically that you were hot and took off your shirt?

MA: *I perhaps might have.*

OD: Do you remember doing the same thing with Miss B., getting hot and taking off some of your clothes?

MA: She took off her sweater so that I could give her a massage.

OD: Do you remember indicating you are hot and taking off any of your clothes?

MA: *I perhaps might have taken my shirt off* because I was hot or because of the massage. *I can't remember.* (CT)

The italicized sentence of 15 shows Matt in a highly agentive positioning: he is the grammatical subject of a transitive verb designating a sexual or intimate act. Yet, Matt's characterization of this act differs substantially from the characterization HL imputes to Connie, that is, *you grabbed her by her hair*. Using the language of love (i.e., *caressing*) rather than the language of violence (i.e., *grabbed, entwined*), Matt mitigates the negative (i.e., violent) nature of this act, constructing himself as an agent of loving and consensual sex.

15   HL: Now . . . she said . . . that you grabbed her by her hair and pulled her face up to yours. Did that happen?

MA: No after uhm she performed oral sex, she voluntarily came up and started kissing me.

HL: Okay she says that during this oral sex you have your hand entwined in her hair? Do you recall that?

MA: *Yeah I was caressing her hair.*

HL: She says you pushed her back down a couple of times.

MA: No. She performed oral sex for twenty minutes and then I ejaculated and that was it.

HL: Okay she said you rolled over and went to sleep, holding her by the hair.

MA: I believe I also said that in my oral testimony that after that we laid down together. There might have been some kissing and whatever and then we fell asleep.

HL: Okay.

MA: And that was it as far as any sexual activity that evening. (UT)

Diffusing agency

Representing the events in question as consensual and reciprocal took still other linguistic forms in Matt's testimony. Consider example 16 where Matt is being questioned by his lawyer (SC) in the criminal trial about events that occurred with Marg. These are the same events described by Marg in 6; in Matt's version, example 16, *she* is responsible for removing her clothes.

16   SC: How is it that she became naked, to your recollection?

MA: She took off her shirt and she pulled down her track pants when I was touching her vagina. (CT)

Example 17 shows Matt and Marg represented as co-agents of the sexually-initiating acts, i.e., getting back into bed and starting to fool around.

17   SC: Can you tell us from that point forward what takes place between you and Marg?

MA: Well, *I went back into bed and then Marg came back into bed and we started to fool around again.* (CT)

Particularly noteworthy in this regard are question/answer sequences between Matt and the prosecuting lawyers in both the criminal trial and the university tribunal that reveal Matt's attempts to diffuse responsibility for initiating acts. In 18 to 20, Matt transforms the utterances of OD and HL from assertions where Matt alone is responsible for the sexual aggression into ones where Matt and the complainant together are the co-agents.[7]

18 OD: Do you remember her saying to you that she was tired and wanted to go to sleep?
   MA: Yes.
   OD: And you didn't let her – well, *you proceeded to touch her anyway*, isn't that correct?
   MA: No, *we started kissing.* (CT)
19 HL: Okay. Now I gather that you did give her a massage and after a couple of minutes *you laid down beside her and kissed her.*
   MA: Well, from what I recall we just laid there for about five minutes and then uh *we started kissing.* (UT)
20 OD: Okay. Despite her clear indications to you, *you then started kissing her and easing her down on the bed and feeling her chest.* Do you remember that?
   MA: I remember that after we had that discussion *that we started to fool around again.* (CT)

In example 18, the alternative version of events is prefaced by what Drew (1992: 487) calls 'an overt correction marker' *no*. That is, before Matt provides an alternative to OD's characterization of the events, he explicitly rejects her version with the overt negative marker *no*. Matt's response in 19 is similarly prefaced by the discourse marker, *well*. While not explicitly denying the content of HL's question, Matt's use of *well* functions to signal a certain disjunction between his response and the original question. Indeed, research on disagreements in ordinary conversation has shown that they differ from agreements in a number of ways (one of which involves discourse markers such as *well*):

> One important respect in which it has been shown that disagreements differ from agreements is that disagreements, unlike agreements, are generally delayed. Such delays may be sequential, as when a speaker who disagrees with something their co-participant has just said does not start speaking at the earliest opportunity after the turn in which the disagreed-with assertion was made, resulting in pausing before disagreeing . . . . Furthermore, disagreements may also be delayed within the design of the turn in which they occur, by being preceded by such

components as agreement prefaces, and by such brief components as *uh* and *well*.

(Drew 1992: 502–3)

In example 20, unlike 18 and 19, Matt does not preface his alternative characterization of events with either an overt correction marker or a contrastive discourse marker; rather, as Drew (1992) points out, in such examples the witness challenges or disputes the lawyer's claims in a more indirect way.

Example 21 shows the transformation seen in 18 to 20 taking place over a number of turns. After overtly denying the truth of OD's proposition twice – that Matt started kissing the complainant – Matt then supplies a different version of events: *we both came and kissed each other mutually*. Not only do we see the same alternation between singular *you* in the prosecuting lawyer's question (i.e., *you started kissing her?*) and *we* in Matt's response (i.e., *we . . . kissed each other*), as in 18 to 20, we also see Matt being very explicit about the mutual nature of the sexual activity in example 21.

21 OD: Okay. *You're the one who started to kiss her first*; is that correct?
    MA: That's incorrect.
    OD: You started kissing her?
    MA: That's incorrect.
    OD: Who started kissing who?
    MA: As I was saying, we were lying in the bed and before coming in, she was lying – and I lied next to her and we laid there for about two minutes and the *we both came and kissed each other mutually*. (CT)

Matt's attempts to diffuse his responsibility for the events under investigation extended beyond sexual events to seemingly innocuous non-sexual ones. In example 22, for instance, Matt performs a great deal of conversational work to represent his dinner with Connie as a mutual endeavour. Asking initially whether Matt is the initiator (i.e., agent) of their contact that night (i.e., *you decided to call Connie?*), HL receives a response from Matt which casts Connie as the agent of the activities (i.e., *Connie asked me if I could call her that evening*). (Notice that this response is not prefaced by either an overt correction marker nor a contrastive discourse marker and thus *indirectly* challenges HL's characterization of events.) Repeating this formulation a couple more times, HL is met with responses from Matt that highlight the mutual nature of their decision to have dinner (i.e., *Well it was a mutual thing and it wasn't me merely asking her*). Finally, over the course of several turns, HL's initial utterance in which Matt is the agent of the activity is transformed into one where the agency for getting together is distributed over both Connie and Matt (i.e., *Well, we agreed to get together to get something to eat*).

22   HL: And at around ten thirty you decided to call Connie?
     MA: Yeah Connie asked me if I could call her that evening.

HL: You you said that you called and asked if she wanted to have a cup of coffee [or something]

MA: [Well it was a] mutual thing =

HL: = Yeah =

MA: = I didn't . . . it wasn't me merely asking her if she =

HL: = Well, I gather she said she'd like to do more that have a cup of coffee. She'd like to get some[thing to eat.]

MA: [She said she was hungry] yes =

HL: = Right okay but is there a big dispute that you heh heh suggested that you get together for coffee?

MA: Well, we agreed to get together to get something to eat. (UT)

Obscuring agency: agentless passives

Still other linguistic constructions conceal or obscure Matt's agency in the initiation of sexual events even further. In examples 23 to 28, Matt employs agentless passives to represent situations in which he is the agent, according to the complainants' testimony, responsible for undoing, unbuttoning, taking off, pushing down the complainants' and his own clothes. Recall that the grammatical process of passivization in English brings the patient or affected participant to the position of grammatical subject; furthermore, an agentless passive involves deletion of the agent, thereby providing no overt information as to the cause of the act designated by the predicate. Some of the italicized examples in 23 to 28 could be considered to be adjectival passives rather than verbal passives (e.g., *were undone* as opposed to *was taken off*) describing states rather than processes, but the effect is the same – to de-emphasize, conceal and/or obscure the actor responsible for these acts.

23 MA: Well, as we were talking *our pants were undone*. (CT)

24 MA: At that point we laid back down on the bed again and, as before, *our pants were unbuttoned* and we began touching each other. (CT)

25 SC: Are her pants still on at this point?
   MA: I think they were not totally off but *they were pushed down* such that I was able to move freely. (CT)

26 MA: I think when I was giving her a massage she had, like, three pieces of clothing on her upper body or two *and one of them was taken off*. (CT)

27 MA: At one point *both of our pants were undone*. I cannot recall if I undid her pants or if she undid my pants. (UT)

28 MA: And as Connie said, you know, *all our clothes at one point were taken off* and we were fooling around. (UT)

In order to contextualize Matt's use of agentless passives, I provide example 29 below which contains the passive already exemplified in 27. In this question–answer sequence, HL reports a couple of times on the complainant's assertion that *Matt* removed *her* pants: *because she says that during this time you were starting to take her pants off* and *she says you pulled her pants off*. Responding to these assertions in which he is the agent of sexual acts of aggression, Matt depicts a scene of consensual sex – a flurry of sexual activity during which it was unclear who removed whose clothes. Set against the background information provided by Matt's passive sentence containing no overt agent, *both of our pants were undone*, this uncertainty about agency and Matt's concomitant construction of consensual sex is made possible.

29 HL: Because she says that during this time you were starting to take her pants off. Is that right?
MA: I believe at one point that . . . well I don't think actually I think in the evening I think she took her pants off.
HL: Okay, what pieces of clothing did you remove of hers?
MA: I think I helped her with her shirt . . . uhm I tried to undo her bra and then she helped me. She took her bra off. Uhm at one point *both of our pants were undone*. I cannot recall if **I** undid **her** pants, or if **she** undid **my** pants.
HL: Okay. She says you pulled her pants off. You don't remember who pulled her pants off?
MA: I'm I don't I mean she might have taken her pants off herself. I might have taken her pants off. She might have taken my pants off. I might have taken my pants off. I don't know. (UT)

Also frequent in Matt's testimony is the occurrence of agentless passives that obscure his role in decision-making processes. From examples 30 to 32, for instance, it is unclear who decided that Matt and Bob would stay overnight in Marg's room; from 33, it is unclear who determined that Matt would stay after he had threatened to leave; and from 34 and 35, it is unclear who determined that Matt and Bob would massage Marg and Melinda and vice versa. All of the agentless passives in examples 30 to 35 have as their subjects the expletive element *it*, an element which has no semantic content; however, the extraposed clauses (e.g., *that the girls would massage u*s) provide the semantic content for these expletive elements. Given that all of the acts represented in these extraposed clauses, for example, mutual massages, could be construed as 'setting the stage' for Matt's unwanted sexual aggression, Matt's use of agentless passives (e.g., *it was decided*), which obscure his role in initiating these acts, is consistent with his overall strategy of representing himself as a non-agent.

30 MA: Well once once their friend had left the room and . . . *it was established* that we were going to stay there. (UT)
31 MA: Then *it was decided* . . . that it would be easier if we all just stayed there overnight. (CT)
32 MA: Well, *it was understood* at the restaurant that we would be staying overnight at Glendon. (CT)

33 MA: I think it was prior to that that when *it was agreed* after I had the
conversation with Bob uhm that *it was agreed* that I was going to stay.
(UT)

34 MA: I got into bed uhm and I think *it was agreed* that they wanted to give
. . . they wanted us to give them a massage first. So we started massaging
them uhm . . . So we were massaging them and it must and well *it was
agreed* like after we massaged them that they were going to give us a
massage. (UT)

35 HL: Then you asked her to give *you* a massage. Is that right?
MA: Well *it was agreed* earlier that the girls would massage us . . . I'm
sorry that *we* would massage them and that the girls afterward would massage us. (UT)

As a grammatical strategy to obscure and conceal responsibility for acts of
sexual initiation and aggression, Matt's use of agentless passives is sometimes
challenged by the prosecuting lawyers. Very striking is example 36 below
which comes from the university tribunal. Here the university lawyer HL
is questioning Matt about something that had arisen earlier in the hearing
– that he had described Connie as a *total bitch*. Through her questioning,
she highlights Matt's use of agentless passives by interrogating him as to
who the agent of *said* was. And, not surprisingly, it is Matt's agency that
has been concealed by the agentless passive, *those words were said*.

36 HL: Would you use the word 'total bitch'?
MA: Total bitch?
HL: Yeah. 'She could be a total bitch at work.'
MA: I believe that at one point I ((laughing)) it might have been at one
point . . . uhm . . . that *those words were said.*
HL: By you?
MA: Pardon me?
HL: You said them.
MA: Yes. (UT)

Eliminating agency: unaccusative constructions

In addition to employing agentless passives to represent his sexual acts of
verbal and physical aggression, Matt also used unaccusative constructions.
I am using the term *unaccusative constructions* here to refer to intransitive
verbs which take as their grammatical subjects non-agents or non-causers
of the actions or processes designated by the intransitive verbs (Haegeman
and Gueron 1999).[8] Consider the following two sentences, which display
the difference between an agentless passage, as in 37a, and an unaccusative
construction, as in 37b.

37 a. The glass was broken.
    b. The glass broke.

The patient or entity acted upon is the grammatical subject in both sentences; in 37b, however, there is no implicit agent. Thus, while agentless passives suggest that an agent is lurking in the background, unaccusative constructions completely eliminate the agent from the representation of the event. Consequently, the causal relationship implicit in agentless passives – that an agent wilfully affected a patient in some way – is absent in unaccusative constructions altogether. Rather, as Toolan (1991: 234) says of these kinds of syntactic forms: 'the affected participant [patient] formerly in object position is now the sole stated participant, occupying subject position, and the former description of a causal relation, what x did to y, is now simply a report of what happened to y, or even, what y "does".' Not only does a sentence containing an unaccusative construction, then, eliminate all reference to the underlying cause of the event designated by the verb, according to Toolan, it can also represent its grammatical subject (i.e., patient or affected participant) as 'doing' something or 'acting' in some sense.

In the italicized sentences of examples 39 to 44, nominalizations representing sexual acts and activities (e.g., *the sexual activity, something sexual, the intimacy*) are the grammatical subjects of unaccusative verbs such as *start*, *begin*, and *go on*. Recall that a nominalization refers to a noun that has been transformed from a verb allowing deletion of the agent, as in the italicized expressions of 38, also from Matt's testimony.

38 MA: Up to this point there wasn't any really major major *sexual activity*, like there wasn't any oral sex. There wasn't any uhm *stimulation* or anything.

Represented as nominalizations, then, the grammatical subjects designating sexual acts in 39 to 44 have no agents. Moreover, as the subjects of unaccusative verbs, they depict their referents as spontaneous sexual events, as happenings that have taken their natural course without any particular cause or agent. Indeed, Talmy (1985), in his taxonomy of verb roots and the different types of causative meanings incorporated into them, calls these unaccusative constructions *autonomous* because they present an event in and of itself without implying that there is a cause.

39 SC: All right. What happens next, please?
    MA: *The sexual activity started escalating even further.* (CT)
40 MA: Well, he knew that *something sexual was going on* in my bed – well, in Marg's bed. He knew there was *something sexual going on*. (CT)
41 MA: So when we got back from the washroom uh Connie was laying down on the bed. . . . I laid down next to her and uhm *the intimacy began* . . . shortly after. (UT)

42 MA: I believe I was nude at that time, I might have had my underwear on I'm not sure. And she was going underneath my underwear. It was just – it was a really – there was *a lot of sexual activity going on* but there was no sexual intercourse. (UT)

43 MA: Well, at the point where I tried to undo her belt and she sat up and said 'I don't think we should be doing this', she expressed to me that her concern – she had no concerns in terms of, you know, *the sexual involvement that was going on*. Her concern was that, you know, 'I know we are involved and we are fooling around here, but I think we have to stop for a second and consider our professional relationship.' (CT)

44 MA: After we had fooled around and she sat up and had reservations because she had told me I believe that she was concerned that I wouldn't speak to her the next day or whatever. It wasn't so much that she was concerned with *the sexual activity that was going on*, it was more in terms of how we were going to deal with each other in the future.

Similar to the italicized sentences of 39 to 44 above are those of 45 to 50 below. What differentiates the two sets of sentences is the nature of their subjects: in 39 to 44, full noun phrases (i.e., nominalizations) assume subject position while in 45 to 50, pronominal elements referring to the sexual activity under discussion do.

45 MA: We were kissing and we I think we did it for you know quite some time not an exorbitant amount of time and then . . . *it started getting more involved and more sexual*. (UT)

46 MA: So at that point what happened . . . we started fooling around uhm she started to feel my genitalia I started to feel hers. Uhm at this point our pants weren't really off, we had just had gone under each others' pants. *Uhm and then it just kept progressing*. (UT)

47 SC: Right. What happened next please?
MA: It became – once we had undone our belts, I did Connie's and then she did mine, and we started fondling each other and became increasingly sexual.
SC: Yes?
MA: Neither of us had climaxed but *it started to heat up* and both of us became really, really aroused and that's, as I said before, that's when she sat up and said, 'I think that we might be going too far.' (CT)

48 MA: Now that we had addressed this and come to a decision that we wouldn't tell our co-workers, she laid back down on the bed and we started to fool around again. And it was after that we fooled around again for quite some time and *it became increasingly sexual*. (CT)

49 SC: Yes. And were you becoming sexually aroused at this point, Mr. A?
MA: I knew that at that point that there was a sexual – that *this is becoming something sexual* because she was next to me without her shirt on and it's a single bed and we were very close in touching up against each other. (CT)

50 SC: All right. What happens next, please?
    MA: So then *it started to escalate* . . . So then this continued for a while and
    then Melinda got up out of bed and wanted to go to the washroom. So
    then Marg got up and both of the girls went to the washroom. (CT)

Containing unaccusative verbs of change of state and movement (i.e., denoting the increasing sexual nature of the activity) the italicized sentences of 45
to 50, like those of 39 to 44, portray the sexual events as 'acting' without
apparent cause. Indeed, I am suggesting that in examples 39 to 50 Matt's
agency is completely removed from the picture; his acts of sexual aggression
are represented as autonomous – as having a force and life of their own.

Matt's representatives: obscuring and eliminating agency

Up to this point I have argued that Matt draws upon a variety of linguistic
resources to mitigate, diffuse, diminish or completely remove his responsibility for the sexual acts that occurred between him and the complainants. In
comparing examples 6 to 10 with 14 to 50, we see that in Matt's narrative
world, sexual events are constructed as consensual through a grammar that
diffuses, diminishes and even removes his responsibility for their enactment.
From examples 51 to 58, all from cross-examination of the complainants, we
see that Matt's lawyer and representative in both the criminal trial and the
university tribunal, respectively, are complicit in this linguistic construction
of the events. This is perhaps not surprising, given that their explicit goal is
to represent their client as innocent and thus to diminish his agentive role in
sexual acts of aggression. In examples 51 to 53, we see the use of nominalizations, *insertion* and *fondling*, which allow for the deletion of Matt, the agent of
these acts.[9] Encoded as nominalizations, not only are these acts of aggression
without a perpetrator, they are also reified – transformed into static objects
that lack the potency of actions.

51 TM: So you do admit that you said nothing to him at that point about *the
    insertion of his finger in the vagina*? (UT)
52 TM: After this incident in which you first indicated *the insertion of his
    finger in your vagina*, uhm you make reference to the fact that Matt was
    really angry. (UT)
53 TM: So at this point you permitted him to go to sleep even after *the second
    insertion of the vagina*? Or *fondling* or whatever? (UT)

Examples 54 and 55 both contain passives. The italicized sentence of 54 is an
agentless passive which thus obscures Matt's role as the remover of the
complainant's pants. By contrast, the italicized passive in 55 includes its
agent; however, as a disembodied hand, even the presence of this agent
obscures Matt's role in an act of aggression, i.e., holding down the complainant's hand.

54 SC: Was there any exchange around this point where *your pants are being removed* where you are asking him or he is telling you 'Do you like me?' (CT)

55 SC: And *were your arms* still in the same position above your head and crossed over and *being held by one hand*? (CT)

Example 56 contains both an unaccusative construction, *your shirt came off*, and a nominalization, *fondling*. Not only do both of these events lack agents or causes, the static agentless condition of *fondling* replaces Matt as the force responsible for the removal of his shirt. We see here how agentless constructions such as unaccusatives and nominalizations allow for the possibility of pseudo-agents such as *fondling* supplanting a true agent such as Matt, thereby severing further the causal link between Matt and his sexual acts of aggression.

56 SC: Well, *your shirt came off* first as a result of *fondling* of the breasts, right? (CT)

Finally in 57 and 58, we see the defence lawyer in the criminal trial transforming Connie's statements, in which Matt is accorded a highly agentive positioning with respect to sexual acts of aggression (i.e., he is the grammatical subject of transitive verbs that designate acts that are wilful and intentional and have consequences for the patient, Connie), into nominalizations that allow the deletion of Matt as agent.

57 CD: At that point is when *he grabbed my hair and wrapped it around his hands and pushed my face down between his legs and gave me an ultimatum.* At that point that became the more pressing matter to get out of that situation more than to get him out of my room.
SC: So in fact was *the fellatio*, was that *the last act of sex* that was between the two of you before everything died down and before Mr. A. went to sleep and you went into the chair? (CT)

58 SC: All right, ma'am. Now, after the *exchange of the fellatio*, . . . I am interested in knowing that at the conclusion of the situation does Mr. A. sort of calm down? (CT)

Moreover, the particular expressions used by SC to represent the violent acts of Connie's testimony depict a scene of nonviolent and reciprocal sex, for example, *the last act of sex . . . between the two of you* and *the exchange of the fellatio*. SC's reformulation of Connie's testimony is emblematic of the defence's (both Matt's and his representatives') linguistic representations more generally: without clear and overt agents, the sexual events under scrutiny seem to 'act' of their own accord, creating the space, as in example 56, for pseudo-agents to replace real agents.

Outcome of the adjudication processes

Having presented the way in which Matt and his representatives actively construct the events under investigation, a question remains as to whether Matt's grammar of non-agency receives validation in these adjudication processes. That is, is Matt's linguistic construction of the events intelligible to the adjudicators? Is it afforded legitimacy and authority? In Capps' and Ochs' terms, does it become the 'official story'? I want to argue that aspects of both decisions were consistent with and thus lent authority to Matt's construction of the events.

The university tribunal

Members of the university tribunal found the defendant's behaviour to have fallen substantially below university standards. More specifically, their decision stated that both complainants were unresponsive to the defendant's sexual advances, that the defendant demonstrated an indifference to the complainants' wishes, and that the defendant's actions were disrespectful and insensitive.

> Both partners were clearly unresponsive to his [Matt's] sexual advances and this should have been a signal to him that he should desist from further activity until such time as his partner clearly expressed interest in engaging in sexual activity. In failing to discharge this duty, Mr. A. demonstrated an indifference to the wishes of the complainant. His actions were disrespectful and insensitive and as such his actions fell below the standard of conduct we must expect from all members of the University community.
> (*In the Matter of M.A: Reasons for Judgement of the University Discipline Tribunal*, p. 22)

In spite of this decision and the university lawyer's recommendation that the defendant be expelled from the university, the tribunal members decided instead to penalize the defendant by restricting his access to the residences on campus where the events under investigation had taken place. Their justification for opposing rustication is provided below:

> First, notwithstanding the actions of Mr. A. with regard to the complainants, there is nothing in the record to suggest that Mr. A. poses a clear and present threat to members of the University Community. . . . Mr. A. was clearly insensitive and disrespectful to the complainants, and *this insensitivity led to harm*; however, I do believe that Mr. A. will be far more careful, caring and sensitive in the future. Considering that we do not find that he poses a threat, it is our view that if there is any institution in which Mr. A. can be sensitized to the need for respecting

the sexual autonomy of women, it would be in a university setting.
Rustication would be counter-productive to the educational mission
that must be part and parcel of the University's disciplinary process.[10]
(*In the Matter of M.A: Reasons for Judgement of the University Discipline*
Tribunal, p. 37)

While restricted access to dormitories on campus may seem a lenient sanction
for two convictions of sexual harassment (in the criminal justice system, this
would be deemed sexual assault), such a penalty corresponds to the putative
cause of the sexual aggression – the somewhat limited and temporary nature
of Matt's insensitivity and disrespect. Acknowledging that Matt was insensitive and disrespectful to the complainants, the tribunal members at the same
time undercut the significance of that insensitivity by excluding the complainants' experience from their determination of Matt's potential threat to
members of the university community (e.g., *notwithstanding the actions of*
Mr. A. with regard to the complainants, there is nothing in the record to suggest
that Mr. A. poses a clear and present threat to members of the University Community).
Moreover, the tribunal members asserted their belief in the transitory nature
of Matt's insensitivity (e.g., *I do believe that Mr. A. will be far more careful, caring*
and sensitive in the future). Of relevance to this discussion is Coates' (1997)
examination of causal attributions – explaining why an accused committed
an offence – in Canadian sexual assault trial judgements. In categorizing
judges' attributions, Coates makes a distinction between internalizing and
externalizing ones, that is, those that discursively locate the cause of the
offence *within* the offender as opposed to *outside* of the offender. Coates
explains:

> Causal attributions that were internalizing focused on the person as a
> freely choosing individual. They frequently described the cause of the
> offender's behavior as a choice (e.g., 'He got drunk' or 'He was out to
> attack'). In these internalizing descriptions, the judge often presented
> the offender as acting upon the world; he was given causal agency. Alter-
> natively, internalizing descriptions also described the offender as some-
> thing (e.g., 'You are a pedophile' or 'He is a rapist'). In either case, the
> attributions tightly connected the offender with the cause and placed
> the cause inside him as a person.
>
> In contrast, causal attributions that served externalizing functions
> depicted the cause of the behavior as something that was external to
> the person's free choice. The cause was cast as something acting upon
> the offender and was typically psychological. . . . In these descriptions, the
> offender himself was not given causal agency. Instead, the personified
> cause of the behavior impelled the offender to commit the crime, for
> example, forces outside of the offender.
>
> (Coates 1997: 286)

A prediction of Coates' research – borne out with respect to offences judges deemed as violent – concerned the relationship between sentencing and externalizing vs. internalizing attributions: when judges attributed the cause of an offence to something external to the individual (e.g., alcohol, sexual drives) as opposed to emphasizing the responsibility of the offender, Coates predicted that sentences would be less harsh.[11] Particularly germane to the tribunal members' decision is the discursive or linguistic criteria involved in Coates' distinction between externalizing and internalizing attributions. Citing the work of Weiner (1979), Coates argues that the categorization of a cause as external or internal depends on its linguistic expression. For example, Weiner points to two expressions of ill health, *I am a sickly person* vs. *The flu bug got me*, arguing that the first categorizes the cause as internal to the individual while the second categorizes it as external to the individual. Like this second expression, some of the tribunal members' comments, specifically the sentence *this insensitivity led to harm*, treats what would typically be construed as an internal state as an external force acting upon the defendant and causing harm to the complainants. Indeed, it is not Matt who is the agent and cause of *harm* in this sentence, but rather the nominalization *insensitivity*. In combination with other comments in the decision declaring that Matt does *not* pose a threat to the university community (e.g., *considering that we do not find that he poses a threat*), this articulation downplays Matt's responsibility. And, consistent with Coates' results, the tribunal members' somewhat lenient penalty for Matt's two convictions of sexual harassment corresponds to their externalizing causal attributions: they locate the cause of his offences in personality traits represented as external to Matt, thereby diminishing his agency in the sexual acts of aggression. In Coates' terms, such attributions do not accord the offender with 'causal agency'.

Criminal trial

Matt was convicted on one count of sexual assault within criminal court (Count 2) and acquitted on the other.[12] The judge convicted Matt on the count involving Marg and cited the corroborating evidence from Marg's witness, Melinda (and even evidence from Matt's witness, Bob) as crucial to such a verdict.[13] Matt was acquitted in the case involving Connie (Count 1). Something that distinguished the two cases, other than the presence of other people in Marg's dormitory room, was the fact that Connie acknowledged in her testimony that she was attracted to Matt and that she engaged in consensual kissing with him. At a certain point, she also reported that she wanted no further intimate contact, yet, according to her testimony, Matt persisted in violent acts of sexual aggression. (Examples 7, 8 and 10 are representative of Connie's version of the events.) Aspects of the judge's decision made reference to this consensual intimate contact between Connie and the accused:

I am content that the offender's conduct [in Count 2] was directed by a refusal to accept 'no' for an answer and wilful blindness in the sense that he expected that he could in the end overcome indications of unwilling-ness to accept his advances. That is the same conduct he exhibited in Count 1, except that in respect of that matter, I was left with a reasonable doubt to the effect really that he may have succeeded in seducing the complainant in that count against her better judgement by persistence. The same persistency took place on Count 2, except that there was never consent on Count 2.

(*Reasons for Judgement in Her Majesty the Queen and M.A.*)

In the judge's words, then, although Matt exhibited the same 'persistence' in both cases, 'there was never consent on Count 2'. Indeed, that some *consensual* intimate activity occurred between Connie and Matt seems significant to the judge's acquittal of Matt on Count 1. Consider other comments from his decision:

Human nature in many respects remains human nature and does not change, especially in the difficult area of sexual conduct and the impulse imbedded in humanity towards the purpose of the continuation of the human race. Young men must be sensitive to a young woman's right to say no, and *young women, in turn, must realize that when a young man becomes aroused during sexual activity beyond a moderate degree there is a danger that he will be driven by hormones rather than by conscience.*

(*Reasons for Judgement in Her Majesty the Queen and M.A.*)

One of the social discourses surrounding male sexuality in the West, and evident in this judge's decision, concerns men's socially-acceptable 'compel-ling' and 'uncontrollable' sexual impulses – what Hollway (1989) has termed the *male sexual drive* discourse. As to the social acceptability of such a view of male sexuality, Estrich (1987: 101) refers to American sex manuals that 'laud[ed] male sexual responses as automatic and uncontrollable' (although also comments on newer ones that 'no longer see men as machines and even advocate sensitivity as seductive'). Constructing male sexuality as driven by a powerful biological imperative, this discourse confers respons-ibility upon women: women who dress 'provocatively', for example, or engage in some intimate activity with men (as in Connie's case) run the risk of setting this powerful and compelling biological drive in motion (Burr 1995). Informed by the *male sexual drive* discourse, the italicized com-ments from the judge's decision call upon young women to realize that, once aroused, young men's sexual urges are uncontrollable. In the terms of Coates' research, the judge employs an externalizing causal attribution. That is, he attributes Matt's 'persistent' sexual aggression to a force outside of Matt: it is not Matt who is responsible for the sexual acts of aggression; rather, it is his hormones. Particularly noteworthy is the linguistic manifestation of this externalizing causal attribution – *there is a danger he will be driven by his hormones rather than by conscience.* In this sentence, italicized in the decision above, *hormones* assumes the role of agent, whereas the generic young man, referred to by *he*, assumes the role of patient – the entity acted upon by hormones. (The corresponding active sentence would read: *there is a danger his hormones will drive him.*) Articulated in this way, the judge's comments resemble the agentless passives and unaccusative constructions that Matt uses throughout his testimony. Sexual acts are represented as having a force and life of their own, uncontrolled by a human agent, only the compelling force of male hormones. Thus, like portions of the tribunal members' decision discussed above, the male sexual drive discourse invoked by the judge discursively locates the cause of male sexual aggression *outside* of the male offender and concomitantly functions to diminish and reduce Matt's culpability and responsibility for the particular sexual assault under investigation (i.e., Connie's).[14] Continuous with Matt's (and his representatives') grammar of non-agency, even in their grammatical properties, these decisions confer authority and legitimacy upon Matt's version of the events in question.

The limits of contextual appropriateness

To the extent that speakers build social identities through talk, I have argued that Matt, given a range of alternatives, draws upon a particular constellation of linguistic features which together construct an identity of innocence: they mitigate, diffuse, obscure or completely remove his responsibility for the non-consensual acts of aggression he allegedly committed. As Duranti (1994: 164) says of the relationship between grammar and sociopolitical processes: 'rather than simply describing an already constituted world, these utterances are at least part of important social acts through which speakers try to affect the world.' While strategically making use of the linguistic system of English to position himself as a non-agent, at times Matt pushes the limits of the very system he draws upon. Consider, for instance, the question/answer sequence below in which Matt is questioned by his defence lawyer in the criminal trial.

59   SC: And then the massage was reciprocated by her giving you a massage, is that correct?
      MA: Yes.
      SC: And how did that all take place?
      MA: Well, *my shirt came off* and I still had a T-shirt on. . . . I lie down on the bed and she proceeded to give me a massage.
      Q: And when you say your shirt came off, how did your shirt come off?
      MA: I mean, *I gather that I took it off.* She took hers off. (CT)

Responding to an open-ended question about how a massage took place, Matt responds with the unaccusative construction – *my shirt came off.* Recall that unaccusative constructions take as their grammatical subjects non-agents or non-causers of the actions their predicates denote; thus, the events represented by unaccusative constructions are often interpreted as autonomous – as having a force or life of their own without an apparent cause. Given what we as speakers and interpreters know about shirts – how they are typically worn and how they typically come off – Matt's autonomous representation of a shirt's removal is somewhat odd in this context, that is, it is pragmatically inappropriate.[15] Because a shirt's coming off typically involves an individual removing their arms (or someone else's) from shirt sleeves, the autonomous depiction of such an event, as in 59, requires a great leap of imagination on the part of interlocutors. Consider an alternative context where the cause of a shirt's removal is more readily accessible: *Matt is wearing a tee-shirt under a pull-over sweater. He takes his sweater off and in the process his tee-shirt comes off*. One could imagine him appropriately uttering: 'Oh, my tee-shirt came off.' By contrast, without the contextual information contained within this scenario (i.e., the removal of a sweater which in turn causes the tee-shirt to come off), the same unaccusative construction within the context of 59 pushes the limits of pragmatic (i.e., contextual) acceptability.

Perhaps indicative of the sentence's inappropriateness in 59 is the defence lawyer's following question: *how did your shirt come off?* That is, in spite of the defence lawyer's complicity in Matt's grammar of non-agency, even he has to inquire as to the cause of an autonomous removal of a shirt. Also driven by attempts to discursively diminish his agency, Matt's next response, *I gather that I took it off*, is equally as inappropriate for the context. The verb *gather* signifies a process by which a conclusion is drawn; however, this process of coming to a conclusion does not involve directly experiencing the specified event. Rather, to *gather* something is to determine it on the basis of indirect evidence often involving some logical deduction or inference. The utterance describing the removal of Matt's shirt, then, functions to distance Matt from the event. By *gathering* that he removed his shirt, he is signfying that he has come to this conclusion by means of indirect evidence, not by experiencing it directly. And, in not directly experiencing the event, Matt diminishes his responsibility for it. Another element in Matt's grammar of non-agency, the use of *gather* in this context also pushes the limits of contextual acceptability. Again, contextualized differently, in a world where Matt, for example, is drunk or on hallucinatory drugs and somewhat removed mentally from his physical activities, the sentence could receive an appropriate reading. Yet, given nothing in the context of 59 to suggest such a scenario, Matt's representation of his shirt's removal as based on an indirect experience of it renders his utterance contextually anomalous.

Conclusion

That a defendant accused of sexual assault attempts to construct an innocent identity in the institutional settings where his case is heard is not in itself unpredictable or surprising. What is perhaps less predictable is the way in which aspects of the adjudicators' decisions are continuous with Matt's representation of himself as a non-agent, even in their grammatical manifestations. The adjudicators lack Matt's strategic imperative (i.e., they are not facing criminal charges); moreover, in Matt's attempts to represent himself as a non-agent his testimony at times pushes the limits of contextual acceptability. In spite of this pragmatic inappropriateness, however, the defendant's testimony is apparently comprehensible and intelligible to the adjudicators. That is, the defendant's characterization of the events is afforded legitimacy in both of the institutional contexts in which this case was heard to the extent that forces represented as external to Matt, and not his own agency, are the putative causes of his sexual aggression (i.e., his insensitivity, his hormones). Recall Capps' and Ochs' comments regarding 'official stories' being determined by the 'plausibility and coherence' of court narratives. Clearly, an institution's assessment of what constitutes a plausible and coherent narrative is not based exclusively on linguistic criteria, that is, on criteria of pragmatic well-formedness. Rather, following Gal (1991: 197), this work suggests that notions of plausibility and coherence within such settings are ideologically-driven ones; a society's institutions are not 'neutral arenas' for talk: 'they are structured along gender lines to lend authority to reigning classes and ethnic groups but specifically to men's linguistic practices.'[16] Indeed, the broader social discourses (e.g., the male sexual drive discourse) that 'frame' these adjudicators' understandings of male violence against women are so powerful and pervasive that the likes of Matt's testimony – testimony that pushes the bounds of contextual acceptability – is recognizable to them.

The intelligibility of the defence's version of events within these institutional contexts also sheds light on the 'rigid regulatory frame' (Butler 1990) within which gender is enacted. As argued in Chapter 1, 'performances' of gender – linguistic or otherwise – are subject to what Cameron calls 'institutional coerciveness': dominant gender ideologies that pre-exist local (linguistic) enactments of gender and structure the kinds of gendered identities that women and men produce. In recognizing and conferring legitimacy upon Matt's grammar of non-agency, the adjudicators in the tribunal and criminal trial were at the same time casting judgement on what constitutes an appropriate and intelligible performance of masculinity. That is, viewed within the interpretive frame of the male sexual drive discourse, for example, Matt's encoding of sexual events in unaccusative constructions – constructions that represent the sexual events as 'acting' of their own accord – constitutes a performance of hegemonic masculinity.[17] And, by attributing the cause of Matt's sexual aggression to factors outside of Matt, the adjudicators licensed a view of male sexuality and masculinity that portrays violent men as not being the 'agents' of their own actions. Consistent with the claims of feminist legal scholars such as Lees (1997) and Crenshaw (1992), then, these decisions do what Crenshaw argues adjudication of male sexual aggression does more generally: 'maintain a considerable range of sexual prerogatives for men' (p. 408). Likewise, Lees (1997: 2) says the following about the treatment of male violence against women within the British criminal justice system: 'the law ostensibly constrains male violence against women but in substance allows such violence to continue.'

To say that the defendant's characterization of himself as a non-agent, and the view of hegemonic masculinity that accompanies such a representation, receive validation in these institutional contexts is not to make the strong claim that Matt's linguistic descriptions directly 'cause' the adjudicators' decisions. As discussed earlier in this chapter, there is psycholinguistic evidence to suggest that violence against women represented in the passive voice (as opposed to the active voice) leads subjects, especially men, 'to belittle the amount of harm suffered by the victim and to lessen the perpetrator's responsibility for the violence relative to the victim's' (Henley *et al.* 1995: 80). In other words, the way that violence against women is linguistically encoded can affect individuals' interpretations of harm and responsibility. At the same time, Coates found that judges discursively located the causes of sexual assault *outside* of the offender (i.e., externalizing causal attributions) in 71 per cent of the decisions she analysed and that these kinds of attributions, because they in some sense reduced the culpability of offenders, were consistently associated with lower sentences. Thus, the kinds of causal attributions found in the adjudicators' decisions analysed here, while continuous with Matt's representation of his sexual aggression, are also consistent with other findings regarding the kinds of judicial reasoning that informs decisions in sexual assault trials more generally. What I want to claim is *not* that Matt's grammar of non-agency 'causes' the adjudicators' decisions but rather that it fails to challenge and concomitantly reinforces the adjudicators' dominant understandings of male sexuality and violence against women. Constituted by gender ideologies, Matt's testimony also functions to reproduce these ideologies in the form of adjudicators' decisions that diminish, deflect and diffuse his culpability. And left unchallenged, such ideologies become 'naturalized', rendered invisible and commonsensical. In a context where participants actively construct, often competing and contradictory, versions of the events under investigation, then, a question arises as to the emergence of alternative representations of Matt's sexual aggression in the 'talk' of these adjudication processes. In the chapters that follow, I consider precisely this – the possibility of discursive challenges to the expressions of sexual violence against women we have seen throughout this chapter.

3 'I see an option . . . I simply want to explore that option with you'

Questions and ideological work[1]

Introduction

Practice theorists such as Bakhtin (1981), Bourdieu (1977) and Volosinov (1973) have all conceptualized language as constituting and embodying ideology.[2] In this view (Philips 1992: 378), language is 'itself material' rather than independent and simply symptomatic of material realities. Scholarship on the language of institutional settings has given this theoretical view empirical substance: researchers have investigated the role of discursive practices in constructing and constituting power relations among professionals and clients, in particular, the interactional mechanisms by which certain ideological or interpretive 'frames' dominate institutional interactions, while others are suppressed (Philips 1992). Todd (1989) and Fisher (1991), for example, document how doctors' medical and technical concerns prevail in interactions with patients, even when patients articulate their problems in social and/or biographical terms. In her comparison of a doctor–patient interaction and a nurse-practioner–patient interaction, Fisher (1991: 162) isolates aspects of interactional structure related to such discursive control: the doctor, much more than the nurse-practitioner, asked questions that 'both allow[ed] a very limited exchange of information and le[ft] the way open for his [the doctor's] own assumptions to structure subsequent exchanges'. By contrast, the nurse-practitioner used open-ended, probing questions which maximized the patient's own 'voice' and interpretation of medical problems. In the context of legal settings, Walker (1987: 79) also comments on the interactional control exerted by questioners. As part of her investigation of linguistic manipulation in legal settings, she interviewed witnesses who reported 'a feeling of frustration at being denied the right to tell their own stories their own way'. While the stories told in court were the witnesses' own, lawyers and judges had the socially-sanctioned prerogative to 'present, characterize, limit and otherwise direct the flow of testimony' such that the frames structuring the stories were often not the witnesses' own. In Fisher's (1991: 162) terms, 'both the questions and the silences – the questions not asked – do ideological work.' Not only was Fisher's doctor–patient interaction structured by the doctor's assumptions (due to questions that allowed a limited exchange of information), but implicit in these assumptions were views about the centrality of the nuclear family to this mother's sense of well-being or ill-health. According to Fisher, the doctor's questions functioned to reinscribe the hegemonic discourse that 'justif[ies] the traditional nuclear family which has at its center a *mother*' (Fisher 1991: 162, emphasis in original).

In this chapter I too consider the 'ideological work' performed by questions in institutional settings. While the previous chapter demonstrated the extent to which adjudicators' decisions can be informed by rape mythologies, this chapter focuses on discriminatory views of violence against women as they (re)circulate within adjudication processes themselves. Indeed, embedded within the questions asked of complainants, rape mythologies become much more insidious, I argue, because of the structuring potential of language. Not only do questions, with their implicit and explicit propositions, frame and structure the complainants' 'talk' about their experiences of sexual assault, they also produce the complainants as particular kinds of subjects – as subjects who are 'passive' in their responses to sexual aggression, as opposed to strategic and active. Fairclough's (1995: 39) comments on his use of the term 'subject' within institutional contexts are relevant here: 'the term "subject" is used . . . because it has the double sense of agent ("the subjects of history") and affected ("the Queen's subjects"); this captures the concept of *subject as qualified to act through being constrained – "subjected" – to an institutional frame*' (emphasis mine). In the terms of this investigation, one manifestation of Fairclough's 'institutional frame' are the questions asked of complainants; that is, the questions' presuppositions embody ideological perspectives which have consequences for the way in which the complainants are 'qualified to act' linguistically.

The idea that linguistic devices (e.g., questions) can be instrumental in the structuring and constraining of interpretive perspectives in discourse has manifested itself in a variety of theoretical works over the last few decades (for example, Bateson 1972, Goffman 1974, 1981, Gumperz 1982a, 1982b). In particular, the concept of *framing*, associated with Bateson, has influenced sociologists, sociolinguists and discourse analysts interested in contextually- and interactionally-based approaches to language. Bateson demonstrated that no interactional move, verbal or non-verbal, could be understood without reference to a broader interpretive perspective (Tannen 1993). Duranti and Goodwin's explication of framing makes this claim more concrete:

> Looking at otters playing in a zoo he [Bateson] made the crucial observation that they were capable of framing their behaviour, so that actions that in other circumstances would be treated as quite hostile and aggressive – nips and bites for example – were here recognized as not serious but playful. Building from such observations, Bateson called attention to

the crucial role that framing plays in the organization of interaction in general.

(Duranti and Goodwin 1992: 24)

According to Bateson, then, the *frame* of 'playing' gave a definition to the otter's nips and bites, communicative acts which otherwise would have denoted hostility. Elucidating the connection between linguistic devices and framing, Tannen points to Gumperz's (1982a, 1982b) concept of contextualization cues, that is, the verbal and non-verbal devices that guide interlocutors' interpretation of linguistic forms and propositional meanings, particularly, in relation to the kind of speech activity within which they are engaged. Conversational code-switching, for example, is a contextualization cue for Gumperz (1982a, 1982b) because it can function to signal a shift in speech activity. Whereas Gumperz is concerned with linguistic devices (i.e., contextualization cues) as they function to define and signal various kinds of *interactional* activities, I am interested in the role of linguistic and discursive structures as they function to define and signal various kinds of *ideological* activities. And just as Tannen uses the term *interactional frame* to refer to the 'metamessage' (Tannen 1993: 3) that defines the interactional activity of a discourse (e.g., teasing vs. expressing hostility), so I use the term *ideological frame* to refer to the metamessage that defines the ideological activity of a discourse.

A powerful example of the role of linguistic practices in 'framing' events can be found in Goodwins' analysis of the Rodney King 1992 criminal trial (Goodwin 1994, Goodwin and Goodwin 1997). Analysing the testimony of expert witnesses, Goodwin shows how their 'professional vision' and concomitant discourse reconstructed the violent beating of Rodney King by four policemen – shown on videotape to the court – as a situation in which King was 'in control of the interaction'. That is, the linguistic choices of expert witnesses constructed the 'meaning' of the videotaped events, 'framing' the events in categories typically used to describe responsible police behaviour. Investigating the way in which discursive practices are 'used by members of a profession to shape events', Goodwin and Goodwin (1997: 292) also comment on the significance of this 'shaping' process: 'the shaping process creates the objects of knowledge that become the insignia of a profession's craft.' Whether examining the 'nips and bites' of otters or the violent beating of an African-American motorist, then, the point is similar – frameworks for interpreting such events are invoked through (among other things) the deployment of particular linguistic and discursive practices.

Ideology

Up to this point, I have discussed, following Fisher (1991), the potential of questions – and silences – in institutional settings to do *ideological* work.

In delineating more specifically how this work is achieved I have pointed to the propositions presupposed in questions and the way in which such propositions can comprise an *ideological* filter or lens (i.e., an ideological frame) through which events under scrutiny in a courtroom, for instance, are interpreted and assigned meaning. Because the term *ideology* may be the most elusive of concepts in the whole of the social sciences (McLellan 1986 cited by Blommaert and Verschueren (1998)), following Woolard (1998), I highlight themes that recur in a wide range of discussions on the topic. First, ideology typically refers to mental phenomena, that is, ideas, beliefs, or consciousness (Woolard 1998: 5). Second, ideology is typically conceptualized as reflecting the interests of a particular social position, even though its perspective is almost always 'naturalized', in other words, perceived as commonsensical, inevitable and universally true. Third, by naturalizing particular social configurations and relations (i.e., rendering them commonsensical), ideology functions to maintain these configurations and relations and thus supports the interests and the power of the social classes from which it derives. While for some theorists, ideology is always associated with dominant groups and their sustaining of asymmetries in power, for others 'ideology may be a tool of any protagonist in the contestation of power . . . subaltern as well as dominant' (Woolard 1998: 7). Like Fairclough (1995), I adopt some version of this latter view, assuming that social institutions are characterized by diverse and potentially competing ideological frames (what Fairclough calls ideological-discursive formations (IDF)) associated with different groups within an institution. For example, the ideological frame that, I claim, is dominant within the sexual assault adjudication processes analysed here is not without contestation. However, given the constraints that a dominant ideological frame places on 'debate' and 'meaning' within these institutional contexts, resistance to the status quo is often difficult to recognize. Thus, I assume, again like Fairclough (1995: 27), that a defining characteristic of an institutionally-*dominant* ideological frame is its capacity to be naturalized – to be accepted as commonsensical. What I explore in this chapter and the next is the extent to which dominant ideological perspectives sustain their dominance or hegemony in these institutional settings, that is, the extent to which they conceal and obscure resistant or counter-hegemonic perspectives and thereby retain their 'naturalized' status.

Ideological frame: the utmost resistance standard

Until the 1950s and 1960s in the United States, the statutory requirement of utmost resistance was a necessary criterion for the crime of rape (Estrich 1987); that is, if a woman did not resist a man's sexual advances to the utmost, then rape did not occur. Estrich (1986: 1122) comments: 'in effect, the "utmost resistance" rule required both that the woman resist to the "utmost" and that such resistance must not have abated during the struggle.' Because women were thought to fabricate accusations of rape, strict – and unique – rules of proof, of which resistance requirements were a part, were imposed upon rape cases in the nineteenth century (Schulhofer 1998). About resistance requirements in particular, Schulhofer (1998: 19) says the following: 'to make sure that women complaining of rape had really been unwilling, courts required them to show physical resistance, usually expressed as "earnest resistance" or even resistance "to the utmost".' He goes on to provide examples of specific judicial decisions in the late nineteenth century and first half of the twentieth century in the United States, which invoked resistance standards in ascertaining that rape did not occur. In 1880, for example, the Wisconsin Supreme Court overturned a rape conviction, arguing that the victim's resistance 'ought to have continued to the last' (Schulhofer 1998: 19) and in 1906 made the resistance requirement even more stringent by requiring that a victim display 'the most vehement exercise of every physical means or faculty within the woman's power'. Commenting on the repetition of such judgements into the middle of the twentieth century, Schulhofer (1998: 20) cites a conviction overturned by the Nebraska Supreme Court: 'only if a woman resisted physically and "to the utmost" could a man be expected to realize that his actions were against her will. "She must persist in such resistance," said the court, "as long as she has the power to do so until the offense is consummated."' While Estrich says that the 'utmost resistance' standard was generally replaced by a 'reasonable resistance' standard by the 1950s and 1960s in the United States, she also cites decisions as late as 1973 which contend that 'rape is not committed unless the woman opposes the man to the utmost limit of her power' (cited by Estrich 1987: 129 from *People* v. *Hughes*).

Within the Canadian context, Busby argues, like Schulhofer (1998), that 'special evidence rules' have been applied to sexual violence cases, focusing far more attention on the complainant's behaviour than is possible in other kinds of criminal cases. She cites John Wigmore (1970: 736), a renowned authority on evidence law, as representative of attempts to justify these special rules of evidence:

> Modern psychiatrists have amply studied the behavior of errant young girls and the women coming before the courts in all sorts of cases. Their psychic complexes are multifarious and distorted . . . One form taken by these complexes is that of contriving false charges of sexual offences by men. The unchaste mind finds incidental but direct expression in the narration of imaginary sex incidents of which the narrator is the heroine or victim . . . The real victim, however, too often in such cases is the innocent man.
>
> (Wigmore 1970, cited by Busby 1999: 275)

In order to protect the 'innocent man' from 'false charges of sexual offences', Canada too has imposed strict rules of proof on sexual violence cases. While degree of resistance is not a requirement which has ever been formally encoded in the Criminal Code of Canada, other such 'special evidence' rules have been. For example, as discussed in Chapter 1, until 1983 the Canadian Criminal Code had a corroboration requirement for rape, which demanded that a complainant's testimony be supported by independent evidence, and a recent complaint requirement, which obligated the complainant to make a prompt complaint in order that her testimony be deemed reliable. Both of these requirements were intended to guard against the false accusations of sexual assault that women ostensibly make against men. Although it would appear that resistance requirements have not been encoded in statutes, resistance requirements have often been operative in the adjudication of sexual violence cases in Canada. Backhouse (1991: 103) argues that a very high standard of resistance was set in the Ontario case of *R*. v. *Fick* in 1866 when the trial judge in this case stipulated that in order for rape to occur 'the woman [must have] been quite overcome by force or terror, she resisting as much as she could, and resisting so as to make the prisoner see and know that she really was resisting to the utmost' (cited in Backhouse 1991: 103). In the 1970s, Clark and Lewis (1977) investigated the characteristics of Toronto-area rape cases leading to perpetrator arrest and prosecutions in 1970 and determined that a victim's testimony of lack of consent was deemed credible only when she resisted her attacker to the utmost of her capabilities. Continuing into the 1990s in Canada, judges have often granted credibility to an accused's defence of 'honest but mistaken belief in consent' and acquitted the accused on the basis of the complainant's lack of resistance.[3] Thus, whether or not strict rules of proof or 'special evidence rules' are actually encoded in law, the adjudication of sexual assault cases can still require such strict rules of proof in order to convict the accused. Indeed, in the remainder of this chapter I argue that the 'utmost resistance standard' is the primary ideological frame through which the events in question and, in particular, the complainants' actions are understood and evaluated. This (re)framing functions to characterize the women as not 'resisting to the utmost' and ultimately (re)constructs the events as consensual sex, thus protecting the interests of the defendant, who in Wigmore's words is 'the real victim'.

Asymmetry in institutional interactions

Of central importance to the idea that institutions are characterized by discursively competitive ideological frames is research on the interactional asymmetry of institutional settings. (See, for example, Atkinson and Drew 1979, Conley and O'Barr 1998, Drew and Heritage 1992, Fisher 1984, Fisher and Todd 1986, Wodak 1996.) Arguing that institutional discourse deviates from 'ordinary' conversation in systematic and institutionally-sanctioned ways, such research has focused both on the distinctive formal properties of the discourse as well as the functions and effects of its formal characteristics. Most notably, institutional discourse exhibits a 'direct relationship between status and role, on the one hand, and discursive rights and obligations, on the other' (Drew and Heritage 1992: 49). For example, as others have noted about courtroom discourse (for example, Atkinson and Drew 1979, Conley and O'Barr 1998, Walker 1987), differential participation rights are assigned to participants depending on their institutional roles: questioners in legal contexts have the right to initiate and allocate turns by asking questions of witnesses but the reverse is not true. Atkinson and Drew (1979) labelled this type of turn-taking system *turn-type pre-allocation*, referring to the fact that the types of turns participants can take are predetermined by their institutional role and institutionally sanctioned. The claim is that the relative rigidity characteristic of turn-type pre-allocation is not found in so-called ordinary conversation as, according to Conley and O'Barr (1998: 21), 'from an everday perspective, it would be very peculiar to limit some speakers so that their only type of turn is asking questions, while restricting others to giving answers to whatever questions they asked.' While the symmetry imputed to 'ordinary' conversation by those proposing this dichotomy between institutional and ordinary discouse is undoubtedly overstated (indeed, McElhinny (1997) critiques the distinction itself),[4] the strict role integrity of questioner (e.g., lawyer, judge) and answerer (e.g., witness) (Walker 1987) has significant implications for whose formulations of events dominate and are dominated in legal adjudication processes. Discussing doctor–patient interaction, Drew and Heritage (1992) note that the question–answer pattern that characterizes most such interactions not only allows doctors to gather information from patients, but can also result in doctors directing and controlling the talk: introducing topics, changing topics, and selectively formulating and reformulating the terms in which patients' problems are expressed. The adversarial nature of both legal and extralegal hearings within the Anglo-American common law system gives question–answer sequences therein a somewhat different character; however, questioners in legal settings probably exert even greater conversational control than doctors because their questioning practices are legally sanctioned.

Adversarial dispute resolution requires that two parties come together formally, usually with representation, to present their (probably different) versions of the dispute to a third party (e.g., a judge, jury, tribunal) who hears the evidence, applies the appropriate laws or regulations to the specific evidence, and determines the guilt or innocence of the parties. Representatives have as their task, then, convincing the adjudicating body that their (i.e., their client's) version of events is the most credible. Apart from making opening and closing arguments, however, representatives do not themselves testify. Thus, through the posing of questions, representatives must elicit from witnesses testimony that will build a credible version of events in support of their own clients' interests in addition to testimony that will challenge, weaken and/or cast doubt on the opposing parties' version of events. Concerned with issues of interactional power and control, most investigations of questions in the courtroom have focused on the latter of these functions. Conley and O'Barr (1998: 21) comment on the power differential that is an integral part of cross-examination:

> This imbalance of power [due to pre-established speaking roles] is present in all courtroom dialogue. However, its consequences are most extreme during cross-examination, when lawyers examine the opposition's witnesses. When lawyers question their own witnesses on direct examination, they typically do so in a supportive manner, allowing friendly witnesses leeway in the form and substance of their answers. By contrast, the cross-examination is a hostile environment for both the lawyer and the witness. The lawyer's objective is to discredit opposition witnesses and minimize the impact of their testimony. And it is in such contexts that lawyers make maximal use of the linguistic power accorded to them.
> (Conley and O'Barr 1998: 21)

The linguistic power afforded lawyers is most apparent, some researchers have argued, in the coercive and controlling questions they ask during cross-examination. Both Danet *et al.* (1980) and Walker (1987) have developed taxonomies of questions used in the courtroom, based on the extent to which the questions constrain or limit the witness's response. The most 'coercive' of question types, for example, in Danet's taxonomy is the *declarative* (e.g., As a matter of fact, she didn't sign it, did she, Doctor?) because its form functions to severely restrict the possible response: it is a question requiring a 'yes' or 'no' answer; furthermore, its declarative form is meant to predispose witnesses to merely confirm the declared proposition. By contrast, the imperative (e.g., Tell us what took place at the meeting with the patient) is the least 'coercive' of question types within Danet's taxonomy because it imposes no particular form on the response. While Danet *et al.* (1980: 228) found coercive questions to be more frequent in cross-examination than in direct examination, the effectiveness of coercive questions in controlling responses was somewhat limited: 'the first general finding to note is that coerciveness of question form apparently influences formal features of responses, but has little or no bearing on more substantive aspects of replies.' That is, although the use of a declarative may be effective in producing a 'yes' or 'no' response (i.e., the question-type constrained the *form* of the response), there seemed to be no correlation between the use of declaratives and the *substance* of the response. A perhaps more important function of 'coercive' questions in legal adjudication processes is associated with questioners' ability to impose their interpretation on the evidence through a strategic use of question forms (Woodbury 1984). Conley and O'Barr (1998), Drew (1992) and Matoesian (1993), for example, have all pointed to the importance of 'coercive' questioning in lawyers' attempts to make damaging comments about witnesses during cross-examination. For Conley and O'Barr (1998: 26), controlling question form, irrespective of the responses elicited, is tantamount to transforming 'the cross-examination from dialogue into self-serving monologue'.

Discursive control

Before considering the 'utmost resistance standard' and its discursive penetration and circulation within the sexual assault adjudication processes under investigation here, I first delineate some of the interactional mechanisms by which discursive control is achieved in my data.

Strategic questioning

Following Woodbury (1984), I adopt a notion of questioners' 'control' that is not related to a questioner's ability to 'produce' a desired answer from an addressee (as Danet *et al.* (1980) and Walker (1987 do), but rather to a questioner's ability to influence and evaluate evidence. That is, for Woodbury (1984: 199), control refers 'to the degree to which the questioner can impose his (sic) own interpretations on the evidence'. Within Woodbury's continuum of control, Wh-questions generally display less control than yes-no questions because Wh-questions ask of 'the addressee that he (sic) provide or specify the questioned item' whereas yes-no questions ask of the addressee that 'he (sic) agree or disagree with the *propositional content* of the question' (emphasis mine, p. 200). That is, a broad Wh-question such as 'And then what happened?' functions to impose little of the questioner's interpretation or words on the testimony: there is no proposition contained within the Wh-question other than the notion that 'something happened'. By contrast, a prosodic yes-no question, (i.e., a declarative sentence containing prosodic cues marking it as a question) as in 1 contains a more substantive proposition – the addressee was attracted to Stephen.

1   You were attracted to Stephen?

Furthermore, not only does question 1 contain the proposition that the addressee was attracted to Stephen, it also expresses *the speaker's (ostensible) belief in that proposition and expectation that the proposition will be confirmed by the addressee.* It is in this respect that yes-no questions are generally more controlling than broad Wh-questions – they function to make available to the adjudicating body (whether it be a judge or jury or tribunal) the questioner's interpretation of events, irrespective of the addressee's (i.e., witness's) answer.

Woodbury's classification of yes-no questions according to the questioner's ability to contribute to or 'control' evidence is ordered below from least 'controlling' to most 'controlling.'

2   Did you enter the house at that time?

3 Didn't you enter the house at that time?
4 a. You entered the house at that time?
   b. You didn't enter the house at that time?
5 a. You entered the house at that time, didn't you?
   b. You didn't enter the house at that time, did you?
   c. You entered the house at that time, (is that) right?
   d. You entered the house at that time, did you?

(Woodbury 1984: 202)

Example 2 is a grammatical yes-no question; 3 is a negative grammatical yes-no question; 4a and 4b are prosodic yes-no questions; and 5a to 5d are tag yes-no questions. Especially important for my purposes is, first, the pragmatic differences between grammatical yes-no questions and prosodic yes-no questions and, second, between prosodic yes-no questions and tag yes-no questions. While grammatical yes-no questions contain a proposition with which the addressee is to agree or disagree, prosodic yes-no questions express the speaker's *belief* in this proposition as well as the expectation that the proposition will be *confirmed* by the addressee. Sharing all of the pragmatic properties of prosodic yes-no questions, tag questions also contain a tag which explicitly elicits a confirmation of the proposition from the addressee. Thus, as questions become more 'controlling', according to Woodbury's continuum of control, questioners express a greater commitment to the truth of the question's proposition and a greater expectation that the proposition will be confirmed. As Woodbury says of prosodic questions, 'because prosodic questions allow lawyers to word the evidence, to signal their beliefs about the truth of the evidence and, in addition, to indicate the answer they expect, these forms provide an important mechanism for communicating with the jury without seeming to address it directly' (p. 217–18). Indeed, if controlling questions have the potential to transform cross-examination into 'self-serving monologue', as Conley and O'Barr (1998: 26) argue, then they are undoubtedly an important site of 'ideological work' (Fisher 1991).

Presupposition

The *presupposition* of propositions provides a further locus for the circulation of ideological frames within the legal settings I am examining. Presupposition is a term used by linguists 'to refer to propositions whose truth is taken for granted in the utterance of a linguistic expression' (Green 1996: 72). For example, the sentence *John realizes that Mary is seriously ill* presupposes the truth of the proposition 'Mary is seriously ill.' That is, in uttering such a sentence the speaker takes for granted that the proposition 'Mary is seriously ill' is assumed knowledge between speaker and addressee, forming the background for the assertion 'John realizes X.' By contrast, the sentence *John thinks that Mary is seriously ill* does not presuppose the truth of the proposition 'Mary is seriously ill.' The speaker who utters such a sentence does not take for granted or assume that 'Mary is seriously ill'; in fact, the sentence could be appropriately produced by a speaker who knows the embedded proposition to be false. What these two examples demonstrate is that certain linguistic constructions (e.g., the predicate *realize* as in *John realizes that Mary is seriously ill*) act to trigger presuppositions whereas others do not (e.g., the predicate *think* as in *John thinks that Mary is seriously ill*). Indeed, a variety of linguistic forms (e.g., words, phrases, syntactic constructions) have been isolated as sources of presuppositions and thus designated as *presupposition-triggers* (Levinson 1983). Existential presuppositions are triggered, for example, by definite noun phrases and possessive constructions: by using expressions such as *the girl next door* or *Mary's children*, the speaker is presupposing the existence of a girl who lives next door and the existence of children whose mother is Mary. Factive presuppositions are triggered by certain factive predicates (e.g., *know, regret, realize, to be aware of*, etc); that is, the complements of such predicates are presupposed (Kiparsky and Kiparsky 1971). And connotation presuppositions are triggered by certain lexical items. Green (1996: 74) explains: 'many lexical items are used in only a subset of the class of situations in which they might conceivably apply, and the restrictions have been claimed to be (or reflect) presuppositions about the situation.' The lexical item, *assassinate*, for example, means 'kill' but there are presuppositions encoded within its meaning that severely restrict the kind of 'killing' that qualifies as *assassination*. First, *assassinate* presupposes that a killing is intended; second, it presupposes that the victim has considerable political power and has been killed in order to thwart that power (from Green 1996: 75). Presupposition triggers are numerous in English and the above examples only begin to illustrate the range of phenomena that has been classified as presuppositional.

One of the defining features of presupposition is its ability to survive negation and interrogation, or put another way, its ability to remain constant or true under negation and interrogation. Thus, like the sentence *John realizes that Mary is seriously ill*, both its negative – *John doesn't realize that Mary is seriously ill* – and interrogative – *Does John realize that Mary is seriously ill?* – versions presuppose the proposition 'Mary is seriously ill.' The fact that presupposed propositions remain constant under negation and interrogation has potential consequences for the 'ideological work' that questions do in legal adjudication processes. While controlling questions (in Woodbury's sense) display a pseudo-declarative or -assertive function, that is, they signal questioners' belief in the truth of the propositions contained within, they do not presuppose or even assert these propositions. By definition, a question always contains a variable or unknown quantity, which the addressee of a question is being asked to supply (Lyons 1977). The act of questioning, then, confers upon the addressee the right to supply this variable – the 'unknown' information. For example, the addressee of a prosodic yes-no question (a controlling question, in Woodbury's sense) has the ability to disconfirm the proposition contained therein even though the question's particular form expresses 'the speaker's expectation that his (sic) belief, whatever it is, will be confirmed' (Woodbury 1984: 203). By contrast, propositions that are *presupposed* by linguistic expressions cannot be denied with the same effectiveness or success. To illustrate I draw upon the following examples from Green (1996: 76):

6 a. The students regret that Mr. D. was late for class.
    b. When Mr. D. was late for class, the students demanded an apology.
    c. If Mr. D. had not been late for class, the students would have done their work.

As Green points out, a speaker uttering any of the sentences in 6 would be taking for granted the fact that 'Mr. D. was late for class.' Given that the three sentences in 6 presuppose this proposition, a denial of the proposition as in 7 is, according to Green, 'not likely to meet with success'.

7 No, he wasn't.

More striking in its pragmatic inappropriateness (i.e., its self-contradictory nature) is a sentence such as 8 where the same speaker presupposes a certain proposition and then immediately denies it.

8 The students regret that Mr. D. was late although Mr. D. was not late.

Because the truth of presupposed propositions is assumed and taken for granted, it cannot easily or appropriately be denied or questioned. Indeed, Graddol and Swann comment on the strategic use of this characteristic of presupposed propositions:

> The incorporation of contentious material into the presuppositional rather than the propositional part of utterances or texts is a well-known ploy of propagandists and advertisers. Presuppositions can, in principle, be taken up by listeners, but pragmatic constraints on discourse make this difficult. Attempts to deny presuppositions are, for example, usually heard as hostile acts (since it suggests that the speaker's assumptions are in error) and may be a difficult activity for a speaker in a subordinate position. In informal conversation each speaker can usually only deal with a single topic in a turn before the conversation passes to another participant and to take up a presupposition may mean that the main proposition remains un-addressed.
>
> (Graddol and Swann 1989: 166)

Witnesses in the courtroom are typically in a subordinate position relative to questioners (especially cross-examiners) and their failure to answer questions and/or to answer them in particular ways can lead to institutional sanctions.

Hence, to deny the truth of a question's presupposed proposition rather than addressing the main proposition of a question is unlikely to meet with success in these kinds of institutional settings, especially in cross-examination. Within the context of legal adjudication processes, then, presupposed propositions may be even more powerful than the pseudo-declarative propositions of controlling questions as a means of influencing and imposing interpretations on evidence. In other words, the 'taken-for-granted' quality that presupposed propositions display makes available a subtle and insidious mechanism for the discursive imposition of ideological frames.

Questions and selective (re)formulations

As others have noted within the context of legal settings (for example, Atkinson and Drew 1979, Drew 1992, Levinson 1992), questions can perform a range of functions and activities given the exclusive rights that questioners have to question witnesses combined with their ability to 'control' evidence through the kinds of questions asked, i.e., controlling questions that are pseudo-declarative in nature and that potentially presuppose various propositions. For example, Drew (1992) highlights the ability of questioners to 'draw conclusions' by strategically designing a series of questions whose propositions (previously gathered from a witness), when juxtaposed in a particular manner, cast doubt on the witness's overall testimony. Here I also focus on actions performed by questions in legal settings – actions that are intimately bound up with the capacity of controlling questions to contribute to and influence evidence – what I am calling *selective (re)formulation*. A notion developed by Garfinkel and Sacks (1970) and Heritage and Watson (1980), formulating refers to 'summarizing, glossing or developing the gist of an informant's earlier statements' (Heritage 1985: 100). Elaborating on this concept in an analysis of question–answer sequences within news interviews, Heritage (1985) points to the *selective* nature of formulations. Formulations can be selective in the sense that interviewers can summarize certain aspects of an interviewee's prior description, while discarding others. Furthermore, given the overarching purpose of news interviews, an interviewer's formulations may be 'designed to commit the interviewee to a stronger (and more newsworthy) version of his position . . . than he was initially prepared to adopt' (Heritage 1985: 110). While the elicitation of *newsworthy* responses is not a goal of cross-examining questioners in trial situations, it is their goal to commit witnesses to descriptions that may be incompatible with previous versions of events. Consider the following selective (re)formulation from a criminal trial.[5]

9   Q: You had what I would call a subjective fear of this man. In other words, you were genuinely scared of him, right?
     A: Yes.

Q: But he didn't do anything overt to cause you to be fearful? By overt
I mean, he didn't do anything outward to make you afraid, never
threatened you?
A: He never uttered any threats.
Q: No. Never punched you or mistreated you physically in any way?
A: No.

This question–answer sequence involves the cross-examining lawyer questioning the complainant about her fear of the accused – fear that she has
expressed a number of times in her previous testimony. Contained within
the lawyer's first question is a characterization of the complainant's fear as
both *subjective* and *genuine*. While seemingly contradictory, these two adjec-
tives are both contrasted with an alternative notion of fear in the lawyer's
second and third question (both prosodic yes-no questions), as indicated by
the contrastive discourse marker, *but* (Schiffrin 1987), which begins the
second question. This contrasting notion of fear seems more limited in its
use: it is warranted only if the fearful subject is overtly threatened or physically abused. And, according to this reformulated characterization of fear, the
complainant is not deemed to be fearful, that is, the accused did not threaten
her nor physically abuse her. Notice crucially how this reformulation results
in a reshaping of the complainant's response. She initially responds that she
has a genuine fear of the accused; over the course of several questions and concomitant reformulations, her responses are reshaped to suggest otherwise.
Especially important to this 'reshaping' are the controlling questions of the
cross-examiner: they have a pseudo-declarative quality which adds discursive
weight to the cross-examiner's (re)formulations. While not designed to produce more 'newsworthy' responses, the selective (re)formulations of cross-
examining lawyers do function to reshape and reconstruct the substance of
witness's answers. And consistent with the goals of an adversarial legal
system, such discursive mechanisms work to challenge and cast doubt on
the opposition's version of events. Hutchby and Wooffitt's (1998: 166)
comments regarding the discursive power of questioners in courtroom interaction are particularly germane to the type of interactional control under
discussion here: 'they [questioners] can define the meaning, the terms and
the upshots of a particular set of answers.'

Ideological work

Previous scholarship on rape trials from a broadly linguistic (i.e., conversa-
tional-analytic) perspective has also focused on their question–answer
dynamics, arguing that the 'ordinary mechanics of cross-examination . . .
simultaneously reflect and reaffirm men's power over women' (Conley and
O'Barr 1998: 37).[6] That is, both Matoesian (1993) and Conley and O'Barr
(1998) have elucidated the power of cross-examiners to 'reproduce rape', in

Matoesian's words, or to revictimize rape victims in the courtroom. Building
on these insightful analyses, I too demonstrate the way in which questioners
exert discursive control. However, I argue that not only do cross-examining
questions have the effect of revictimizing complainants, they also perform
substantive ideological work. Specifically, through the pseudo-declaratives
and presuppositions embedded in questions – many of which were reformulations of complainants' previous propositions – the defence and the tribunal
members in both the tribunal and criminal trial imposed interpretations on
evidence. That is, although the complainants described their experiences as
sexual assault, they were discursively represented and produced as 'passive'
and 'ineffectual' agents, their so-called lack of resistance being construed as
tantamount to consent. What follows is an analysis of the various propositions
that emerge in question–answer sequences between cross-examining questioners, including the so-called neutral tribunal members, and complainants.
Taken together, I argue that these propositions 'frame' the way the events
come to be understood: they function as an ideological filter through which
the complainants' acts of resistance are characterized as 'inaction' and the
events generally are (re)constructed as consensual sex.

Options and choice

The 'ineffective' actions of the complainants and their witness was an over-
riding concern of one of the tribunal members, GK, who asked numerous
questions about the women's *options* in the face of Matt's sexual aggression.
Examples 10 to 12 all include questions in which GK inquires about options.
While in 11 this is a yes-no question which allows Melinda, the addressee, the
possibility of denying the existence of options, in 10 and 12 these are
Wh-questions, which presuppose the truth of the propositions contained
therein. Specifically, GK's questions *What might have been your option?* in 10
and *Tell me . . . what options you might have had to tell Bob something* in 12 presuppose the propositions 'You might have had options' and 'You might have
had options to tell Bob something' respectively. Encoded as presuppositions
in 10 and 12, GK's ideas about the complainants' options have a taken-for-
granted status within the discourse: they are difficult to deny or question.
Moreover, following GK's Wh-question in 10, she *asserts* quite boldly the
existence of an option (i.e., *I see an option*) that, through further questioning,
she *explores* with Marg.[7]

10 Tribunal
   GK: Uhm . . . now this is a question. I realize that . . . that you were under
   certain stress, but in your story I heard the men left the room twice on two
   different occasions =
   MB: = Right.
   GK: And you and Melinda ((the other woman in the room)) were in your
   room alone. *Uhm what might have been your option? I see an option. It may not*

have occurred to you but I simply want to explore that option with you. Uhm did it occur to you that you could lock the door so that they may not uh return to your room?

MB: It did, but it didn't. Now it does. I mean looking back. Everyone was telling me that nothing's going on. Don't worry about it. Forget about it. When your friends are telling you nothing's going on, you start to question . . . maybe nothing is going on. I just . . . I couldn't think.

11 Tribunal

GK: But in spite of Marg telling you that he was trying things that she didn't want, were you . . . I mean I don't know how to phrase this uhm . . . *did you feel you had some options to do something for Marg?* [or did you feel]

MK: [Well, I] wanted to do something for her but I didn't know what to do. I was afraid that if I said anything to Matt or tried to do anything that he would hurt me or hurt Marg for trying to stop it. And everything was happening so fast, I didn't even think about knocking on the neighbour's door or anything.

12 Tribunal

GK: I mean . . . that evening did you ever feel you knew Bob enough to get him involved because I think you were intimidated?

MK: Yeah. I was close enough with Bob to =

GK: = to tell him you know 'get up and do something. I hear some noises.' Or you didn't feel that there was anything really going on. I don't want to put words in your mouth. Tell me how you felt please.

MK: I felt towards Bob? And how =

GK: = how – *what options you might have had to tell Bob something* and what =

MK: = Well, I tried to. The incident in the bathroom when I asked Bob to go talk to Marg . . . was the only thing I could think of . . . to get someone to tell Matt to stop it. I thought well Bob and Matt are friends. He'll listen to Bob but they didn't get the opportunity. I kind of think that Bob is very much influenced by Matt. . . . I think he's scared of Matt. I think Matt is a very intimidating person. He scares a lot of people . . . the way he talks.

Through the repeated use of the word *option*, GK not only conveys her belief that the complainants had an alternative course of action, but also that their failure to pursue other alternatives was a *choice*. Indeed, intrinsic to the meaning of *option* is the notion of choice, as demonstrated by the following entry from the *Funk & Wagnalls Canadian College Dictionary*:

option n. 1. The right, power, or liberty of *choosing*; discretion. 2. the act of opting or *choosing*. 3. The purchased privilege of either buying or selling something at a specified price within a specified time. 4. A thing that is or can be *chosen*. (emphasis mine)

Even more explicit about the *options* and *choices* the complainants had was Matt's cross-examining representative, TM, in his questioning of Connie.

13 Tribunal
>   TM: So I guess my my question to you is uh *you had a choice* at this point even though you say in your your oral testimony that you **didn't** have a choice. *Everybody has a choice* . . . and your choice was that you could have asked him to leave. So I'm wondering why you didn't ask him to leave? *We all have free will.* Let me rephrase the question or put another question to you then in the absence of an answer of that one. Why did you let uh what you say happened happen?
>   CD: ((crying)) I didn't let it happen.
>   TM: But *you had certain options.* You could have left the room. By your admission there was a time when he was asleep. You could have called through a very thin wall. Uh you actually left the room to go to the wash-room. Uh *you had a number of options here and you chose not to take any of them.*

More often in the form of declaratives than interrogatives, TM's comments echo and elaborate upon GK's. While pointing to the specific *options* and *choices* Connie ostensibly had, TM also makes assertions about the free will and choices that we all enjoy. One is reminded here of the classic liberal subject – the rational, autonomous, and freely-choosing individual. Yet, as socialist feminists, among others, have argued, such a view denies the socially-structured inequalities among individuals that shape and restrict so-called options. In an analogous way, TM's and GK's talk about options, choice, and freedom fails to acknowledge the power dynamics that can shape and restrict women's behaviour in the context of potential sexual violence.

Numerous and unlimited options

In keeping with this view of the complainants as unconstrained by socially-structured inequalities, many of the question–answer sequences involving complainants (and cross-examiners or tribunal members) focused on the seemingly numerous and unlimited options that they did not pursue. In 10 above, for example, with the question *Uhm did it occur to you that you could lock the door so that they may not uh return to your room?* GK presupposes that Marg could have locked the door to prevent Matt's return. That is, the phrase *did it occur to you* presupposes the truth of the proposition embedded within it. As already stated, the italicized Wh-question in 12 presupposes that one of Melinda's options might have been telling Bob. And in 13, TM, in addition to asserting that Connie had options, illustrates a few of them: leaving the room, calling through a thin wall. Example 14 also displays a delineation of options not pursued: GK lists (i.e., asserts) a series of actions that Marg did not perform – *You never make an attempt to put him on the floor* . . .

to close the door behind him or . . . to lock the door – and then asks whether they were offensive to her. GK's use of *only* in *You only have to cross the room* is indicative of her own view of such actions: Marg could have *easily* performed them.

14 Tribunal

GK: What I'm trying to say and I I realize what I'm saying is not going . . . You never make an attempt to put him on the floor, or when he leaves the room to close the door behind him, or you know you have several occasions to to lock the door. You only have to cross the room. Or to move him to the floor, but these things are offensive to you?

MB: I was afraid. No one can understand that except for the people that were there. I was extremely afraid of being hurt. Uhm: as for signals, they were being ignored. I tried I mean maybe they weren't being ignored I don't know why he didn't listen to them. I shouldn't say they were being ignored but he wasn't listening. And I kept telling him, I kept telling him, I was afraid to ask him to sleep on the floor. It crossed my mind but I didn't want to get hurt. I didn't want to get into a big fight. I just wanted to go to sleep and forget about the whole entire night.

Examples 15 to 23 below illustrate in more detail the many options that the cross-examining questioners and tribunal members deemed as appropriate and possible for the complainants to pursue.

Seeking help

In example 15, TM asserts over a couple of turns that *cry{ing} out* or *yell{ing} out* is a *natural* and *appropriate* way of responding to *real trouble*, thereby undermining Connie's claim that she was in trouble.

15 Tribunal

TM: Why is it that you made no attempt to scream? Can you explain what you mean by 'I really didn't want anybody to know?' If you were in such difficulty, if you felt threatened, if you felt that an assault was taking place, *it strikes me as only natural to cry out and that help probably was available as that wall was extremely thin* . . . Could you tell the panel what was in your mind?

CD: I was afraid. I was ashamed that I had lost control of the situation. I was embarrassed and above that, I honestly can't tell you why I didn't scream.

TM: I would submit, though I understand your embarrassment, if your story is correct, the fact is that help overrides embarrassment and *if you really were in trouble then the only appropriate way to protect yourself was to yell out.* Embarrassment would have been the last thing on your mind at the time if you were in real trouble.

Examples 16 and 17, from the criminal trial, also show the cross-examiner suggesting that 'seeking help' was a reasonable option for Connie.

16 Trial

> Q: And I take it part of your involvement then on the evening of January 27th and having Mr. A. come back to your residence that you felt that you were in this comfort zone because you were going to a place that you were, very familiar; correct?
>
> CD: It was my home, yes.
>
> Q: *And you knew you had a way out if there was any difficulty?*
>
> CD: I didn't really take into account any difficulty. I never expected there to be any.
>
> Q: I appreciate that. *Nonetheless, you knew that there were other people around who knew you and obviously would come to your assistance, I take it, if you had some problems*, or do you know? Maybe you can't answer that.
>
> CD: No, I can't answer that. I can't answer that. I was inviting him to my home, not my home that I share with other people, not, you know, a communal area. I was taking him to my home and I really didn't take into account anybody else around, anybody that I lived near. It was like inviting somebody to your home.
>
> Q: Fair enough. And I take it from what you told us in your evidence this morning that it never ever crossed your mind when this whole situation reached the point where you couldn't handle it, or were no longer in control, to *merely* go outside your door to summons someone?
>
> CD: No.

17 Trial

> Q: What I am suggesting to you, ma'am, is that as a result of that situation with someone other than Mr. A., you knew what to do in the sense that if you were in a compromising position or you were being, I won't use the word harass, but being pressured by someone you knew what to do, didn't you?
>
> CD: No, I didn't. Somebody had suggested that, I mean, I could get this man who wasn't a student not be be permitted on campus and that's what I did.
>
> Q: What – *but I am suggesting that you knew that there was someone or a source or a facility within the university that might be able to assist you if you were involved in a difficult situation, isn't that correct, because you went to the student security already about this other person?*
>
> CD: Yeah, okay. If you are asking if I knew about the existence of student security, yes, I did.

The italicized sentences in examples 16 and 17 are 'controlling' questions in Woodbury's sense: two prosodic yes-no questions in 16 and a tag question in 17. In producing such questions, then, the defence attorney is signalling his (ostensible) belief in the truth of their propositions and his expectation that the propositions will be confirmed by the addressee. Moreover, these questions all contain the factive predicate *know*, a predicate that presupposes the truth of its complement. More specifically, what is taken for granted and assumed in the cross-examiner's remarks is the 'fact' that help was readily available on the university campus for those in trouble; what is 'declared' – in the form of controlling questions – is Connie's awareness of these sources of help. Like TM's comments in example 15, the juxtaposition of these propositions has the the effect of implicitly undermining Connie's claim that she was sexually assaulted. That is, if it is established in the discourse that help was available and that Connie was aware of its availability, then her 'failure' to seek assistance casts doubt on her credibility. The final question of example 16 further undermines the charges of sexual assault – *It never ever crossed your mind . . . to merely go outside your door to summons someone?* – in so far as the word *merely* characterizes the seeking of help as unproblematic and effortless.

Saying something different

Examples 18 and 19, both from the criminal trial, show the judge and the cross-examining lawyer asking Connie and Marg, respectively, why they didn't utter other words in their various attempts to resist Matt's sexual aggression. Connie reports saying 'Look, I don't want to sleep with you' at a certain point that night and Marg recounts one of several incidents when she attempts to elicit Bob's help, saying 'Bob where do you get these persistent friends,' yet these expressions of resistance are problematized by the questioners. Both of the italicized questions in 18 and 19 are negative Wh-questions. First, then, they presuppose the fact that the complainant has not uttered the words suggested by the questioner: 'Don't undue (sic) my bra' and 'Why don't you knock it off' in 18 and 'Bob, he was doing it again, please help me' in 19. More significantly, however, negative questions signal a speaker's surprise at/conflict with the presupposed proposition contained therein (Lyons 1977, Woodbury 1984). Hence, when the judge and the cross-examining lawyer produce utterances of the form 'Why didn't you say X', they are subtly communicating their surprise at/opposition to the complainants' failure to produce the suggested utterances. Indeed, Lyons (1977: 766) argues that negative questions are 'commonly . . . associated, in utterance, with a prosodic or paralinguistic modulation indicative of *impatience or annoyance*' (emphasis mine). Of added import is the fact that in example 18, it is the judge – the ostensibly neutral adjudicator – who is expressing his impatience or annoyance with the complainant's 'inaction'.

18 Trial
> Q: And in fact just raising another issue that I would like you to help us with if you can, this business of you realizing when the line was getting

blurred when you said 'Look, I don't want to sleep with you', or words to that effect, yes, you remember that?

CD: Yes.

Q: Well, when you said that, what did that mean or what did you want that to mean, not to have intercourse with him?

CD: Yeah, I mean, ultimately, that's what it meant. It also, I mean . . .

THE COURT: *You didn't want to sleep with him but why not, 'Don't undue (sic) my bra' and 'Why don't you knock it off?'*

CD: Actually, 'I don't want' – 'I don't want to sleep with you' is very cryptic, and certainly as he got his hands under my shirt, as he took off my shirt, as he undid my bra, as he opened my belt and my pants and pulled them down and I said, 'Please don't, please stop. Don't do that. I don't want you to do that, please don't', that's pretty direct as well.

19 Trial

MB: And then we got back into bed and Matt immediately started again and then I said to Bob, 'Bob where do you get these persistent friends?'

Q: Why did you even say that? You wanted to get Bob's attention?

MB: I assumed that Bob talked to Matt in the hallway and told him to knock it off.

Q: You assumed?

MB: He was talking to him and came back in and said everything was all right.

Q: Bob said that?

MB: Yes.

Q: But when you made that comment, you wanted someone to know, you wanted Bob to know that this was a signal that Matt was doing it again?

MB: Yes.

Q: A mixed signal, ma'am, I suggest?

MB: To whom?

Q: What would you have meant by, 'Where do you get these persistent friends?'

MB: Meaning Bob is doing it again, please help me.

Q: *Why didn't you say, 'Bob, he was doing it again, please help me'?*

MB: Because I was afraid Matt would get mad.

Q: You weren't so afraid because you told Bob, 'Where do you get these persistent friends?' Did you think Matt would be pleased with that comment because it was so general?

MB: I didn't think about it but I thought that was my way of letting Bob know what was going on.

Asking Matt to leave

In examples 20 and 21 the option of 'asking Matt to leave' is explored by the questioners. The italicized sentence in 20 contains the matrix clause *it's quite obvious that*, which presupposes the truth of its embedded clause. Thus, what is taken for granted by the defence lawyer is that it never occurred to Connie that she might tell Matt to leave. The italicized sentence in 21 displays the same presuppositions as the italicized sentence in 20 in addition to possessing other pragmatic properties. As a negative Wh-question, not only does it presuppose the truth of its proposition – 'You did not ask him to leave', it also expresses the speaker's surprise at/conflict with this proposition. The preceding negative question in 21, *did you not have a choice?*, has similar effects: the cross-examining questioner expresses his surprise at Connie's failure to pursue options that would seem to be 'freely-chosen'.

20 Trial

Q: I am not trying to be critical here. We weren't there, you were, but when you talk about I think instinct, ma'am, the muscle memory was there when Matt had already offered to leave once, and I take it *it's quite obvious that it never crossed your mind at that point to tell him to leave* and in fact he never did?

CD: No, the context was certainly different. Before I could even think of him leaving I wanted him to stop. I mean, that came first.

21 Tribunal

TM: My question to you is although you say you have no choice . . . uh did you not have a choice? You could have asked him to leave at this point. *Why did you not ask him to leave?*

CD: Because . . . I wanted to explain to him why I wanted him to stop. I wanted him to understand I didn't want him to be angry. I didn't want him to be offended, I wanted him to understand.

Physically resisting

In response to many questions about options not pursued, both complainants would sometimes make reference to the fact that they were physically incapable of carrying out the suggested actions. In 22 below, for example, Connie explains that she was *underneath* Matt at a certain point in time and cites her immobility as the reason she did not leave, did not pick up a phone, etc.: *I mean, before I could be in a position to pick up a phone to, to leave, I had to be in a position to move and I wasn't.* In spite of her assertions throughout example 22 (this example continues immediately after example 20) that she was underneath Matt, that she couldn't move, that she couldn't get her arms free, the cross-examiner continues to ask Connie about her acts (or lack thereof) of physical resistance: whether she tried to push him off (*Did you try to push him off?*) and whether she sat up to express her resistance verbally (*Did you ever sit up at the point that he was trying to remove your pants and say, 'What's going on here? Look at the two of us, how far we have gone here?'*). Such questions are reminiscent of Schulhofer's (1998: 20) description of a 1947 Nebraska Supreme Court decision, which applied the utmost resistance standard to a woman's charge of rape: 'only if a woman resisted physically and "to the utmost" could a man be expected to realize that his actions were against her will.'

22 Trial

Q: And all of this happened fairly quickly. Again, I realize it's ridiculous to suggest that you are looking at a watch, but I take it that we've got this ongoing behaviour, that it's so physical that you are in no position to leave or do anything?

CD: That's right. I mean, before I could be in a position to pick up a phone to, to leave, I had to be in a position to move and I wasn't. So before thinking of I have to pick up the phone and I have to walk out the door, I had to think of how am I going to get out from underneath this man.

Q: Right. *Did you try to push him off?*

CD: Yes, I did.

Q: You weren't able to?

CD: No, I wasn't.

Q: Is that because you weren't able to get your arms free or because he was on top of you?

CD: I couldn't get my arms free and I couldn't push him off.

Q: At one point you were naked?

CD: Yes.

Q: At what point was that?

CD: I can't even pinpoint a specific time.

Q: Well, your shirt came off first as a result of the fondling of the breasts, right?

CD: Yes.

Q: And Mr. A. started to undue (sic) your belt and try to take your pants and try to take them down to which you responded 'don't' and all of that other stuff?

CD: Yes.

Q: And yet he was still able to do that with your other pants?

CD: Yes.

Q: And were your arms still in the same position above your head and crossed over and being held by one hand?

CD: Yes. I am not sure at what point exactly he let go of them.

Q: But I take it, whatever he did, if he let go of your hands they went to another part of your body that rendered you incapable of getting out from under?

CD: Yes.

Q: Ma'am, *did you ever sit up at the point that he was trying to remove your pants and say, 'What's going on here? Look at the two of us, how far we have gone here', nothing like that.*

A: Everytime I tried to sit up, I got pushed back down.

Example 23, from the tribunal, also shows the cross-examining questioner posing questions to the complainant, Marg, about physical acts of resistance. (This question–answer sequence concerns Marg's responses to Matt's attempts to put his toe in her vagina.) A negative Wh-question, the first italicized sentence, presupposes the proposition 'Marg didn't get up,' and, in addition, signals the speaker's surprise at/conflict with such a proposition. Moreover, the word *just* in *Why didn't you just get up?* expresses the speaker's belief that such an action could have been performed easily and unproblematically by Marg. Further on in the example, we see that the questioner asks two more questions about Marg 'getting up': a negative tag question – *You did not get up. Is that correct?* – and a negative prosodic yes-no question – *And you still did not get up?* Both continue to express the cross-examiner's (ostensible) surprise at her 'lack of action'; furthermore, the word *still* suggests that the act of getting up was long overdue. Despite the fact that several of Marg's responses point to a physical act of resistance she did perform – pushing Matt's toe away – this act was clearly not 'vehement' enough to satisfy the cross-examiner's standard of resistance.

23 Tribunal
    TM: It's after that point that you're sitting on a windowsill and now comes a rather bizarre incident according to you.
    MB: Yeah.
    TM: Uh . . . he attempts to stick his toe =
    MB: = Right =
    TM: = in your vagina?
    MB: Yes.
    TM: Uh: . . . now you were very upset the previous night when a total stranger whom you picked up in a bar took your hand and put it on his . . . uh crotch. Uh::m . . . yet you don't deny that you continue to sit there at the windowsill while this is going on.
    MB: I didn't sit there and let him do that. I was sitting in the fetal position, he kept trying to put his toe there and I kept pushing it away.
    TM: *Why didn't you just get up?*
    MB: **I didn't know what to do. You don't understand. The whole entire time. I didn't know what to do. I was not thinking clearly. Where would I have gone?**
    TM: You've now had a whole night's experience with this young man according to you =
    MB: = And I [still didn't know what to do.]
    TM: [And you're still prepared] to uh to to tell this panel that you are sitting there allowing his kind of bizarre [behaviour to go on?]
    MB: [No I wasn't allowing it.] I kept pushing his foot away and telling him that I did not want to go to his house.

TM: *But I come back to the fact you did not get up. Is that correct?* When he first began to do this?
MB: No I pushed his foot away.
TM: And then he continued to do it?
MB: Right.
TM: *And you still did not get up?*
MB: I . . . don't think so.

Ineffectual agency and passivity

Repeatedly posing questions that presupposed and (pseudo)asserted the complainants' access to unlimited, freely-chosen options, I am suggesting that the defence and the supposedly neutral tribunal members transformed the complainants' strategic responses to sexual aggression into ineffective acts of resistance. This characterization, while somewhat implicit in the previous examples' focus on options not pursued, is more explicitly depicted in the examples that follow: the complainants' 'ineffectual agency' is represented in examples 24 to 26; their so-called inaction in example 26 to 28.

Example 24 focuses on one of Connie's attempts to get rid of Matt – telling him that she had a class the next morning. The two italicized sentences are prosodic yes-no questions, both of which characterize this attempt as woefully inadequate. Connie is first asked if this was the *only* effort she made, signifying the limited nature of her resistance, and second whether this was *the best she could come up with*, suggesting that there were better ways to resist. While disconfirming the proposition of the first prosodic yes-no question, in response to the second italicized question Connie adopts the formulation of the questioner (i.e., *it was the best I could come up with*) thereby supporting his characterization of the evidence, i.e., her attempts at resistance could have been better. Example 25 is similar to 24 in the sense that Marg's acts of resistance (e.g., talking to Melinda and Bob, telling Matt she wanted to go to sleep) are represented as not forceful enough – *And that's as far as you went though?* And example 26 reiterates this theme: Marg is described as *holding back* with Melinda. What emerges from these examples is a portrayal of the complainants as ineffective in their attempts to resist Matt; their acts of resistance are acknowledged, yet characterized as weak and limited.

24 Trial
Q: *So do I take it then – correct me if I am wrong – that the only effort that you would have made to try and jolly him out of this or have him leave was to say that, 'I have a class in the morning so you'll have to leave', or words to that effect?*
CD: No. That was not the only effort I made with regards to making him stop doing what he was doing. It may have been the only time that I outright said, 'Now you have to leave', but I certainly did make it clear beforehand.

Q: But, ma'am what I am getting at is this: You, according to what I heard you say in your evidence today, you must have been outraged by what he was doing to you at this point?

CD: I hadn't got to outrage.

Q: You were still stunned, were you?

CD: Yes.

Q: *And the best you could come up with I suggest is, 'I've got a class in the morning, you better leave'?*

A: At the time it was the best I could come up with.

25   Trial

Q: And if I understand you also told us that you never clearly gave that message to Matt. It was like a broken telephone line. You were trying to tell Melinda and Bob what Matt was doing?

MB: No. I told Matt that I wanted to go to sleep. When you want to go to sleep, that means you don't want to do anything.

Q: *And that's as far as you went though?*

MB: No. I also said, 'No I don't want to do anything.'

26   Trial

Q: But this was Melinda, not some person you ran into in the hall. *Why would you hold back with her if you wanted her to help you?*

MB: I wasn't holding back. I was telling her what happened and asking her for help.

Q: And you said, 'Matt is touching me', and not 'Matt is putting his fingers in my vagina. What's going on?'

MB: It's not something you blurt out. It's kind of humiliating.

Q: Even to Melinda?

MB: Even to anybody.

Q: Even to Melinda?

MB: Yes, even to Melinda.

Q: *Well, I suggest to you it's no wonder she didn't know what to tell you because you didn't really tell her anything?*

MB: Sir, I said Matt was touching me and I didn't want him to.

Initially describing Marg as *holding back* with Melinda, in example 26 the cross-examiner goes on to (re)formulate this proposition in the second italicized prosodic yes-no question – *you didn't really tell her anything?* What intervenes is a series of questions that challenge Marg's claim that she was too embarrassed and humiliated to describe the graphic details of Matt's aggression to Melinda. Having undermined the motivation for Marg's 'inexplicit' cry for help, the cross-examiner then (re)constructs her communications with Melinda as being without content – Marg didn't really tell Melinda anything.

More extreme characterizations of the complainants as passive – as having done nothing – are found in 27 and 28 below. The italicized question in 27 transforms Marg's preceding response, in which she cites a verbal act of resistance, into a proposition that presupposes (i.e., takes for granted) that Marg said nothing – *So you do admit that you said nothing to him at that point about the second insertion of the vagina?* This prosodic yes-no question signals the speaker's (ostensible) belief in its proposition and his expectation that the proposition will be confirmed. More importantly, however, the predicate *admit* is a factive predicate and therefore presupposes the truth of its complement. What is taken for granted and assumed within the discourse, then, is the proposition 'You said nothing to him about the second insertion of the vagina.'

27 Tribunal

> MB: At that point I did not respond at all. Like I said I was in shock I wasn't sure what to do . . . so I got out of the bed. I went and I asked Melinda to come in the hallway or in the washroom and talk to me and I told her what had happened. I went back into the room and I said 'I just want to go to sleep.'
> TM: *So you do admit that you said nothing to him at that point about the second insertion of the vagina?*
> MB: And I did not respond in any way.

Example 28, a continuation of example 13 above, involves an interchange between Matt's representative in the university tribunal and one of the tribunal members, BW. BW is trying to extract a *question* from a series of TM's assertions. He summarizes TM's remarks in the following way: *Uh the only question that emerged out of the long statement Connie is whether or not you can explain why at this juncture you didn't do anything?* Presupposed in the embedded Wh-question BW poses is the proposition that 'Connie didn't do anything' at a particular juncture in time. The difficulty of denying presupposed material is manifest in Connie's response: she responds to the questioned proposition, 'can you explain', leaving the presupposition intact.

28 Tribunal

> TM: But you had certain options. You could have left the room. By your admission there was a time when he was asleep. You could have called through a very thin wall. Uh . . . you actually left the room to go to the washroom. Uh you had a number of options here and you chose not to take any of them. Subsequent to that you chose not to tell anybody for a number days including the police or the campus security and it was only some days later . . . that you chose to make a decision about this. And then only in concert with Marg. Let's let's move on.
> BW: I don't think you're asking a question [and]
> TM: [well yes I think I was] my question was I asked asked her very specific questions =
> BW: = Okay okay. But let me let me interrupt. Uh the only question that emerged out of the long statement Connie is *whether or not you can*

explain why at this juncture you didn't do anything?
CD: Well I can't explain.

Reformulating fear

The most frequent response to questions concerning the complainants' and the witness's so-called passive or ineffectual behaviour in spite of 'options' was that they had been motivated by fear, as in examples 11, 12, 14, 15, and 19. Indeed, when asked throughout the tribunal and the criminal trial why they didn't pursue certain avenues of resistance, both the complainants and their witness typically pointed to Matt's frightening and intimidating presence. Consider example 29 from Marg's direct testimony:

29 Tribunal

HL: Is there anything else that you haven't told us that you want to?

MB: (long pause) Only that hh . . . I know everything . . . the night that was dumb. It was dumb of me to invite Matt to stay well in my bed eh – heh but in residence everyone is like your brother like I said and you don't imagine that that could happen uhm and that. Well, I have definitely learned from this. But I didn't yell I didn't . . . I didn't do anything because I didn't know what to do. I mean everyone kept telling me just forget about it, just go back to bed, just go to sleep. And I figured you know if I yelled . . . Melinda and Bob weren't going to help me. I mean hh they were just lying there. Like I kept telling Melinda and I told Bob that what he was doing and . . . and they they didn't obviously care. After Bob had talked to Matt when we were laying in bed that Matt tried something again and I said to Bob you know 'Where did you get these persistent friends' to let Matt or let Bob know that Matt was doing it again and Bob said 'Oh I don't know, you know.' It's that was it – he didn't care. *Uhm so I figured you know if if he if he hits me I mean they're not going to stop him and the door was locked so like I hh he's a scary guy I mean hh he is very intimidating. If he intimidated Bob not to get out of the bed or or to go with him and he made Melinda afraid that he was going to hit her. I mean I didn't want I didn't want to get hit, I didn't want to get raped, but I didn't want to get hit. I just didn't know what to do.* ((voice trembling)) ((sniffling))

After the complainants' and witnesses' numerous expressions of fear, the cross-examiners and tribunal members generally followed with questions attempting to deconstruct the cause or source of the fear. This can be seen in 30 below where the chair of the tribunal, BW, is questioning Connie.

30 Tribunal

BW: In your statement, I think, twice, you mention 'he was sounding very angry' and 'I was scared' and I was wondering if you could elaborate on what you mean by that? What was he saying that you found scary?

If you remember anything specific or whether it was an impression.

CD: It was just rough. It was mostly . . . he just . . . it was demanding. I didn't feel like I had any more choice. And whatever he said was no longer a request. It was a demand.

BW: So, in your statement when you say he said 'I paid for dinner and you invited me up so what did you expect' . . . that was something you perceived as demanding and rough? It wasn't like a joking comment in your mind?

CD: No, it wasn't a joke at all.

BW: Did he raise his voice? Or was it just very emphatic?

CD: No, he didn't raise his voice but it was very blunt, very . . .

BW: Okay.

Here we see the tribunal member trying to get at the precise causes of Connie's fear: What was it about Matt that was frightening? Was it something he said? Was it his tone of voice? Similar kinds of questions, probing the exact origins of Melinda's fear, are evident in example 31. (This example follows directly after example 12 in which Melinda has just described Matt as *a very intimidating person*.)

31 Tribunal

BW: Could you explain that? Because we've heard that twice and in your story the *only* time you mention about being scared of Matt was with the eavesdropping incident . . . that he was very scary. He was insisting that you tell him. Were there other things that he did or is it a general demeanor? What do you mean by he's very scary?

MK: He's . . . the way he . . . it seems to me if his way . . . it's either his way or no way. The way he was talking to Bob like even his friend Bob when I asked Bob to come to the bathroom, Matt said 'No, don't go.' And Bob hesitated not to go which sort of led me to believe that Bob was scared of Matt and maybe Bob knows a history of [Matt]

BW: [Well,] let's just stick to what you know. The two times in that evening that you found Matt scary would be the eavesdropping incident and with Bob . . . how insistent he was about Bob. You saw a side of him that scared you. Anything else than those two things?

MK: No.

Again BW tries to isolate the specific aspects of the defendant or the defendant's behaviour that were frightening to the witness. I suggest that the attempt to pinpoint so precisely and exactly the causes of the women's fear has the effect of reducing or minimizing it. Indeed, in the second line of example 31, BW comments that the *only* time the witness has expressed her fear of the defendant is in relation to the eavesdropping incident, signifying the limited range of the witness's fear. It seems that it was not sufficient for the complainants simply to report that the defendant was a *scary guy* or *a very intimidating person {who}* . . . *scares a lot people*. Through this tribunal member's questioning and his attempts to impute the women's fear to very specific aspects of the defendant's behaviour, its potential impact on the women's actions is called into question. In the last part of example 31, we see the tribunal member cutting Melinda off and reformulating her comments about her fear of Matt. Thus, what begins as a description of how intimidating the witness found the defendant (*I think Matt is a very intimidating person*) is transformed into the witness feeling frightened only twice over the course of events (*The two times in the evening that you found Matt scary*). That is, after producing fairly detailed descriptions of Matt's scariness, Melinda's final response in 31 confirms that there were only two things about Matt that scared her. Expressed more generally, BW's reformulation of Melinda's fear functions to reshape her own description of it, its final articulation being much diminished from the original formulation.

Conclusion

This chapter has analysed the questions asked of complainants in sexual assault adjudication processes under the assumption that the questions asked – and the questions not asked – in institutional discourse 'do ideological work' (Fisher 1991). Constituted by and constitutive of cultural ideologies of gender, these particular types of institutional settings are fertile grounds for the (re)circulation of discourses that disadvantage and discriminate against women. As a number of feminist theorists have said of the legal adjudication of rape, rather than protecting the sexual autonomy of women, the rape trial can be seen 'as a public mechanism for the control of female sexuality' (Lees 1997: 88) and concomitantly a forum in which a considerable range of men's sexual prerogatives are protected (Crenshaw 1992: 408). I have attempted to give empirical substance to these claims. By considering the way in which cross-examining questioners, including so-called neutral tribunal members, control evidence through their questioning, I have identified a number of propositions that are presupposed or (pseudo)asserted within this discourse. When taken together these propositions form a powerful ideological frame through which the events under investigation are understood. First, it is presupposed and/or 'declared' that the complainants had choice and options when confronted with the threat of sexual aggression. Second, the complainants are depicted as being unconstrained in their choice of appropriate avenues of resistance. Indeed, viewed within the context of 'numerous' and 'unlimited' options, the complainants' responses to Matt's sexual aggression come to be construed as ineffectual and passive. Third, then, the women's 'lack of resistance' is established: because they did not pursue readily available and numerous options they did not resist to the utmost. Finally, through questions that discount the paralysing and pervasive nature of the women's fear, the motivation for their 'inaction' is eliminated. Thus, although no longer codified in law, the utmost resistance standard circulates discursively within these adjudication processes, (re)constructing the events in question as consensual sex. That is, without utmost resistance on the part of the complainants, according to this standard, rape did not occur.

In presupposing resistance to be unproblematic for the complainants and their fear, irrelevant or inexplicable, the cross-examining questioners and tribunal members, through their questions, were implicitly judging the complainants' behaviour against the standard of the 'normal' subject of legal discourse – the rational, autonomous, freely-choosing individual of classic liberal theory. That such a subject permeates the legal doctrine of the Anglo common law system is a claim articulated by both feminists and critical legal theorists; the following excerpt from an introduction to a collection of articles on feminist legal theory is representative:

> The Anglo-U.S. legal system presupposes what is essentially a mythical being: a legal subject who is coherent, rational and freely choosing, and who can, in ordinary circumstances, be held fully accountable for 'his' actions. Thus, legal doctrines generally assume that an individual acts with clear intentions that are transparently available to himself and to others, on the basis of suppositions about what a 'rational person' would do in similar circumstances.
>
> (Bartlett and Kennedy 1991: 7)

Focusing on sexual assault legal doctrine specifically, Lacey (1998: 117) makes a similar critique of the legal concepts of consent and sexual autonomy: 'in focusing on an individualised notion of consent, rather than the conditions under which choices can be meaningful, the prevailing idea of sexual autonomy *assumes* the mind to be dominant and controlling, irrespective of material circumstances' (emphasis in original). That is, constructing complainants as freely-choosing, autonomous individuals, as legal doctrine does, precludes a consideration of the material conditions under which their consent is 'meaningful': conditions in which the victims' fear and paralysis (and not their minds) can be 'dominant and controlling', given the unequal power dynamics that potentially characterize male/female relations in situations of unwanted sexual aggression. While Lacey's critique is focused on legal *statutes*, what we have seen throughout this chapter is the discursive penetration of legal categories such as the 'autonomous subject' and an 'individualised notion of consent' within the adjudication process itself. Moreover, given the pervasive form in which these categories are expressed – as *presupposed* propositions – their presence in the discourse remains relatively invisible and common-sensical, 'naturalizing' a version of events that represents the complainants as having made bad choices in the context of unlimited options. To underscore the insidious nature of the ideological frame of 'utmost resistance' in structuring our understanding of the complainants' behaviour, I return to Bateson's example of otters. Just as the 'frame' of playing defined the otter's nips and bites as playful, and not hostile, so the ideological frame of utmost resistance defined the women as passive and lacking in resistance, and not strategic and active. More specifically, such a lens (re)constructed the women's acts of resistance as ineffective and weak or rendered them imperceptible and unrecognizable as acts of resistance. Analysing the linguistic features of the complainants' and their witness's testimony, the next chapter elucidates further the transformative ideological work performed by questions: how the complainants' strategic agency is (re)produced as ineffectual agency.

4 'I didn't yell . . . I didn't scream'

Complainants' ineffectual agency or strategic agency?[1]

Introduction

Co-constructing an ideological 'frame' that characterized the complainants and their witness as autonomous, self-determining subjects, unconstrained by the socially-structured inequities that can shape women's responses to male sexual aggression, I have argued that the cross-examining questioners, including the 'neutral' tribunal members, (re)presented the events in question as consensual sex. This is not to say, however, that the complainants and their witness subscribed to this same interpretation of events. In example 30 from the previous chapter (and repeated below), we see the complainant, Connie, asserting that Matt's utterances were demands, not requests; that is, from the complainant's perspective, there were no 'options' to choose from.

1 Tribunal
   BW: In your statement, I think, twice, you mention 'he was sounding very angry' and 'I was scared' and I was wondering if you could elaborate on what you mean by that? What was he saying that you found scary? If you remember anything specific or whether it was an impression.
   CD: It was just rough. It was mostly . . . he just . . . it was demanding. *I didn't feel like I had any more choice. And whatever he said was no longer a request. It was a demand.*

Likewise, example 2 indicates that, for Connie, the sexual activity was not consensual.

2 Tribunal
   BW: We know that you don't know but is it possible I guess is the question. Is it possible that he . . . saw the events differently . . . than you perceived them?
   CD: I suppose it's possible. But . . . I don't see how, I mean . . . hhh how many times do you have to say 'no I don't want to do this'? You know, how many times do you have to push a hand away? How many times does this have to come back and for you to push it away again?

How many times do you have to say 'No, please don't' before somebody understands.

Given the complainants' understanding of these events as sexual assault, and not consensual sex, this chapter considers the extent to which the ideological frame of utmost resistance was absolute and seamless in its ability to define the nature of the events under investigation. That is, to what extent was there struggle over the interpretation and representation of events in these adjudication processes and, if so, whose meanings prevailed?

Of relevance to the idea that institutional interactions are potential sites of ideological struggle is Fairclough's discussion of the 'institutional subject'. For Fairclough (1995: 39), as discussed in Chapter 3, the double sense of the term, subject, as both 'agent' and 'affected' 'captures the concept of the subject as qualified to act through being constrained – "subjected" – to an institutional frame'. Indeed, according to Fairclough, one of the ways in which institutional frames constrain their subjects is through discourse: institutions 'impose ideological and discoursal constraints upon them [subjects] as a condition for qualifying them to act as subjects' (p. 39). Expressed in the concrete terms of this investigation, the complainants (i.e., subjects) are 'qualified to act' (i.e., speak) but do so within constraints. What I have been calling the ideological frame of utmost resistance functions as a discursive constraint, restricting the complainants' 'talk' about their experiences and producing them as particular kinds of subjects – as *ineffectual* agents, that is, as agents whose so-called passivity and lack of resistance is considered tantamount to consent. In other words, not only do the kinds of questions analysed previously characterize the complainants as 'passive' and 'lacking in resistance', they also constrain their *own* representations/productions of themselves. In Chapter 1, I suggested, as others have, that because gender is an organizing principle of cultural institutions, the 'institutional cooerciveness' (Cameron (1997: 31) that Fairclough refers to above will manifest itself along gendered lines. Accordingly, in Chapter 2 I demonstrated how dominant notions of male sexuality informed the decisions of adjudicators in these adjudication processes and afforded legitimacy and authority to Matt's testimony, in particular, his representation of himself as a non-agent of sexual aggression. Consistent with the idea that institutional frames, whether manifest in judicial decisions or the talk of adjudication processes, constrain and shape *gendered* identities, I suggest in this chapter that the complainants' representation of themselves as 'passive' and 'ineffectual' is an institutionally-*coerced* performance of stereotypical femininity: the complainants are 'thrust into' this particular subject position. That is, if one looks beyond the constraints that the ideological frame of utmost resistance imposes upon their talk, and hence upon the (gendered) identities they are allowed to produce, one locates evidence of active and strategic resistance on the part of the complainants. Thus, after delineating the complainants' grammar of ineffectual agency produced in these proceedings by questions that presuppose the inadequacy of their actions, I turn to the complainants' expressions of *strategic* agency – expressions often obscured and rendered invisible by the ideological frame that discursively dominates these adjudication processes.

A grammar of ineffectual agency

Illustrating the interactional control exerted by questioners, I have in the previous chapter identified specific question–answer sequences where the complainants and their witness contribute to a discursive portrayal of themselves as passive and/or ineffectual agents. In 28, for example, the complainant's final response *well I can't explain* leaves intact the presupposed information of the previous question, that is, that the complainant didn't *do anything* to resist the accused's sexual acts of aggression. And in example 31, the witness's final response confirms the tribunal member's *reformulation* of her previous assertions – that she was *only* frightened twice over the course of events. While previously focusing, then, on the complainants' implicit and explicit confirmations of questioners' presupposed or (pseudo)asserted propositions, in what follows I turn to the complainants' linguistic characterizations of their own behaviour as they respond to (i.e., are subjected to) the barrage of questions delineating the numerous and unlimited options available to them. Example 3 is representative:

3   Trial
Q: Guess I am just asking you did you have it in your mind that your room at some point might be a place that you can go, particularly when you started to get into trouble with Mr. A?
MK: That didn't even enter my mind.
Q: Why didn't it enter your mind?
MK: Because as things were happening they were happening so fast and I didn't have a lot of time to think about what to do, what to do. Everything clouded over on me.
Q: Right. I know it did, but what about from 4.30 in the morning until 10 or 11 in the morning, it still didn't cross your mind?
MK: No.
Q: You know your roommate was there because you said 'I am home', or words to that effect?
MK: Yes.
(a few intervening questions)
Q: It never crossed your mind to go back and speak to Wayne again since that was his job?
MK: No.
Q: Did it ever cross your mind?
(a few intervening questions)

Q: You didn't think that he might be a safe person to help you out of your dilemma?

MK: I wasn't thinking. I wasn't thinking clearly and I didn't know what to do.

Q: Is it because of your exhaustion you don't know what to do now? You sure seemed to know what to do when the car was towed and the fact that you wanted to get back up to see Bob and that suggests a presence of mind you have?

MK: I have never been put in a situation like that and, as I said, things were happening quickly and I was at a loss of what to do. I have never been put in that position. I am not experienced with that. I just didn't even think about it.

Implicitly claiming that Melinda has 'failed' to seek help for Marg, the defence attorney asks a number of questions about possible sources of help. Melinda is questioned about whether she thought of her residence room as a safe refuge and whether she enlisted the help of her roommate or the residence adviser, Wayne. Faced with repeated questions about her 'failure' to pursue such options, Melinda responds by referring to her inability to think clearly under the circumstances. Indeed, this is one 'stroke' in the portrayal of ineffectual agency – a portrayal produced in the 'talk' of the complainants and their witness in the process of being 'subjected . . . to an institutional frame' (Fairclough 1995: 39). Contributing to the realization of this depiction are a variety of grammatical forms (illustrated in example 3), used by the complainants and their witness, that emphasize their inability to *act* in ways that effectively express their resistance to Matt's sexual aggression. That is, when questioned about the 'numerous' and unlimited 'options' that they were 'free' to pursue, the complainants and their witness did not generally respond by casting themselves in the roles of agents and actors, that is, as individuals who 'purposefully intiate[d] or cause[d] actions' (Capps and Ochs 1995: 67). Rather, when they did represent themselves as initiators or causers of actions (i.e., as agents or actors) their causal role was severely diminished; otherwise, they represented themselves as experiencers of cognitive or emotional states or as patients – entities that were acted upon. Specifically, the complainants and their witness: (1) referred to themselves as agents or actors of negated actions, that is, actions that were *not* performed, (2) referred to themselves as agents or actors of unsuccessful actions, (3) referred to themselves as agents or actors of actions, the force of which was diminished by adverbial or adjectival phrases, (4) referred to themselves as experiencers of negated cognitive states, (5) referred to themselves as experiencers of fear, and (6) referred to themselves as patients, that is, entities that were *acted upon*.[2] I use terms such as agent, actor, experiencer and patient to refer to the semantic roles that referents designated by noun phrases assume in relation to the verbs they are predicated of. *Agent* and *actor* refer to the intentional initiator of an action. If this action has consequences for an object or animate patient, then the intentional initiator is referred to as an agent; if not, it is referred to as an actor (Duranti 1993). *Experiencer* refers to one who experiences some psychological or cognitive state (e.g., feeling or thinking) and *patient* refers to a person or thing undergoing an action. Consider the following four sentences in which the noun phrase *the woman* assumes the semantic role of agent, actor, experiencer and patient, respectively.

4   a. The woman resisted her attacker.
    b. The woman escaped from her attacker.
    c. The woman was extremely frightened as a result of the attack.
    d. Fear overcame the woman as she realized her attacker had returned.

Examples 4a and 4b depict *the woman* as exercising agency, given her repre-sentation as a wilful and purposeful initiator of the actions. In example 4c, by contrast, the woman is represented, not as an initiator of an event, but rather as an experiencer of an affective state, fear; indeed, example 4d repre-sents the woman as an entity *acted upon* by the force of this emotion.

The examples that follow are generally drawn from, and are representative of, answers that the complainants and their witness provided to questions of the type illustrated in Chapter 3 – that is, questions asked by the cross-examining questioners or the tribunal members that presupposed and (pseudo)asserted the complainants' ready access to a variety of options in the face of (potential) sexual aggression. Whenever the examples below have been drawn from responses to questions asked in *direct* examination this is expli-citly indicated. (The posing of questions in direct examination is an issue I return to later in this chapter.)

Negated actions

In examples 5 to 10, the italicized sentences display the complainants and/or their witness as the agents or actors of grammatically-negated acts. Generally, then, all of the italicized predicates designate actions that were *not* caused or initiated by the referents of their subjects. In 5 to 7, we see a number of vocal actions that were not realized, for example, yelling, scream-ing or saying something while in 8 to 10 it is cognitive events that are repre-sented in this way, for example, formulating an idea or thinking of a way of seeking help. Two of the italicized sentences (in 5 and 7) are even more extreme expressions of inaction on the part of the complainants – *I didn't do anything*.

5   I just sat there, and I didn't – *I didn't do anything. I didn't say anything.* (CD, Trial)
6   *I didn't fight and I didn't scream. I didn't say anything.* (MB, Trial)
7   I have definitely learned from this . . . but *I didn't yell* I didn't . . . *I didn't do anything* because I didn't know what to do. (MB, Tribunal, direct)

8 *I never even formulated the idea that I can't handle this by myself.* I thought that I could get control of the situation back and I thought that – I just didn't think about it. (CD, Trial, direct)

9 It crossed my mind that if I can't get him out, then, you know what do I do? *But I never really formulated into a coherent this is what I have to do next.* (CD, Trial)

10 And everything was happening so fast, *I didn't even think about knocking on the neighbour's door or anything.* (MK, Tribunal)

Unsuccessful actions

In a similar way, the italicized sentences in examples 11 to 14 all represent the complainants as agents or actors of actions that were *not* performed. In these examples, however, the acts are represented as 'attempted' but 'unsuccessful', given the presence of the main verb *try*. More specifically, example 11 represents a failed cognitive act; examples 12 to 14, various failed attempts at verbal acts of resistance; and examples 15 to 18, unsuccessful acts of physical resistance.

11 I was too busy *trying to figure out how to make him stop.* I thought I could do it. (CD, Trial)

12 Well, *I tried to* [talk to Bob about Matt's aggression]. The incident in the bathroom when I asked Bob to go talk to Marg . . . was the only thing I could think of . . . to get someone to tell Matt to stop it. (MK, Tribunal)

13 I was afraid. No one can understand that except for the people that were there. I was extremely afraid of being hurt. Uhm: as for signals, they were being ignored. *I tried* [to give signals of non-consent] I mean maybe they weren't being ignored I don't know why he didn't listen to them. (MB, Tribunal)

14 I told Matt, I said if the circumstances would have been different different, maybe. It was a lie but I mean it was another way *for me to try to tell him 'no'.* . . . It wasn't getting through so *I tried different approaches.* (MB, Tribunal)

15 *I tried to get out of the bed and go talk to Melinda* about what had been said at the door. *I tried to get out.* (MB, Tribunal)

16 *I kept trying to move away and push my head back up* but he had my hair and every time – *every time I tried to,* he just pushed me back down. (CD, Trial)

17 Everytime *I tried to sit up,* I got pushed back down. (CD, Trial)

18 *I tried to get out of the bed* . . . he pulled me back down. *I tried to get out of the bed* he pulled me down again. (MB, Tribunal)

Actions with limited force

Whereas examples 5 to 18 represent actions *not* caused or initiated by the complainants and/or their witness, examples 19 to 25 do depict the women as agents or actors of actions. The italicized sentences in 19 to 25, however, contain adverbial or adjectival phrases that diminish the force or effectiveness of these actions. The adverbial *just* modifies the events represented in 19 to 22, signifying that the actions were minimal or limited in some way. Likewise, in 23 and 24 CD's use of the phrase – *the best I could come up with* – suggests that there were *better* ways of resisting Matt. (In 24 CD seems to be adopting the phrasing of her questioner; however, example 23, where she also uses this phrasing, occurs before 24 in the course of the trial.) Finally, the use of the adverbial *even* in example 25 represents the idea of *knocking on the neighbour's door* as an obvious and unproblematic option to pursue. Having not pursued it, then, Melinda represents her efforts as limited.

19 Q: And going somewhere this time or contacting someone at this time?
    MB: No, sir, *we just went outside* and I grabbed our cigarettes and sat outside the door. (MB, Trial)
20 Q: Right. So what, so you did what?
    MB: So *I just sat there* and desperately hoped he would leave. (MB, Trial)
21 Q: And you didn't encourage that and said, (sic) 'Thanks for coming fellows, see you around', anything to jolly him out?
    MB: I was afraid and *I just sat there staring* I was so afraid. (MB, Trial)
22 *I just sat there*, and I didn't – I didn't do anything. I didn't say anything. (CD, Trial)
23 Q: So you didn't sort of then say, okay try plan 'B'. You didn't say, 'Matt, I want you to leave.' That would have been clear as a bell.
    CD: I didn't really have a well thought out plan 'A' and plan 'B'. I was running on I think instinct and is *the best I could come up with was 'Don't, stop, no, please don't.'* (CD, Trial)
24 Q: And the best you could come up with I suggest is, 'I've got a class in the morning, you better leave'?
    CD: At the time *it was the best I could come up with*. (CD, Trial)
25 And everything was happening so fast, *I didn't even think* about knocking on the neighbour's door or anything. (MK, Tribunal)

Experiencers of negated cognitive states

Like many of Melinda's utterances in example 3, examples 26 to 35 show the complainants as experiencers of negated cognitive states. First, then, the women are not representing themselves as purposefully or wilfully initiating actions. Second, they are not representing themselves as experiencers of *positive* cognitive states, that is, as having ideas and/or knowledge about possible actions. On the contrary, the italicized sentences in 26 to 35 depict the complainants as unable to act purposefully or wilfully because they lack knowledge or are unable to think clearly.

26 Which is why *I wasn't sure what to do.* (MB, Trial)
27 Because I was in shock everything started coming in on me and *I didn't know what to do.* I was tired and *I wasn't sure what to do.* (MB, Trial)
28 *I didn't honestly know what else in my mind to do at that time.* (MB, Tribunal)
29 I am telling you that *I didn't know what to do.* (MB, Trial)
30 I had trusted him and then he started doing this and I didn't understand where it was coming from which is *why I didn't know what to do.* (MB, Trial)
31 All I wanted was to take – someone to take control of the situation and help me because *I wasn't thinking of what to do for myself.* (MB, Trial)
32 Because as things were happening they were happening so fast and *I didn't have a lot of time to think about what to do, what to do.* (MK, Trial)
33 *I didn't know what to do.* You don't understand. The whole entire time time . . . *I didn't know what to do.* I was not thinking clearly. (MB, Tribunal)
34 He seemed very angry and I realized I had lost control of the situation and *didn't really know what to do about it* and *couldn't really think straight* at this point other than wanting him to stop. (CD, Trial)
35 *I didn't know what to do.* I just felt overwhelmed, I was so tired. I felt so helpless. *I didn't know what to do.* (CD, Trial)

Experiencers of fear

By far, the most frequent response to questions concerning the complainants' and their witness's 'failure' to pursue the numerous options presented to them was that they had been motivated by fear. Many such expressions of fear appear in the examples of Chapter 3 and in the examples presented previously in this chapter. I provide the following question–answer sequence as a further representative example:

36 Trial

Q: And you didn't encourage that and said, (sic) 'Thanks for coming fellows, see you around', anything to jolly him out?
MB: *I was afraid and I just sat there staring I was so afraid.*
Q: You were afraid that Mr. A. was saying to Bob, 'Let's go out of here, let's leave'?
MB: No. *I was afraid because he was mad* because I didn't want to do anything with him so he was mad with me, *so I was afraid that he was going to physically hurt me* because I didn't want to do anything with him.
Q: Right. So what, so you did what?
MB: So I just sat there and desperately hoped that he would leave.
Q: And you felt that if you tried to keep the momentum up of having him leave or open the door or something he might turn on you and say, 'Oh, no, not so fast'?

MB: I hoped that he would forget and I know that doesn't make sense, but forget that I was there and carry on his conversation with Bob and leave. *I was afraid to make a noise* that they might turn and realize that I was there and then Matt take it out on me.

Patients or entities acted upon

Using grammatical constructions that even further diminish their agency, the complainants and their witness at times represented themselves as entities that were *acted upon*. That is, not only did they not portray themselves as initiators of events, they represented events or psychological states as controlling *them*. Connie's utterance in 37 is an explicit statement about her increasing sense that she was not in contol.

37 From that point that I realized that it had gotten out of control. (CD, Trial)

Examples 38 and 39 represent this same complainant as an experiencer of unrealized cognitive states (e.g., knowing how to react, being logical and coherent). Indeed, Connie is both patient and experiencer in these two examples; the events are represented as happening *to her* too quickly to allow for careful reflection.

38 I mean actions were happening too fast for me to know how to react to them, for me to know what to do, and be logic and coherent about what the next move would be. (CD, Trial)
39 Everything was happening too quickly for me to react to it. (CD, Trial)

The idea that the women's thoughts were not within their control has a more explicit grammatical realization in examples 40 to 42. Their minds are depicted in the semantic role of *patient* – as entities that were subjected to certain thoughts and not others.

40 Q: Guess I am just asking you did you have it in your mind that your room at some point might be a place that you can go, particularly when you started to get into trouble with Mr. A?
   MK: *That didn't even enter my mind.* (MK, Trial)
41 Q: Why didn't you say 'Look, you can't do this to me', whatever. 'I've got a class in the morning', why did that come to your mind? . . . Were you still worried about his feelings?
   CD: No. I don't know why *that's the first thing that came to my mind.* (CD, Trial)
42 *It never even crossed my mind of anything sexual happening.* (MB, Tribunal)

Examples 43 to 45 also show the women as acted upon, either by the force of emotions or by the overwhelming strength of the events. That the italicized portions of examples 40 to 45 all have verbs of motion further reinforces this representation: the women are controlled by potent and *active* forces.

43 I was like . . . I was so confused and *so so many emotions running through me* that I didn't know what to do that I just rolled over. (MB, Tribunal)
44 Because I was in shock and *everything started coming in on me* and I didn't know what to do. I was tired and I wasn't sure what to do. (MB, Trial)
45 But as things were happening they were happening so fast and I didn't have a lot of time to think about what to do, what to do. *Everything clouded over on me.* (MK, Trial)

Overwhelmed by uncontrollable forces, Marg, in examples 46 and 47, expresses a desire for help, again casting herself in the semantic role of patient. As she so eloquently articulates her plight, someone has to act upon her (i.e., help her) because she no longer can think (or act) for herself.

46 I was waiting for or hoping *somebody would help me* and say, 'Let's leave.' (MB, Trial)
47 All I wanted was to take – *someone to take control of the situation and help me* because I wasn't thinking of what to do for myself. (MB, Trial)

The cumulative effect of the grammatical forms delineated in this section can be seen in the question–answer sequence of example 3. Responding repeatedly to questions about help she did *not* seek, Melinda is produced, not as a purposeful initiatior of actions that would solicit help, but as an entity acted upon by paralysing emotions (e.g., *Everything clouded over on me*) or as an experiencer of cognitive states that yielded no action (e.g., *I wasn't thinking clearly, I just didn't even think about it*). Set against a landscape peopled by autonomous subjects whose 'choices' are unencumbered by socially-struc-tured inequities, this portrait of Melinda renders her purposeful acts (i.e., her agency) as weak, unsuccessful or non-existent. Returning to Fairclough's notion of the 'institutional subject', we can view the complainants and their witness as subjects 'acting through' discursive constraints, producing themselves as ineffectual agents. They are 'entered' involuntarily into this subject position (Hirsch and Lazarus-Black 1994) by questions that accomp-lish ideological work – questions that not only represent their actions as passive and ineffectual but also 'produce' them as such.

Potential sites of resistance

Following Foucault, recent approaches to contemporary feminist scholarship have abandoned a conception of power as essentially 'repressive or prohibitive' in favour of one that is 'continuous, subtle, and productive' (Davis and Fisher 1993: 8). According to this view, power does not rely on violence and 'the barrel of a gun' for its enforcement nor is it simply imposed in a top–down fashion by a capitalist-patriarchal state. Rather, 'it is a force and effect which exists and circulates in a web of social interaction' (Cameron *et al.* 1992), exerting its authority through socially and historically-constituted domains of knowledge that create, for example, categories of 'normality' and 'deviance'. Bordo (1993) offers an illuminating discussion of Foucauldian ideas about power in relation to her own work on the female body. Illustrating the way in which power can work 'from below', Bordo (1993: 27) describes eating disorders within the contemporary context 'as arising out of and reproducing normative feminine practices of our culture, practices which train the female body in docility and obedience to cultural demands while at the same time being *experienced* in terms of power and control' (emphasis in original). Cultural definitions of female beauty, then, are not imposed and policed by coercive and violent measures, but rather achieve their force through 'individual self-surveillance and self-correction to norms'. Thus, for feminists critical of the totalizing tenet of radical feminism – that women are essentially (i.e., universally and transhistorically) oppressed by men – and its solution – dismantling patriarchy – understanding power as operating through multiple and local forces offers possibilities for understanding the workings of hegemony and resistance in what Fraser (1989) calls the 'politics of everyday life'. While sexual assault adjudication processes may not constitute 'everyday life' for most of us, the microanalysis of this particular kind of discursive practice resonates with attempts to bridge the gap between structural and systemic notions of power and Foucauldian ones. Hirsch and Lazarus-Black explain:

> Although . . . many feminists draw on Foucauldian approaches to discourse and the microlevel of power dynamics, most also offer the critique that theorizing power primarily in multiple local contexts tends to elide more systematic domination, particularly the oppressive effects of patriarchal institutions on women. . . . Accordingly, these scholars emphasize that power operates discursively *and* materially in many contexts, *including* state institutions, an innovation that puts the bite back into new concepts of power. (emphasis in original)
>
> (Hirsch and Lazarus-Black 1994: 3–4)

Assuming that the 'oppressive effects of patriarchal institutions' such as the legal system manifest themselves at the microlevel of interaction, I have identified the ideological frame of utmost resistance as one of patriarchy's discursive reflexes. A 'capillary' circulating throughout the discourse, its power is exercised interactionally at the most local of levels (e.g., question–answer sequences). And because power operates 'at the lowest rather than the topmost extremities of the social body' (Fisher 1991: 176), in Foucault's terms, it creates the potential for multiple sites of resistance: 'resistances . . . are formed right at the point where relations of power are exercised' (Foucault 1980: 142). The dilemma that this section takes up, then, is how to focus on the ideological frame that discursively delimits and constrains the expressions and concomitant subjectivities of the complainants and their witness, while at the same time investigating potential sites of resistance – sites where the complainants and their witness successfully exercise and represent their agency.

To adequately capture the multiple dimensions along which power can be exercised and thus resisted in these kinds of adjudication processes, I return to a distinction made in Chapter 2. Hale and Gibbons (1999: 203) distinguish between 'two intersecting planes of reality' in the courtroom: the reality of the courtroom itself – what they call the 'courtroom reality' – and the reality that comprises the events under investigation in the courtroom – what they call 'the external reality'. Given that our access to 'the external reality' in these cases is mediated exclusively by the language of 'the courtroom reality' – language that I have claimed frames the complainants' actions as 'passive' and 'ineffectual' – our ability to see resistance in 'the external reality' depends to a large extent on resistance being possible in 'the courtroom reality'. That is, if the complainants' are able to reveal their strategic agency or resistance in 'the external reality', they must be able to impose their own interpretations on events as they are represented in 'the courtroom reality'. Thus, below I consider the possibility of resistance within 'the courtroom reality' – in both cross-examination and direct examination.

Interactional resistance in cross-examination?

As discussed previously, a defining characteristic of institutional discourse is its interactional asymmetry: differential speaking rights are assigned to participants depending on their institutional role. In legal contexts, as we have seen, questioners have the right to initiate and allocate turns by asking questions of witnesses but the reverse is not true. Witnesses are prohibited from asking questions, which in turn means that they have difficulty controlling topics and, concomitantly, imposing interpretations on evidence. Indeed, Walker (1987: 79) argues that even informed witnesses, that is, 'those prepared by their own counsel, carefully educated in what is about to happen in the legal adversary interview', are without any real power because they are restricted to the role of responder. Supportive of Walker's claims are comments made by Hutchby and Wooffitt (1998: 170) in a review of conversational analytic work on talk in institutional settings. They say that a high proportion of CA studies of asymmetry in institutional interactions demonstrate the power that differential participatory resources bestow upon the participant who asks questions or takes up the first position in a conversational turn. Nonetheless, in keeping with Foucauldian notions of power, they caution against simply viewing power as monolithic and primarily repressive. It is in this spirit that I consider here the extent to which the question–answer sequences of the adjudication processes under investigation constitute sites of resistance for the respondents. While in previous examples I have highlighted questioners' ability to reformulate responders' answers and ultimately to reshape their subsequent responses, below I focus on instances where the complainants seem to challenge the questioners' characterization of events.

In examples 48 and 49, TM asks questions that presuppose (in 48) and assert (in 49) that Marg said nothing the first time Matt put his finger in her vagina. While not disputing this presupposition/assertion, in both examples Marg implicitly provides an alternative way of understanding the significance of her behaviour: the *absence* of a response on her part conveyed her non-consent. TM's subsequent turns interrogate Marg's formulations in the form of controlling questions (a negative yes-no question in 48 and a prosodic yes-no question in 49) which signal his belief in the truth of the proposition that 'saying nothing could signal consent' and his expectation that such a proposition will be confirmed. Thus, although Marg does impose her own interpretation on the events in question (i.e., that not responding signals non-consent) the cross-examining questioners' immediate reformulations of these interpretations may have the effect of, at best, neutralizing them and, at worst, discounting them.

48 Tribunal
   TM: So you do admit that you said nothing to him at that point about the insertion of his finger in the vagina?
   MB: And I did not respond in **any** way.
   TM: Alright. I . . . would ask you another question. Do you not think, knowing what I assume you know about young men, that if you said nothing to him . . . that he would . . . think . . . that it might be wanted as opposed to not wanted?
49 Tribunal
   TM: Since my last question . . . since you did not tell him the first time that it was unacceptable to you to put his finger in your vagina, does it not stand to reason that he saw no reason not to fondle you the same way this second time?
   MB: First of all I did not react. I've already gone over this. I did not respond. I didn't do anything. I just lied there.
   TM: Well that could be conceived as consent could it not?

Unlike 48 and 49, example 50 shows the complainant, Connie, *explicitly* challenging the (pseudo)assertions of the defence attorney's questions. (This is example 24 from Chapter 3.) That is, Connie quite forcefully disconfirms the proposition that is (pseudo)asserted in the preceding prosodic yes-no question: *No. That was not the only effort I made with regards to making him stop doing what he was doing.*

50 Trial
> Q: So do I take it then – correct me if I am wrong – that the only effort that you would have made to try and jolly him out of this or have him leave was to say that, 'I have a class in the morning so you'll have to leave', or words to that effect?
>
> CD: No. That was not the only effort I made with regards to making him stop doing what he was doing. It may have been the only time that I outright said, 'Now you have to leave', but I certainly did make it clear beforehand.

Although resisting the questioner's characterization of her efforts as weak and limited in her response of example 50, Connie goes on in example 51, a couple of turns later, to adopt her questioner's formulation of these same efforts – *it was the best I could come up with*. What intervenes between these two quite different representations of her resistance is a question from the defence attorney in which he (pseudo)asserts Connie's outrage at Matt's sexual aggression. Juxtaposed with outrage, Connie's verbal acts of resistance become (re)framed as weak and ineffective by the defence lawyer.

51 Trial
> Q: But, ma'am, what I am getting at is this: You, according to what I heard you say in your evidence today, you must have been outraged by what he was doing to you at this point.
>
> A: I hadn't got to outrage.
>
> Q: You were still stunned, were you?
>
> A: Yes.
>
> Q: And *the best you could come up with* I suggest is, 'I've got a class in the morning, you better leave'?
>
> A: At the time *it was the best I could come up with*.

Thus, what begins as an explicit rebuttal of the questioner's 'assertion' is transformed over a couple of question–answer sequences into an utterance where Connie echoes her questioner's characterization of her verbal behaviour.

Perhaps the most extreme example of interactional resistance in my data can be seen in example 52. Not only does Marg ask a question of the defence attorney, she is also granted permission to comment on his version of events. Her comment challenges the attorney's suggestion that she gave *mixed messages* to Matt; by contrast, she emphasizes the *unequivocal* nature of her verbal acts of resistance. TM's next question functions simultaneously to 'close off' the topic of Marg's comment and to introduce a new topic – whether Marg was wearing Matt's shirt during the course of the events.

52 Trial
> Q: You never asked Mr. A. to leave?
>
> MB: No.

Q: I am suggesting that's another mixed message. You said that you wanted to ignore this?

MB: Can I comment on that?

Q: Sure. If I am suggesting something to you I think you are entitled to do that.

MB: If you are suggesting by my telling Matt not to leave was a mixed message, 'I just want to go to sleep', not responding to him and saying, 'No I don't want to do anything', and 'Good night everybody', is a pretty loud message to me and I am sure it would be to any person that chose to listen to it.

Q: Did you say yesterday that you wore his shirt in the course of all this going on?

Whether such a topic shift succeeds in diminishing the impact of Marg's previous remarks is an open question; what is clear, however, from examples such as 48 to 51 (and many others in this book) is the discursive power accorded to questioners. In Sack's (1964) words (cited in Drew 1992: 507), 'What we find . . . is that the person who is asking the questions seems to have first rights to perform an operation on the set of answers.' At times throughout these adjudication processes, the complainants and their witness implicitly and explicitly challenged and rebutted the characterization of events presupposed or 'asserted' by the cross-examining questioners and the tribunal members. Yet ultimately, in the role of responder, they were subject to the capacity of the questioners to 'perform an operation on the set of answers'. As Walker (1987: 79) says of legal settings specifically, 'it is in the hands of the questioner that the real power lies'.

Direct testimony as a site of resistance?

In her comparison of a doctor–patient interaction and a nurse-practioner–patient interaction, Fisher (1991) found that the nurse-practitioner, much more than the doctor, used open-ended questions. While the doctor's more 'controlling' questions 'both allow[ed] a very limited exchange of information and le[ft] the way open for his [the doctor's] own assumptions to structure subsequent exchanges', the open-ended questions of the nurse-practitioner 'maximize[d]' the patient's voice and encouraged her to interpret/contextualize her medical problems in her own terms. Within the context of legal adjudication processes, open-ended questions are more frequent in direct examination than in cross-examination. Because they allow witnesses greater latitude in formulating answers, they are not often used by lawyers questioning witnesses for the opposition. Furthermore, because the primary focus of direct examination is the developing of new information, 'leading' questions, or in our terms 'controlling' questions, are prohibited (presumably because of their 'controlling' nature). Finally, Woodbury (1984: 211) points to a strategic reason for the use of open-ended questions in direct examination:

Broad Wh-questions allow the witness to break into narratives that give an authentic ring to testimony. The jury can take this in and at the same time see that the lawyer can trust his (sic) witness.

Whatever the particular motivation for open-ended questions in direct examination, their more frequent occurrence should create the space for witnesses to 'maximize' their own voices and to impose their own interpretations on evidence. Indeed, the following open-ended questions from the criminal trial allow both Connie and Marg to represent themselves in the semantic role of agents and actors, predicated of verbs that designate their resistance to Matt's sexual aggression. Contrast these representations with those of 5–47.

53 Trial

> Q: Okay. So after he had your pants or your jeans off, what happened next?
>
> CD: He put his fingers into my vagina.
>
> Q: Okay. And how long did he do that for?
>
> CD: I don't know.
>
> Q: Okay. And did you say anything to him about this?
>
> CD: By then somehow, I and don't remember how, but by then my hands, like I could move my hands. My hands were free and he wasn't holding them any more and *I kept pushing his hand away and I kept telling him to stop and I physically would push his hand away* and would try and get up, but he was still on top of me and I couldn't get up but every time I pushed his hands away they would go right back.

54 Trial

> Q: So after he puts his fingers inside of your vagina he gets on top of you?
>
> MB: Yes, while he is still doing it.
>
> Q: And then what happened?
>
> MB: *And I said, 'Melinda', I said, 'I need to talk to you out in the hallway.' And I sat up and kind of pushed him off of me* and then Melinda got up and we went out in the hall and we were talking and *I said, 'Matt is touching me and I don't want him to, I don't know what to do.'*

Although at times permitting an alternative version of events to emerge, the direct examiners in both the criminal trial and the university tribunal – lawyers representing the state and the university, respectively – seemed 'controlled' in their ability to radically redefine the defence lawyers' and tribunal members' representation of events. Put within the terms of this analysis, their capacity to recontextualize, or reframe, the 'meaning' of the events within an alternative interpretive framework seemed somewhat limited. Influenced by ideas from Herman and Chomsky (1999) and Chomsky (1989), I conceptualize the 'debate' that occurred within these adjudication processes as 'constrained within proper bounds'. That is, for Herman and Chomsky (1988), democratic societies are characterized by 'debate' that is itself an object of control: 'controversy may rage as long as it adheres to the presuppositions that define the consensus of the elites . . . thus helping to establish the very condition of thinkable thought, while reinforcing belief that freedom reigns' (Chomsky 1989: 48). The idea that the direct examination of these adjudication processes was itself framed by the presuppositions underlying the 'utmost resistance standard', and thus 'constrained within proper bounds', finds some support in the following two examples. Example 55 is representative of the kinds of questions asked during the criminal trial by the Crown attorney (representing the state) in re-direct examination, that is, once the defence attorney had completed his cross-examination of each of the complainants and their witness. Notice that what the Crown focuses on in this question–answer sequence is the strength, the forcefulness, and the volume of Connie's verbal acts of resistance. Continuous, then, with questions that presupposed the inadequacy of the complainants' and their witness's acts of resistance, the Crown's questions in 55 can be viewed as articulated within the terms of the prevailing 'debate', that is, whether the complainants resisted to the utmost.

55 Trial
> Q: Counsel asked you as far as you were concerned when you indicated 'Please don't, please don't, stop, I don't want you to do that' – you were telling him that you were repeating that type of comments to him when he was touching you, and Mr. C. said to you something to the effect do you know if he even heard that, referring to the comments that you were making to him. What I want to ask you is how you were saying that to him? Were you saying it to him very quietly, medium, very loudly? Can you comment on that?
> CD: I wasn't screaming but it was certainly loud, serious, I mean, and I don't think –
> Q: Sorry, I didn't hear that.
> THE COURT: 'I don't think', and she hasn't finished.
> CD: No. It was in a forceful tone of voice loud enough to be heard without screaming.
> Q: From your observations of what was going on is there any reason from what you could tell that he would not have heard what was being said? Given that you said it in a forceful tone and loud enough is there any reason, as far as you know, that he wouldn't be able to hear your comments?
> A: No, I don't see how he couldn't have heard them.

It is significant in this context to point out that within the Canadian criminal justice system, as is the case in all systems deriving from English common law, Crown attorneys represent the state; that is, they do not represent complainants, who assume the role of witnesses for the state. Furthermore, with the exception of personal records applications, complainants cannot have independent legal representation in criminal cases. Busby elaborates on the lack of agency complainants exercise within the criminal justice system:

> While some Crown attorneys are sensitive to the experience of trauma complainants, it is not their role to counsel complainants. Moreover, many Crown attorneys have such high caseloads that they have little time to prepare witnesses for trials (often they see the file the night before the trial), and even less time to keep complainants informed about the progress of the prosecution. Plea bargains . . . usually occur without any input from complainants, and they may not even be informed that a guilty plea has been entered and a sentence pronounced. . . . If an acquittal is entered, the complainant has no say in determining whether it should be appealed and, if an appeal is made, she cannot participate in the appeal. In law's Official Version, a complainant has no interest in the outcome of criminal proceedings.
>
> (Busby 1999: 267–8)

Lees (1997: 57) makes similar comments about complainants' status within the British criminal justice system:

> The complainant is only a witness for the prosecution so has no separate representation in court, whereas the defendant can consult with his defence lawyer before the case comes to trial. The complainant, as the main prosecution witness, is not allowed even to speak to the prosecution counsel, indeed she may not even know which of the barristers he is.
>
> (Lees 1997: 57)

Even more significant perhaps than the limited representation and advocacy that complainants receive from prosecuting lawyers are the ideological perspectives that they themselves embrace or embody on behalf of the state. Lees (1997: 57), for example, suggests that prosecuting lawyers in Britian are 'inept at countering myths and prejudices about women' put forth by defence lawyers; indeed, according to Lees, 'they often share them'. The ideologies of prosecuting lawyers notwithstanding, given that such individuals are representatives of the state, and not the complainants, their ability to transform or reframe the terms of debate in sexual assault trials may be constrained by the standards and values of the state – standards and values that do not serve the interests of many groups of women.

Further evidence of the 'framing' influence of the utmost resistance standard in structuring the 'talk' of these adjudication processes can be seen in example 56. Like example 55, the question–answer sequence in example 56 occurs during re-direct examination. In fact, it is the final question asked of Marg by the university lawyer during the course of the tribunal proceedings. Despite the generality and the open-endedness of the university lawyer's question, Marg seems to be responding to the many questions asked of her throughout the tribunal about her so-called 'lack of resistance'. That is, what is significant about this response is its dialogic nature (Bakhtin 1981).

56 Tribunal
> HL: Is there anything else that you haven't told us that you want to?
> MB: (long pause) Only that hh . . . *I know everything . . . the night that was dumb. It was dumb of me* to invite Matt to stay well in my bed eh – heh but in residence everyone is like your brother like I said and you don't imagine that that could happen uhm and that. Well, I have definitely learned from this. *But I didn't yell I didn't . . . I didn't do anything because I didn't know what to do.*

Highlighting the dialogic, as opposed to the monologic or singly-authored quality of texts, Bakhtin (1981) theorized texts 'as the products of previous, current, future, and hypothetical dialogues with other interlocutors' (Jacoby and Ochs 1995: 173). Understood in this way, Marg's response in example 56, while seemingly an answer to the university lawyer's immediately preceding question, is the the product of previous dialogues (i.e., question–answer sequences) within the tribunal proceedings – and arguably elsewhere. Moreover, like her answers to questions from the defence and tribunal members that presupposed the inadequacy of her responses to Matt's sexual aggression, Marg here is 'called into' a subject position of ineffectual agency. She casts herself in the semantic role of actor, predicated of verbs designating actions that she did not perform (i.e., *But I didn't yell I didn't . . . I didn't do anything*). Furthermore, she attributes her lack of action to her lack of knowledge (i.e., *I didn't know what to do*) or her stupidity (i.e., *I know everything . . . the night that was dumb, It was dumb of me*). Hence, not only does this example display the dialogism and intertextuality that Jacoby and Ochs (1995), following Bakhtin, claim characterize all discourse, it also attests to the force of certain ideological presuppositions in the discourse – a force to which the complainant is compelled to respond.

Resistance at the margins: strategic agency

Functioning as a lens that obscures or makes unrecognizable the complainants' acts of resistance, the frame of utmost resistance also poses problems for the analyst: that is, how do we distil representations of agency and action on the part of the women without an alternative contextualizing framework? In introducing a collection of essays that explore the tensions between structural and systemic forms of domination and women's agency, Davis and Fisher (1993: 17) argue that 'women's location at the margins of the structural and symbolic order' provides an ideal site from which to investigate this relationship. I have argued that the complainants and their witness are 'produced' as ineffectual agents as they respond to the barrage of questions that presuppose the inadequacy of their actions in the context of what is construed as numerous, readily-accessible, freely-chosen options. What is foregrounded, then, in their responses to such questions is their failure to perform actions that are deemed possible and appropriate by the questioners. Conversely, what is backgrounded, or relegated to the margins, is their performing of acts that are deemed insignificant or ineffectual by the questioners. It is in these metaphorical margins, then, that evidence of the complainants' agency may surface. Incorporating insights from Capps' and Ochs' (1995: 80) analysis of the discourse of an agoraphobic woman, I suggest that 'crucial causal threads' in the complainants' and their witness's narratives are hidden or marginalized by the causal structure of the adjudication processes' prevailing narrative – a discourse of individualism that posits the individual as the locus of action. That is, what drives (i.e., causes) the women's actions is *not* the free will of an autonomous individual, but rather the strong emotions of fear, shock, and confusion engendered by Matt's sexual aggression. Traces of this causal connection are grammatically manifested in examples 38 to 47, where the women often assumed the semantic role of patient acted upon by strong emotions or paralysing thoughts; the causal connection is also evident in the question–answer sequences that follow. Both come from direct examination in the criminal trial and both are illustrative of the complainants' extreme fear and its role in motivating the women to adopt certain strategic responses to Matt's sexual aggression, and not others.[3] In 57, Marg recounts lying to Matt about her willingness to 'do it' on Sunday as a way of forestalling more sexual violence in the moment. Likewise, Connie reports performing oral sex on Matt as a way of preventing more serious or prolonged instances of physical violence.

57 Trial
Q: And what happened next?
MB: And then – just let me think for a second, I want to make sure that I get it right. And then I said, I looked at him and I said, 'I don't want to do anything. I am going to sleep. Leave me alone.' And I rolled over and then he grabbed my arm and he pulled me back down again and he said 'What are you doing on Sunday?' And I thought that was a really unusual comment and I said, 'Well, why? What did you mean?' And he said, 'What are you doing on Sunday?' And I said 'I don't know.' And he said, 'Well, you are coming to my house and we'll do it then.' And I said 'Pardon?' and then he grabbed my arm tighter and said, 'You are coming to my house and we'll do it then.' And I thought that if I agreed at that second and said yes, that he would leave me alone, that I would be safe, that if I could just push it off. I had no intention of going there Sunday but if I could get him out of my room to leave me alone, Sunday was another day and he won't be there, so I figured I would be safe. . . . And then he grabbed my arm and said 'Promise me.' And I said 'I promise.' And then he grabbed my arm really tight again and he said, 'I want you to promise me. And I said, 'I promise.' And he grabbed me even tighter and he said, 'You

better not go back on your promise.' And I said, 'I won't, I won't, Sunday we'll do it.' And he said, 'Well, I don't know, maybe we should just do it now.' And I said, 'Sunday would be better, Sunday is better.' And then he said, finally he agreed and he said, 'All right, then.' And he just rolled over and cuddled up to me and went to sleep and I just laid there the whole time just waiting for him to leave.

58 Trial

Q: Okay. And then what happened next?

CD: I performed oral sex on him.

Q: Why did you do that? Did you want to do that?

CD: No.

Q: Why did you do it?

CD: Because I was scared and I really didn't feel that I was being given any choice in the matter.

Q: What did you think would happen if you didn't do what he told you?

CD: I don't know. I don't think I really gave much thought to what would happen if I didn't, except that I was afraid not to.

Q: What were you afraid of or what were you afraid would happen if you did not do the oral sex that he told you to?

CD: I was afraid that he would hurt me.

Q: When you said that you felt you had no choice, what did you mean by that?

CD: I felt that I had to do it or get hurt.

Caught within a situation of escalating violence, the complainants *acted* in ways that (they believed) would minimize the risk of further sexual aggression and/or physical violence and injury. Thus, it is not that their behaviour is lacking in resistance; rather, they can be seen as considering possibilities for action given the restricted options available to them and actively negotiating relations with the accused in order to prevent further and more extreme instances of violence – from Matt or from someone else. Davis's (1988: 87–8) discussion of Giddens (1976) is useful in conceptualizing the complainants' exercising of agency in the context of restrictive and dangerous circumstances:

> Any agent possesses a range of causal powers, which she deploys in the course of her everyday activities. This does not mean that interactants share equal resources, but rather that, even in asymmetrical interaction, the weaker party can exercise some power. . . . By positing a logical connection between agency and power, the possibility is rejected that actors can ever be completely determined by their circumstances. Even when their activities are severely restricted or where the power imbalance is extreme, there is always a sense of *could have done otherwise.* (emphasis in original)
>
> (Davis 1988: 87–8)

Faced with the threat of continued and/or more severe expressions of sexual and physical violence from Matt, the complainants' situations were 'severely restricted'. Yet, in spite of these severe restrictions, examples like 57 and 58 capture the complainants' active deployment of strategies intended to increase their likelihood of survival. Thus, even though 'the weaker party', they are exercising some aspect of their 'causal powers'. As researchers on violence against women have asserted, submitting to coerced sex or to physical abuse can be 'a strategic mode of action undertaken in preservation of self' (Lempert 1996: 281).[4] That is, if physical resistance on the part of victims can escalate and intensify violence, as some research shows (Dobash and Dobash 1992) and many women believe – and are instructed to believe – then submission to coerced sex is undoubtedly the best strategy for survival. Indeed, example 58 shows Connie explaining her actions in precisely this way.

Hidden and obscured by the prevailing narrative of the court, then, are the causal connections that the complainants establish between the situation of Matt's escalating physical and sexual violence and the fear and immobility that such violence engendered in them. As Lacey (1998: 117) has said of sexual assault legal doctrine, 'the liberal discourse of autonomy appears to leave no space for the articulation of the affective and corporeal dimensions of *certain* violations of autonomy' (emphasis in original). I have previously demonstrated in Chapter 3 that the 'talk' of these adjudication processes 'left no space' for the complainants' expressions of fear – an 'affective dimension' of their response to Matt's sexual aggression. Arising from that fear are the kinds of strategic responses the complainants describe in 57 and 58; and these strategic responses are also marginalized or (re)framed by notions that circulate within the discourse: 'the rationally-choosing subject' whose mind is 'dominant and controlling' (Lacey 1998: 113). Consider example 59 below, repeated from Chapter 3 (example 19):

59 Trial
> MB: And then we got back into bed and Matt immediately started again and then I said to Bob, *'Bob where do you get these persistent friends?'*
> Q: Why did you even say that? You wanted to get Bob's attention?
> MB: I assumed that Bob talked to Matt in the hallway and told him to knock it off.
> Q: You assumed?
> MB: He was talking to him and came back in and said everything was all right.
> Q: Bob said that?
> MB: Yes.
> Q: But when you made that comment, you wanted someone to know, you wanted Bob to know that this was a signal that Matt was doing it again?
> MB: Yes.
> Q: A mixed signal, ma'am, I suggest?
> MB: To whom?

Q: What would you have meant by, 'Where do you get these persistent friends?'

MB: Meaning Bob is doing it again, please help me.

Q: *Why didn't you say, 'Bob, he was doing it again, please help me?'*

MB: Because I was afraid Matt would get mad.

Q: You weren't so afraid because you told Bob, 'Where do you get these persistent friends?' Did you think Matt would be pleased with that comment because it was so general?

MB: I didn't think about it but I thought that was my way of letting Bob know what was going on.

What this example displays is yet another kind of strategic response adopted by the complainants to Matt's sexual aggression. When Matt begins his sexual aggression once again, Marg attempts to attract Bob's attention. Rather than saying 'Bob, he is doing it again, please help me?', as the defence lawyer suggests, Marg employs a somewhat more indirect formulation: 'Bob where do you get these persistent friends?' Asked by the defence lawyer why she uses what he characterizes as a mixed signal, Marg responds that she was afraid Matt would get mad. Like many of the question–answer sequences analysed in Chapter 3, the defence lawyer here employs a multi-step discursive tactic to undermine the credibility of Marg's behaviour. That is, in addition to characterizing her utterance as a 'mixed signal' (i.e., as weak and ineffective), he also discounts the fear she claims motivated this particular formulation. Viewed within an alternative contextualizing framework, Marg's utterance could be construed as a strategic response to her fear of Matt's escalating violence; yet, within the context of example 59, representative of much of the discourse of these adjudication processes, it is (re)constructed as 'passive' and 'lacking in appropriate resistance'.

Adjudicators' decisions

To what extent were the adjudicators' decisions consistent with the representations of the complainants and their witness that were prevalent in the discourse of the adjudication processes and exemplified in this chapter and Chapter 3? Consider excerpts from the tribunal members' decision. (Recall that the tribunal members deemed Matt's behaviour to fall below university standards, but, at the same time, imposed upon the accused a somewhat lenient penalty for two convictions of acquaintance rape.)

At the outset of their interaction with Mr. A., both complainants were very clear as to their intentions. They clearly set the limits at the very beginning but *their resolve became somewhat ambiguous as the night progressed.* Did their actions leave Mr. A. with the impression that they had changed their minds later in the evening? There is little doubt that *both* complainants did not expressly object to some of the activity that took place that evening. It is also clear that *their actions at times did not unequivocally indicate a lack of willing participation.* For example, the actions of Ms B. [Marg] in constantly returning to bed may have left Mr. A. with the impression that she was interested in continuing the sexual touching. Further, much was made of the fact that Ms D. [Connie] voluntarily attended a pub with Mr. A. the very evening after the incident, and that she even slow danced with Mr. A.

(In the Matter of M.A: Reasons for Judgement of the University Discipline Tribunal, p. 19)

Continuous with the ideological frame that structured the adjudication processes, this excerpt suggests that the complainants' protests were too unclear and equivocal to send the message to the defendant that they were not consenting to the sexual activity. Particularly noteworthy are the italicized sentences above. In describing the complainants as *not expressly object{ing} to some of the activity*, their resolve as *somewhat ambiguous* and their actions as *not unequivocal*, the tribunal members continue their representation of the complainants as 'weak' and 'ineffective' in resisting Matt's acts of sexual aggression. Indeed, they remark that Marg's constant returning to her *own* bed may have signalled to Matt that she was consenting to sexual activity. That is, like the discourse of the adjudication processes, it is the 'equivocal' nature of the complainants' behaviour (i.e., they are not resisting to the utmost) that potentially transforms sexual assault into consensual sex, according to the tribunal members' decision.

Following this assessment of the complainants' behaviour, the tribunal members go on to comment on the complainants' *own* characterization of their actions.

Both complainants conceded in their testimony that they did *not* take the most *sensible* and available steps to prevent the sexual touching from continuing. They both agreed that in hindsight their actions were *irrational* and ineffective. At a minimum they both agreed that they should have unequivocally asked Mr. A. to leave their rooms when the activity escalated beyond the limits they initially set; however, they asserted that at the time they were in shock and confused and they did not wish to offend Mr. A. considering that he had helped them with personal problems.

(In the Matter of M.A: Reasons for Judgement of the University Discipline Tribunal, pp. 19–20)

Their identities shaped and constrained by the innumerable questions that presupposed the inadequacy of their response to Matt's sexual aggression, here the complainants are criticized for precisely these self-representations.

That is, while the complainants' expressions of 'ineffectual agency' documented earlier in this chapter are 'produced' in part by the tribunal members'
questions, here they are also deployed in service of the tribunal members'
views. Moreover, the affective states that might have motivated the complainants' actions (e.g., fear, shock, confusion) are characterized negatively
in this excerpt: the complainants are described as *not sensible* and *irrational*.
Like the questions asked of the complainants in both the tribunal and the
criminal trial, this aspect of the tribunal members' decision discounts and
eliminates the complainants' fear, confusion and shock as a legitimate cause
for what becomes construed as ineffective behaviour on their part. Within
the criminal trial, the rationale (repeated below) that the judge provides for
Matt's acquittal on Count 1 of sexual assault (i.e., Connie's case) is also
suggestive of the complainant's ineffective behaviour.

> Young men must be sensitive to a young woman's right to say no, and
> young women, in turn, must realize that when a young man becomes
> aroused during sexual activity beyond a moderate degree there is a
> danger that he will be driven by hormones rather than by conscience.
> (*Reasons for Judgement in Her Majesty the Queen and M.A.*, p. 828)

In calling upon young women to realize that, once aroused, young men's
sexual urges are uncontrollable, the judge is implicating young women in
the control of men's sexual drives. What is evident in both decisions, then,
is an emphasis on the women's behaviour and actions and an interrogating
of their role in resisting/controlling Matt's sexual aggression. Not only
does the frame of utmost resistance dominate and structure the 'talk' of
these sexual adjudication processes, it also informs, perhaps constrains, the
kind of reasoning that underlies these decisions and verdicts.

Unlike juries, the adjudicators in the university tribunal were not an overhearing, *non-speaking* audience (Atkinson and Drew 1979). That is, the
tribunal members not only adjudicated the hearing but also asked questions –
questions that, combined with the questions of the defence, performed substantial ideological work. Thus, to the extent that the tribunal members'
questions contributed to the ideological frame that dominated the proceedings, the consistency of the two discourses (the talk and the adjudicators'
decision) within the university tribunal is not altogether surprising. By
contrast, the judge in the criminal trial was essentially an overhearing,
non-speaking audience. While authorized to ask questions of witnesses,
this was a rare occurrence. Can we say, however, that the judge's decision
was influenced by the linguistic representations I have argued dominated
these proceedings? Put another way, what is the relationship between the
'talk' of these adjudication processes and the adjudicators' decisions? As I
suggested in Chapter 2, I am not making the strong claim that the linguistic
representations of the adjudication processes 'cause' the adjudicators to reason
and decide in the way they do. On the other hand, given the absence of

representations that challenge culturally-dominant notions of sexual violence against women, the 'talk' of the adjudication processes may reinforce and perpetuate such notions. With respect to the representation of the complainants specifically, a plethora of rape myths are blaming of victims, as is the ideological frame that dominates both the criminal trial and the university tribunal analysed here. As Lazarus-Black and Hirsch (1994: 12–13) say of the identities constituted in legal discourse, 'the subject position from which one enters the legal process or is "entered" involuntarily influences the success or failure of the struggle'.

Conclusion

In a discussion of representations of violence against women in the mainstream media, Chancer (1997: 227) cites Stuart Hall (Hall *et al.* 1978) on the difficulty of alternative 'voices' emerging within such contexts: 'what debate there is tends to take place almost exclusively *within the terms of reference* of the controllers . . . and this tends to repress any play between dominant and alternative definitions.' I have argued similarly that the 'debate' evident within these adjudication processes tended to be 'framed' almost exclusively by a culturally-dominant ideological perspective that presupposed the complainants' behaviour to be lacking in appropriate resistance – this lack of resistance being equivalent to consent. Yet, the *interactional* (i.e., question–answer) quality of these adjudication processes (i.e., they are literally dialogic) had consequences for the particular potency with which alternative perspectives were submerged in these contexts. While Chancer (1997: 227), following Hall *et al.* (1978), argues that 'viewpoints which challenge dominant perspectives seldom shine in the spotlight of contemporary mass culture',[5] my data show that linguistically-encoded dominant ideologies acted as a constraint on the complainants' *own* linguistic practices. That is, not only did the dominant perspectives obscure and/or render invisible the complainants' acts of strategic agency (i.e., did not allow them to 'shine'), they also *produced* them as subjects who had not acted strategically. Questions, as we have seen, can mould or exert control over the forms of answers. And, in response to innumerable questions whose presuppositions and (pseudo)assertions embodied the utmost resistance standard, the complainants were cast as agents who were ineffectual: their performances of strategic acts within 'the external reality' were transformed into performances of ineffectual acts of resistance within the linguistic representations of 'the courtroom reality'. And, without effectual and appropriate resistance, the dominant discourse (re)framed the sexual activity as consensual.

The kinds of 'coerced' identities that I have claimed the complainants and their witness produced in these institutional settings, in large part due to the institutionally-sanctioned strict role integrity of questioner and respondent, are, like the perpetrator's identity described in Chapter 2, subject to interpretation and reception along gendered dimensions. Matt's representation of himself as a non-agent of sexual aggression described in Chapter 2, for example, becomes intelligible as a gendered way of being when understood against the background of the male sexual drive discourse – a discourse that absolves men of their responsibility and agency for sexual aggression, attributing it instead to their uncontrollable sexual drives.

Likewise, the complainants' representation and production of themselves as 'ineffectual agents' is intelligible in so far as it reinforces and perpetuates stereotypical images of women as weak and passive. Particularly pervasive in the area of male/female sexual relations are stereotypes of 'active and aggressive masculinity and passive and victimised femininity' (Lacey 1998: 100), images confirmed by the representations (self- and other-generated) of the complainants. Different about the identities constituted in these contexts is the degree of institutional *coerciveness* involved: while Matt's representation of himself as a non-agent was afforded legitimacy by the adjudicators, the complainants and their witness were 'called into' their subject positions involuntarily by a dominant discourse that constrained their possibilities for representing their strategic agency. Indeed, the discursive constraints imposed upon the complainants within the adjudication processes mirrored the highly restrictive circumstances surrounding the sexual assaults. Just as the complainants and their witness had few opportunities to challenge the prevailing narrative of the court, so they had few possibilities for action within the context of Matt's intimidating and frightening demeanour and his escalating sexual and physical violence.

5 'The signals . . . between men and women are not being read correctly'

Miscommunication and acquaintance rape[1]

Introduction

With the aim of theorizing a transformed ideological frame that renders visible the complainants' subaltern perspectives, I turn in this chapter to a relatively new cultural explanation for acquaintance rape, and gender struggle more generally – male/female miscommunication. Although a miscommunication account of rape has been heralded 'as a progressive alternative to the victim precipitation model with its associated victim-blaming' (Crawford 1995: 123), I suggest that its particular manifestation in these adjudication processes does not eliminate victim-blame. On the contrary, fragments of this new model are incorporated seamlessly into more traditional ideologies surrounding sexual violence, leaving intact the overarching assumption that women are responsible for rape. For example, while not held accountable for rape on the basis of their 'provocative' dress or their 'promiscuous' sexual past, the complainants discussed in this study were nonetheless held account- able for not communicating their lack of consent clearly and unambiguously. Indeed, the miscommunication model of date rape, as it is manifest in these adjudication processes, is the utmost resistance standard in disguise: because the complainants' signals of non-consent did not take particular forms, their resistance to Matt's sexual aggression was deemed as weak and equivocal – such equivocation being tantamount to consent.

At the root of a miscommunication account of rape is the *difference* or *dual-cultures* theory of communication between women and men. Initially applied to gender relations by Maltz and Borker (1982), the dual-cultures model has its origins in work by Gumperz (1982a, 1982b) on the nature of cross-cultural or inter-ethnic communication. Demonstrating that communication between interlocutors from different cultural groups can be problematic due to differences in the conversational norms of groups, Gumperz showed that interlocutors themselves often did not perceive this kind of conversational difficulty as rooted in 'linguistic' differences; rather, on the basis of such difficulty, they made value judgements about interlocutors' personality characteristics and/or interpreted their behaviour through the lens of racist and ethnocentric ideologies. One of Gumperz's points concerns the imperceptibility of conversational norms: despite genuine attempts to communicate on the part of interlocutors, their unwitting violation of unrecognized norms at times functioned to reinforce and perpetuate negative cultural stereotypes. Applying Gumperz's account of problematic cross-cultural communication to male–female communication, Maltz and Borker (1982) and later Tannen (1990), in her popularized and best-selling version of this model – *You Just Don't Understand: Women and Men in Conversation* – suggest that women and men, like members of different cultural groups, learn different communicative styles because of the segregated girls' and boys' peer groups they play in as children. This segregation results in inadequate or incomplete knowledge of the other groups' communicative norms, which in turn leads to miscommunication. A crucial point for Tannen (1990: 47) in her articulation of this dual-cultures model is the legitimacy of both men's and women's conversational styles: 'misunderstandings arise because the styles [women's and men's] are different' and 'each style is valid on its own terms'. In fact, it has often been the so-called innocence of the communicative differences underlying male–female miscommunication that has been critiqued by scholars advocating a 'dominance' rather than a 'difference' approach. (See, for example, Freed (1992), Henley and Kramare (1991), Troemel-Ploetz (1991), and Uchida (1992).) That is, in arguing that women's and men's styles are separate but equal (as Tannen does above), Tannen ignores the power or *dominance* relations within which men's and women's conversational styles are developed – power relations that help to *shape* the particular forms that these styles take. It is not merely an accident, for example, that men, more than women, interpret questions as requests for information or interpret problem-sharing as an opportunity to give expert advice. (These are claims made by Tannen (1990) about men's speech styles.) As Crawford (1995: 96) says of these: they 'can be viewed as prerogatives of power. In choosing these speech strategies, men take to themselves the voice of authority.' Put another way, locating explanations for women's and men's different communicative styles (to the extent that they actually exist) in their so-called separate peer groups obscures the effects of power on the particular way these styles come to be constituted.

Critiques of her work notwithstanding, Tannen (1992: 252) is very explicit about the fact that her version of the dual-cultures model of miscommunication is only meant to explain 'quotidian conversational frustrations' and not more serious instances of gender struggle: 'there is no reason . . . to think I would seek to explain away rape, domestic violence, sexual harassment or sexual abuse as conversational misunderstandings.' Nonetheless, as Crawford (1995: 123) argues, miscommunication has become the dominant cultural model for explaining acquaintance rape: 'the miscommunication framework has become the culturally dominant explanation for acquaintance rape among helping professionals, educators, and the college students whose behavior the model seeks to explain.' Indeed, in what follows I show that miscommunication models of acquaintance rape have also entered legal and extralegal arenas, where arguably they have more serious consequences. In the university tribunal analysed here I show that Matt and two of the tribunal members invoked a miscommunication model of male–female communication as a way of explaining what transpired between Matt and the complainants. While at times the explanatory framework deployed could be characterized as a separate-but-equal model of miscommunication, more often it was what Crawford (1995) calls a *deficiency* model of miscommunication. That is, both the accused in his testimony and the tribunal members through their questioning communicated that neither Matt nor the complainants interpreted the other's verbal and non-verbal communicative acts accurately, primarily because the complainants were 'deficient' in their attempts to signal non-consent. As a reconstituted manifestation of the utmost resistance standard, I show that this particular framing of the events succeeds in characterizing the complainants' behaviour as lacking in appropriate or utmost resistance, thereby affirming the sexual prerogative of the defendant.

Matt's (re)definition of consent

Whereas Chapter 2 showed Matt to construct his innocence through a grammar that mitigated, diffused and obscured his responsibility for sexual acts of aggression, examples 1 to 5 below focus on how the defendant constructs his innocence by redefining what constitutes consent on the part of the complainant, Marg. According to the defendant, unless the complainant showed strong resistance after each sexual advance, his sexual aggression was welcome. In other words, if the complainant did not resist each of the defendant's advances as soon as it was initiated and if these signals of resistance did not take particular (strong) forms, the defendant interpreted the complainant's behaviour as conveying consent. Consider example 1 below in which Matt is questioned by the university counsel, HL, in the university tribunal.

1   MA: Uhm she was just reciprocating and we were fooling we were fooling around. This wasn't . . . heh this wasn't something that she didn't want to do.
     HL: How did you know?
     MA: How did I know?
     HL: Yeah.
     MA: Because she never said 'no', she never said 'stop' and when I was kissing her she was kissing me back . . . and when I touched her breasts she didn't say no.

This example shows the defendant explaining how he knew when the complainant was expressing consent – because she didn't say 'no' and didn't say 'stop' in response to each of his sexual advances ('when I was kissing her', 'when I touched her breasts'). Examples 2 to 5 are further expansions on this theme. Especially noteworthy in examples 2 to 5 is how temporality becomes crucial to the defendant's notion of consent. In each example, there is explicit acknowledgement on the part of the defendant that the complainant has expressed lack of consent at some previous point in the interaction; however, because she did not communicate her protests in the wake of each of his acts of sexual aggression, he understood her to be 'consenting.' In example 2, the university counsel questions the defendant about events that took place after Marg left the dormitory room (to tell Bob that Matt was taking advantage of her). The university lawyer is trying to determine why the defendant continued with his sexual advances after hearing of the complainant's feelings:

2	MA: I still wanted to clarify this because this was I felt	1
	that this was really abnormal. So I asked her I said	2
	['do you']	3
	HL: [What was abnormal?]	4
	MA: Well that she goes and tells Bob that I'm taking	5
	advantage of her and then she comes =	6
	HL: = Did you ever think for a moment that she that she	7
	felt you were?	8
	MA: Well at that point for her to say to say that I was	9
	taking advantage of her when she let me kiss uh kiss	10
	her, when she never said 'no', when she never said 'stop',	11
	when she never got up out of the bed and said 'Bob and	12
	Melinda, Matt is taking advantage of me. Help me.' Uh for her	13
	to go for her just to say uh you know 'I couldn't do	14
	anything and I was just lying there' and uh, and then	15
	sort of like she can't do anything and then she escapes	16
	and then goes to Bob and says 'Matt took advantage of	17
	me' uh, and then and then after saying that, she gets	18
	back into bed with me.	19
	HL: But it was her bed. ·	20
	MA: Yeah but if somebody takes advantage, if I was if I	21
	was a woman =	22
	HL: = Yeah =	23
	MA: = Okay? And I was in bed with somebody =	24
	HL: = Right =	25
	MA: = And this person and two other people were next	26
	to me, okay? And this person started to take advantage	27
	of me and was doing things I didn't want to do, okay? I	28
	would get up out of bed, I would ask this person to	29
	leave, I would tell the two other people and I would	30
	deal with it then.	31
	HL: Right	32

MA: I don't understand the logic of . . . no I'm sorry. I do   33
not think that it's appropriate to get back into a bed   34
with somebody who you claim was taking advantage of   35
you.   36
HL: So you felt when she got back into bed that that   37
was a consent to other activities?   38
MA: At that point when she comes back to bed, at that   39
point I wasn't even looking for consent.   40
(defendant's representative interrupts)
HL: You at that point you didn't believe that she didn't   41
want you to do this?   42
MA: Of course not.   43

While Matt acknowledges that Marg felt he was taking advantage of her, he attempts to discredit and undermine this charge by pointing out in lines 10 to 13 that 'she never said no' ('when she let me kiss her'), 'she never said stop', 'she never said Matt is taking advantage of me' at previous points in the encounter. We see here how the timing of acts of resistance is an integral part of Matt's definition of consent: only if Marg were to protest *then*, at the very moment Matt initiated a sexual advance, would he hear her as expressing a lack of consent. The question of timing is also operative in Matt's response to questions about why he resumed sexual activity after Marg's comments to Bob. Matt focuses on Marg's subsequent act, that is, 'getting back into bed', in justifying his interpretation of consent. Indeed, Matt's repeated use of temporal expressions referring to previous points in the interaction (e.g., *then, at that point* in lines 6, 9, 15, 16, 18, 31, 39–40) indicates the importance of temporality to his definition of consent. It seems that every new point in the interaction provides a new opportunity for Matt to ascribe consent or lack of consent to the complainant's behaviour.

Examples 3 and 4 contain further questioning of the defendant by the university's counsel. Example 3 shows Matt claiming that, at some point during the night, Marg indicated that under different circumstances she might willingly engage in sexual activity:

3   HL: Yeah so she told you under different circumstances [she]
    MA: [Yeah]
    HL: might be willing to engage in sexual activity with you.
    MA: Under the circumstances which she explained to me =
    HL: = Right with everyone in the room.
    MA: Well yeah I mean the =
    HL: = So she did tell you at some point that she didn't want to have sexual activity with you with everyone in the room. Am I right?
    MA: At that point she did.

Like 2, example 3 demonstrates the importance of *each* of Marg's responses to Matt's successive acts of aggression in his determination of consent. When confronted with evidence of Marg's non-consent, Matt again invokes the issue of timing: from his perspective, Marg's expressed lack of consent at one point in this encounter does not preclude her consenting to his advances at a subsequent point. Example 4 describes events that occurred after those represented in 3.

4   MA: She was like caressing and like we were fooling around and I was caressing her and everything.
    HL: She already told you that under different circumstances she might do it. Right?
    MA: She had said earlier in the washroom =
    HL: = Yeah. So this is after =
    MA: = Yeah but the thing, I knew, I know what you're saying but the thing is this, whenever I was engaged with sexual activity with Marg, okay? If Marg or anybody for that matter, if if that person at that time when I'm doing something, say if I'm lying in bed with them and reach over and grab their breast and, I had already done something with this person and they consented with it and, they did not move my hand away or anything and didn't say 'no', didn't say 'stop', didn't say uh uh uh, jump up and say 'No I want you to leave', I am assuming, okay? Uhm that if a person does not resist to anything when they, that that that is consent.
    HL: Okay.
    MA: I never heard and I don't . . . I never heard from uh this instance you're referring to. I never uh heard at that time her refuse to engage in whatever we were engaged in.

In this example, the defendant is quite explicit about his definition of consent: 'If Marg or anybody for that matter, if . . . that person at that time that I'm doing something . . . didn't say "no", didn't say "stop", didn't . . . jump up and say "No I want you to leave", I am assuming, okay? . . . that is consent.' In short, Matt seems to be saying that since Marg did not express resistance in response to each of his advances, she 'consented' to his sexual aggression.

Whereas my discussion of examples 1 to 4 has focused on the *temporal* aspect of Matt's definition of consent, example 5, from a tribunal member's questioning of the defendant, shows that his understanding of consent rests also on the *strength* of expressions of resistance:

5   GK: One last question, if Marg was asleep and there's testimony that says that she's asleep and we have testimony that says it's debatable whether she was asleep =
    MA: = Mhmm =
    GK: = Uh why do you continue caressing her?

MA: Well as I said last week what occurred was that we had gotten back into bed and we started kissing and she said that she was tired, you know, she never said like 'no', 'stop', 'don't', you know, 'don't do this' uhm 'get out of bed'.

Matt acknowledges that Marg has said that she is tired; he does not construe this as resistance – she did not say 'no' 'stop' 'don't', etc. We see almost identical comments by the defendant about the strength of signals of resistance in examples 1 and 2, for example, 'she never said "no"', 'she never said "stop"' (in line 11 of example 2). Moreover, in example 2 Matt makes reference to gender (in line 22): he hypothesizes how he would convey non-consent if he were a woman, raising the possibility that signals of resistance are expressed differently by women and men. And, as a woman in Marg's situation, Matt would produce signals of nonconsent that were strong and forceful ('I would get up out of bed', I would ask this person to leave', 'I would tell the two other people') and that were expressed at a particular point in time ('I would deal with it *then*'). In sum, examples 2 to 5 all contain Matt's acknowledgments that Marg has expressed lack of consent at some point during the course of their encounter. However, because Matt defines 'consent' as the absence of vehement expressions of resistance in the wake of every sexual advance, he contends that his escalating sexual aggression is justified.

One way of understanding Matt's (re)definition of consent is in terms of the socially-conditioned process by which linguistic forms are endowed with meaning. As argued in Chapter 1, a woman may say 'no' with sincerity to a man's sexual advances, but the 'no' gets filtered through a series of cultural beliefs and attitudes that transform the woman's direct negative into an indirect affirmative, for example, 'she is playing hard to get, but of course she really means yes' (McConnell-Ginet 1989: 47). From examples 1 to 5, we see that, for Matt, 'no' is reconstructed as 'yes' in the absence of aggressive and frequent expressions of resistance on Marg's part. Perhaps relevant to Matt's (re)construction of 'consent' (out of the absence of strong and frequent enough expressions of resistance) is a feature of hegemonic masculinity already discussed in Chapter 2 – the male sexual drive discourse. Recall that in acquitting Matt of the sexual assault involving Connie, the judge in the criminal trial made reference to this discourse in his decision. That Matt himself invokes the male sexual drive discourse is shown in example 6: here the university counsel, HL, is asking him why he continued with his sexual advances towards Connie when earlier he had indicated that he was not interested in her sexually.

6 HL: Okay . . . Then you – she said you said 'I changed my mind about not wanting to sleep with you.'
    MA: Okay, there was a point . . . and this is the, I believe second time in the evening that she said she did not want to have sex. Uhm we were fooling around and then I stopped and I said I wanted to discuss something

with her, but I was very reserved. Then I told her, well . . . cause we were fooling around I had become aroused and that . . . uhm . . . uh . . . that I was . . . yeah that I was sexually aroused and that I had desires to want to have sex. And I had expressed to her earlier that I . . . didn't want to and . . . it was more because we were involved in such . . . heavy sexual activity that I changed my mind.

Given that Matt's sexual advances towards the two complainants seem to depend on whether he is sexually aroused from one moment to the next, it is perhaps not surprising that he claims to interpret Marg's expressions of resistance as also variable from moment to moment. Put another way, Matt's interpretation of 'consent' relies on culturally-dominant values and beliefs (or discourses) that form the background for the interpretation of linguistic utterances, including how a woman's 'no' is interpreted. Changing one's mind about wanting sex is completely consistent with the male sexual drive discourse which says that once aroused, men's sexual urges are 'compelling' and 'uncontrollable'. And, I am suggesting that Matt's interpretation of Marg's expressions of resistance as variable and as not definitive relies on such views of hegemonic masculinity.

The deficiency model of miscommunication

In a critique of the dual-cultures or difference model of male–female miscommunication, Eckert and McConnell-Ginet (1992a: 467) problematize the passive role it ascribes to women and men in the construction of gendered identities: 'the emphasis on separation and resulting ignorance misses people's *active engagement* in the reproduction of or resistance to gender arrangements in their communities' (emphasis mine). Citing the example of a man interpreting a woman's 'no' to mean 'yes' in the context of potential sexual relations, Eckert and McConnell-Ginet argue that this 'reading' is possible not because of the man's mistaken belief in shared communicative norms, but rather because he is actively exploiting ideas about gender differences in communication to rationalize a certain interpretation. In a similar way, I am arguing here that the defendant's discursive (re)definition of consent strategically invokes notions about 'gendered' miscommunication in his justification of sexual assault. It is not that Matt mistakenly believes that women's expressions of non-consent are variable and not definitive; rather he strategically relies on dominant notions of masculinity (e.g., resistance is expressed strongly and forcefully) and of male sexuality (e.g., the male sexual drive is compelling and overpowering) in interpreting Marg's signals of resistance in this way. Moreover, the defendant's characterization of these events as consensual sex is legitimized by a more general 'framing' of the tribunal proceedings in terms of a difference or dual-cultural model of miscommunication.

In examples 2 and 4 above, we see that Matt makes reference to his interpretation of Marg's behaviour, specifying the particulars necessary for him to understand her as refusing his advances. If he were a woman, he says (in example 2, lines 21 to 31), his resistance would be vehement and unequivocal, occurring precisely after a sexual advance. Two of the tribunal members were even more explicit than Matt in articulating the idea that miscommunication was operative on the night of the alleged sexual assault. For example, in questioning Marg and Connie at the closing of the tribunal, BW raised the possibility that Matt perceived the events differently than the complainants did. This is illustrated in examples 7 and 8.

7   BW: If I can . . . sort of . . . put a question to the women, both of you. Uh . . . it's always hard to respond . . . without just saying that the other person is lying uh: . . . but I'm just wondering . . . are you able to answer this? Is it possible . . . we've heard two different stories, you being here the entire time, we know your story. You've heard Matt's story. Is it possible that he could have perceived events differently than you? Reflecting back on that evening or . . . is your explanation that he's simply distorting the events?

8   BW: All that we were trying to flush out is for you to comment on . . . Are we talking here about a situation in which you basically are saying that Matt is not telling the truth about these things, or is there a possibility that two people could have had different perceptions about what was going on? Sort of a vague question, but what we're trying to understand is whether you're telling the tribunal that in your mind Matt is lying to us, or in your mind you could actually say maybe he could understand this a certain way?
CD: I . . . I honestly don't know what's going on in his mind. I don't know if he's making it up. I don't know if he just doesn't understand what happened. I I don't know =
BW: = We know that you don't know but is it possible I guess is the question. Is it possible that he . . . saw the events differently than you perceived them?
CD: I suppose it's possible.

Notice in example 8 that the tribunal member does not accept 'I don't know' as an appropriate response to his questions about the defendant perceiving the events differently than the complainants. Instead, the complainant is enjoined to acknowledge that misperception and miscommunication were possible ways of understanding the unwanted sexual aggression. Here we see again how questioners have the power to reformulate a respondent's answer: the tribunal member's questioning has the effect of restructuring the propositional content of the complainant's responses (i.e., from 'I don't know' to 'I suppose it's [miscommunication] possible').

Even more insistent about 'gendered' miscommunication as an explanatory model for the events under scrutiny is the woman faculty member, GK, when questioning Marg:

9   MB: I kept saying 'let's just go to sleep.' I didn't honestly   1
    know what else in my mind to do at that time. For me   2
    that was all I could do to tell him I didn't want to do   3
    anything.   4
    GK: And did it occur to you through the persistent   5
    behaviour that maybe your signals were not coming   6
    across loud and clear, that 'I'm not getting through what   7
    I want and what I don't want?' Does it occur to you 'I   8
    need to stand up and say something', 'I need to move   9
    him to the floor?' This is the whole thing about getting   10
    signals mixed up. We all socialize in one way or the   11
    other to read signals and to give signals. In that   12
    particular context, were you **at all** concerned your   13
    signals were not being read exactly and did you think   14
    since signals were not being read correctly for you,   15
    'should I do something different with my signals?'   16
    MB: I did. He made me feel like I wasn't saying   17
    anything, that I wasn't saying 'no' and that's **why** I   18
    asked to talk to Bob, thinking if I couldn't tell him   19
    maybe Bob could tell him. Bob came in the room and   20
    said everything was okay just to forget about it and go   21
    back to sleep. I tried that. I told Matt, I said if the   22
    circumstances would have been different, maybe. It was   23
    a lie but I mean it was another way for me to try to tell   24
    him 'no'. I mean obviously I just wanted to go to sleep.   25
    It wasn't getting through so I tried different   26
    approaches. And in my mind I hoped that they were   27
    getting through, I mean, I was making it as clear as I   28
    could. I'm not sure if that answers your question or not   29
    but   30
    GK: No, it's because right from there to the end you,   31
    you had felt that you hadn't made it clear because at   32
    the end you said you were willing to lie and give him   33
    this phone number and get rid of him. So all along the   34
    way you felt your signals were not read correctly. But   35
    the whole thing is, you know, that concerns all of us is   36
    that the signals of, you know, between men and women   37
    are just, are not being read correctly and I'm not   38
    debating who's lying and who's telling the truth   39
    because it's not mine to say that. The substance is why,   40
    that signals, do you feel at that time your signals were   41
    not being read correctly?   42

Note that, on lines 10 to 16, GK contends that signals are bound to get mixed
up because 'we all [are] socialize[d] in one way or the other to read and give

signals'. Furthermore, lines 37 and 38 show GK invoking *gender* socialization as an explanation for this differential interpretation of 'signals': 'the signals . . . between men and women . . . are not being read correctly'. This tribunal member seems to subscribe to a 'different-but-equal' model of miscommunication in lines 38 to 39: 'I'm not debating who's lying and who's telling the truth'. In other words, it is not a question of one person lying and the other telling the truth; rather, 'signals' are interpreted differently by these individuals. In lines 5 to 16 and 31 to 35, however, she seems to subscribe to a 'deficiency' model of miscommunication (Crawford 1995) – one in which the complainant is represented as deficient in her attempts to communicate lack of consent. For example, she first asks on lines 12 to 14 whether Marg was concerned about the interpretation of her 'signals': 'In that particular context, were you **at all** concerned your signals were not being read exactly?' and then assumes (or presupposes) in lines 15 and 16 (in the clause introduced by *since*) that the 'signals' were not being read correctly: 'did you think since signals were not being read correctly for you, "should I do something different with my signals?"' Moreover, in lines 31 to 35 the tribunal member asserts that Marg must have known her signals were not being read correctly 'all along'; otherwise, she would not have lied to the defendant. Implicit in the tribunal member's questions, then, is the claim that Marg was responsible for 'do[ing] something different with [her] signals', given that she knew Matt wasn't interpreting them correctly.

Though GK suggests in 9 that Marg has not adequately or appropriately signalled her non-consent, she does not generally focus on questions of appropriateness when she asks Matt about his interpretations. In examples 10 and 11, we see GK questioning the defendant, Matt:

10 GK: You said often that it was important to you that   50
        Marg had never said 'no' to you or that 'she didn't like   51
        you', but you read into her actions, but you were   52
        always looking at non-verbal signs from her to   53
        understand that it was consensual. The fact that she   54
        invites you into into her bed, well maybe that may be   55
        verbal, the fact that she stays in bed with you, the fact 56
        that she doesn't leave and so on, uh some of them were   57
        not, most, a lot of them I see as non-verbal signals.   58
11 GK: I'm trying to gather from this is that you read more   59
        verbal signals than non-verbal signals [and I'm trying   60
        and I'm trying to]   61
    MA: [that she likes me?]   62
    GK: Yes so that your paying attention to her, according   63
        to your testimony, to her non-verbal signals. It is really 64
        hard you see, the point is when when the idea 'no   65
        means no' when when when people are – tend to give   66
        people signals in different ways and I'm just trying to   67

> interpret for [myself these signals.]   68
> MA: [Yeah I know there's there's a communication   69
> thing.]   70

Here, we see the tribunal member again expressing her understanding of the events in terms of a difference or dual-cultures model of miscommunication: she asserts, on lines 66 and 67, that 'people . . . tend to give people signals in different ways' and wonders, on lines 59 and 60, whether Matt 'read more verbal signals than non-verbal signals'. Not surprisingly, the defendant echoes her characterization of the events: 'Yeah I know there's there's a communication thing.' In contrast to GK's questioning of Marg, however, there is no suggestion in her questioning of Matt that he had other ways of interpreting Marg's 'signals': the tribunal member is 'just trying to intepret these signals [for herself]'. Like example 11, example 12 shows GK concerned with Matt's verbal and non-verbal 'signals'.

> 12 GK: Uh and you say 'I can't read her mind' at some   71
>   times. Now I'm concerned that there's certain verbal   72
>   signals you pick up and certain non-verbal signals you   73
>   pick up =   74
>   MA: = Mhmm =   75
>   GK: = Uh and then there's certain very clear verbal   76
>   signals and non-verbal signals that you choose not to   77
>   pick up or you don't pick up and it's really hard for me   78
>   to know.   79

While GK does focus on 'signals' from Marg that Matt did not 'pick up', there are no direct assertions in example 12 about Matt knowing that his interpretations were faulty. (Consider, by contrast, GK's assertion to Marg on lines 34 and 35 of example 9: 'So all along the way you felt your signals were not read correctly'.) Nor does GK assert that Matt should have or could have considered other interpretations. (Again, compare example 12 to GK's questioning of Marg in example 9, lines 8 to 10: 'Does it occur to you "I need to stand up and say something, I need to move him to the floor"'.) Thus, although the complainant was criticized for not making her signals clearer and not changing her signals, Matt is not generally criticized for what might be faulty or inaccurate interpretation of signals. Indeed, when GK questions Matt about 'mixed signals' in 10 to 12 it seems to be her assessment of the situation that is at issue. For example, as already noted, on lines 67 and 68, she 'is just trying to interpret for [herself] these signals' and on line 78 'it's very hard for [her] to know' about the signals that Matt does or does not 'pick up' on.

In addition to the types of questions found in 10 to 12, GK's questioning of Matt also focused on Marg's behaviour, specifically, the 'signals' that she did not use. That is, in 13 and 14 below, we do not see GK questioning Matt about *his* behaviour or interpretations; rather, GK is attempting to confirm that Marg did not pursue avenues of resistance that GK seems to regard as appropriate. Beyond GK's noting 'that [Marg] stays in bed . . . , that [Marg] doesn't leave', consider her comments in examples 13 and 14:

13 GK: Uh when you left the room, as you left the room several times, was the lock ever used?
    MA: The lock was never used =
    GK: = Was the lock ever used when you were inside the room?
    MA: The lock was never used.
14 GK: Okay. And as you said earlier and I want to make sure that I understand correctly, at no point were you asked to go on the floor?
    MA: No.

Like examples 9 to 12, 13 and 14 reflect GK's preoccupation with Marg's behaviour, even when she is questioning the accused.

The idea that women, and not men, are deficient communicators in the context of potential sexual relations has been characterized previously as a deficiency model of miscommunication between women and men (Crawford 1995). Such a model does not assume separate-but-equal communicative styles; rather, women are blamed or held responsible for failing to signal their lack of consent clearly and unambiguously. Crucially, such an interpretive frame functions to deflect men's responsibility for rape; instead victims are held responsible for being deficient in their attempts to communicate. In the examples above, we have seen that a 'different-but-equal' model of miscommunciation is quickly replaced by one in which the woman is held responsible for miscommunication. That is, talk about 'difference' only thinly conceals the assumptions that truly underlie the tribunal member's questions – androcentric assumptions that legitimize the defendant's defence of weak and equivocal 'signals' on the part of the complainant. In characterizing the complainants' signals as inappropriate and inadequate, as GK does here and in questioning exemplified in Chapter 3, the tribunal member affirms the defendant's definition of the situation and, in particular, a stereotypically-masculine code of behaviour in which 'real' resistance is expressed aggressively and directly. If, indeed, GK subscribed to a dual-cultures or difference model of miscommunication (as her comments sometimes suggest), then one might expect her to apply different interpretive standards or codes to the defendant's and the complainants' testimony. Reference to 'signals' the complainants could have or should have chosen (e.g., standing up, saying something, moving Matt to the floor), however, suggests that GK viewed the complainants' communication of resistance as 'deficient', in line with Matt's assessment of their behaviour as indirect and equivocal. Indeed, aspects of the tribunal members' decisions cited in Chapter 4 characterize both complainants as *somewhat ambiguous* and *not unequivocal* in responding to Matt's sexual aggression. The non-neutral interpretive codes adopted by the tribunal members are in keeping with Henley and Kramarae's (1991: 41–2) comments regarding the 'metastructure of interpretation' in the context of men's dominance and women's subordination: 'the accepted interpretation of an interaction (e.g., refusal versus teasing, seduction versus rape, difference versus inequality) is generally that of the more powerful person, therefore [the man's interpretation] tends to prevail.' Moreover, in endorsing Matt's interpretation of the complainants' signals as weak and unforceful (i.e., deficient), the tribunal members at the same time lend credence to the hegemonic norms of masculinity that Matt's interpretations rely upon.

I suggested earlier that the miscommunication model of acquaintance rape is a reconstituted version of more traditional ideologies surrounding sexual violence. Certainly, as it was manifest in the university tribunal, it displayed close affinities with the utmost resistance standard. While not emphasizing Marg's lack of physical resistance, GK took issue with the form her signals of non-consent took, subtly suggesting that she had not resisted Matt's aggression adequately or appropriately. As noted previously, women's responses to men's sexual aggression typically occur in a context where physical injury is a threat to women and where physical resistance can escalate the possibility of violence. I have pointed throughout this book to the complainants' frequent expressions of fear in the face of Matt's sexual violence; moreover, in Chapter 4 I identified aspects of the complainants' testimony which were suggestive of the strategic responses they adopted to this sexual aggression. Examples 3 and 4 of this chapter illustrate further the nature of these strategic responses: Marg tells Matt that under different circumstances she might be willing to engage in sexual activity with him. From other parts of Marg's testimony, we learn that this was a ploy on her part to prevent further sexual acts of aggression in the moment. Yet, in line with Matt's interpretation of this signal as not forceful enough, the tribunal members, in their discourse of questioning and adjudicating, also characterize such a signal as deficient, equivocal and ambiguous. Thus, what 'difference' or 'dual cultures' models of communication fail to capture are the structural and systemic inequalities that engender difference – the inequalities, for example, that led Marg, out of fear of the defendant, to couch her signals of non-consent in delicate and tactful terms. In Cameron's (1996: 44) words, this is a case of 'difference arising in a context of unequal gender relations'. That is, the consistent reference to gender differences and miscommunication within the university tribunal had the effect of obscuring and neutralizing the power dynamics between women and men that undoubtedly shaped the complainants' responses to Matt's sexual aggression. And, like other discourses of the tribunal and the criminal trial, the discourse about gender difference functioned to deflect the accused's accountability for sexual assault.

Transforming the ideological work of questions

In beginning to theorize an ideological frame that takes seriously victims' perspectives, and concomitant communications, within the context of (potential) sexual aggression, I consider in this section how different questions, with different presuppositions, might structure acquaintance rape adjudication processes. For Fisher (1991: 162), recall that it is 'both the questions and the silences – the questions not asked' that 'do ideological work'. Hence, how might we excavate the 'silences' of these proceedings, or what has been submerged or relegated to the margins, to build an interpretive framework that did not construct the complainants' behaviour as deficient and their 'inadequate' resistance as tantamount to consent? Since I have shown how power relations help *constitute* the communicative behaviour of women and men in situations of sexual violence, an adequate account of acquaintance rape must begin with the presupposition that women's and men's differential expressions and interpretations, to the extent that they exist, are shaped by social inequities. Given the extent to which interlocutors' communicative acts are embedded within the social landscape, I turn first to some theoretical and analytic concepts from linguistic pragmatics as a way of explicating the contextual nature of utterance production and interpretation.

Linguistic pragmatics and conversational implicature

A primary goal of pragmatics is to explain the discrepancy between sentence meaning and speaker meaning or, put another way, to provide an explicit account of how speakers manage to mean more than they say (i.e., more than is expressed by the literal sense of the linguistic expressions produced). The most notable of the interpretive principles proposed for this purpose is *the cooperative principle*, first introduced by Paul Grice in a series of lectures given at Harvard in 1967 (and partially published in 1975 and 1978). By assuming that interlocutors impute cooperation and rationality to the communicative behaviour of others, Grice attempts to explain how listeners interpret utterances that are superficially unintelligible. That is, the presumption of cooperation among interlocutors gives rise to inferences or, what Grice calls, conversational implicatures. Listeners assume that superficially uncooperative utterances are cooperative at some fundamental level and impose intelligibility and coherence where, from a literal point of view, there is none. Consider the following example:

15 A: What time is it?
   B: Well, the mailman's already been here.

While B's response, interpreted literally, does not answer A's question, the cooperative principle would hold that B's interlocutor performs the necessary inferential work to interpret B's response as being an answer to the question asked. Speaker A thus concludes that it is later than 10 o'clock, for example, because 10 o'clock is the time the mailman typically comes. Consider a similar example, where A and B are on a camping trip without watches or clocks.

16 A: What time do you think it is?
　　 B: Well, the sun's directly above us.

Again we see that B's response, from a literal point of view, does not answer A's question. However, because, according to Grice, A will assume rational and cooperative behaviour from B, A will draw inferences, or conversational implicatures, that establish a connection between A's question and B's response. Grice's point is not that speakers are always cooperative in their communicative behaviour; rather, his argument is that the presumption of cooperation on the part of listeners gives rise to inferences. As Levinson (1983: 102) notes 'inferences arise to preserve the assumption of cooperation; it is only by making the assumption contrary to superficial indications that the inferences arise in the first place.'

Note that in both of examples 15 and 16 it is not just the presumption of cooperation that gives rise to implicatures or inferences; the precise inferences drawn depend on assumed knowledge within the local context (i.e., the time the mail is delivered) or within the culture or world more generally (i.e., how the sun's position relates to time). That is, in making inferences or, in Grice's terms, calculating implicatures, interlocutors draw upon assumed cultural and world knowledge. That general cultural knowledge is involved in the calculating of implicatures is also evidenced by the well-formedness of the following sequence of sentences.

17 Fred got the picnic supplies out of the car. The beer was warm.

Such a sequence can be interpreted as coherent (i.e., as a 'text' as opposed to a randomly-ordered set of sentences) because interlocutors have access to general cultural knowledge that includes the proposition 'picnic supplies can include beer'. Without such knowledge to draw upon, an interlocutor, in spite of imputing cooperative behaviour to the producer of 17, could not easily impose coherence on the sequence. Indeed, the following comments from Grice (1975: 50) indicate that the cooperative principle must be supplemented by contextual information and background knowledge in the process of calculating conversational implicatures:

> To work out that a particular conversational implicature is present, the hearer will rely on the following data:
> (1) the conventional meanings of the words used, together with the identity of any references that may be involved
> (2) the Cooperative Principle and its maxims

(3) *the context, linguistic or otherwise, of the utterance*
(4) *other items of background knowledge*
(5) the fact (or supposed fact) that all relevant items falling under the previous headings are available to both participants and both participants know or assume this to be the case. (emphasis mine)

(Grice 1975: 50)

Social inequalities and utterance interpretation

Implicit in Grice's formulation above is the assumption that successful utterance interpretation depends upon interlocutors having access to the *same* contextual information and background knowledge. That is, in 5 above Grice claims that the calculation of implicatures is possible to the extent that interlocutors have access to the same linguistic and extralinguistic information. Liang's (1999) discussion of conversational implicature and lesbian and gay identities complicates this assumption. According to Liang, lesbians and gays face a dilemma: they risk dangerous consequences (ostracism, violence, discrimination) if they directly communicate their identities (at least, in contexts where they are unclear about the their addressees' views on homosexuality); on the other hand, concealing their identities can be experienced as deceitful, compromising, hypocritical, etc. Confronted with this double bind, some lesbians and gays have devised what Liang calls gay *implicatures* – communication strategies that indirectly and ambiguously convey their identities. Liang (1999: 301) elaborates: 'their [gay implicatures'] covert meanings – though misleadingly worded for "credulous," that is, straight listeners – can be inferred only if listeners disabuse themselves of the default assumption of heterosexuality.' For example, the avoidance of gendered pronouns in designating intimate partners is a strategy, according to Liang, designed to generate a gay implicature, that is, to identify a speaker as gay or lesbian. Consider example 18 taken from Liang. Whereas a naive heterosexual interlocutor like B does not calculate A's gay implicature (i.e., that A is a lesbian), an interlocutor knowledgeable about gay and lesbian identity could infer from A's avoidance of a gendered pronoun or noun phrase that the 'ungendered' referent is a woman.

18 Scenario: A lesbian speaker (A) is conversing with her naive heterosexual female co-worker (B), to whom she has not disclosed her sexuality.
   A: I'm looking forward to the weekend.
   B: You doing anything special?
   A: Well, I'm having a visitor.
   B: Ooh . . . that kind of visitor? Does he come in often?
   A: Actually, yes . . .
   B: Is this someone special?
   A: I think so . . . we'll see.

(Liang 1999: 302)

Put another way, gay implicature exploits the ambiguity and indeterminacy of linguistic expressions, and this ambiguity relies crucially on the differential access that addressees have to particular kinds of cultural knowledge. In Liang's words, 'a naive hearer may fail to calculate a gay implicature . . . , where the community as a whole had exposure to lesbians and gays, the speaker's continued use of gay implicature over the course of an interaction may lead the hearer to make the correct inference' (Liang 1999: 306). What is significant for my purposes in Liang's work is her demonstration that the varying social locations of interlocutors can determine the nature of the cultural knowledge brought to bear upon the production and interpretation of utterances. Gays and lesbians, according to Liang, may convey their identities (to certain interlocutors, at least) in indirect and ambiguous ways given their cultural knowledge about the pervasiveness of homophobia. In turn, the interpretation of their identities as gay and lesbian will depend upon the cultural knowledge to which interlocutors have access, specifically, interlocutors' knowledge about gay and lesbian identities and communities.

A question that arises from the previous discussion concerns the extent to which women and men might draw upon different background assumptions in interpreting sexual acts of communication. Indeed, this question lies at the heart of feminist critiques of the 'reasonable person' standard as a measure for evaluating charges of sexual harassment. Since the early twentieth century, courts in Canada and the United States have found it useful to invoke the notion of a *reasonable person* in considering whether certain kinds of behaviour should be deemed as harmful or offensive and thus punishable. The reasonable person is supposed to represent community norms; thus, whatever would offend or harm a reasonable person is said to be more generally offensive or harmful. Some feminist legal scholars (e.g., Abrams 1989) have recently challenged the generalizability of a reasonable person's experiences, arguing that men and women may experience sexual advances differently. Indeed, there is extensive evidence to suggest that women are more likely than men to perceive sexual behaviour as sexual harassment. That is, while there is much variation among women as to the kinds of behaviour they believe constitutes sexual harassment, it is nonetheless the case that sexual harassment is a term used substantially more by women to describe their experiences than by men. Kitzinger and Thomas summarize the empirical research:

> Women consistently define more experiences as sexual harassment than do men, and the factor which most consistently predicts variation in people's identification of what constitutes sexual harassment is the sex of the rater (see, for example, the overview by Riger, 1991). Overall, men tend to label fewer behaviours as sexual harassment (Kenig and Ryan, 1968; Powell, 1986) and, in particular, are less likely to see behaviours such as sexual teasing, looks or gestures as harassment (Collins and Blodgett, 1981; Adams *et al.*, 1983).
>
> (Kitzinger and Thomas 1995: 33)

In response to this kind of evidence, some state courts and lower federal courts in the US have modified the reasonable person standard and introduced a *reasonable woman* standard for evaluating charges of sexual harassment.[2] One such US court (*Ellison* v. *Brady* 1991) justified introducing the reasonable woman standard in the following way:

> We realize that there is a broad range of viewpoints among women as a group, but we believe that many women share common concerns which men do not necessarily share. For example, because women are disproportionately victims of rape and sexual assault, women have a stronger incentive to be concerned with sexual behavior. Women who are victims of mild forms of sexual harassment may understandably worry whether a harasser's conduct is merely a prelude to violent sexual assault. Men, who are rarely victims of sexual assault, may view sexual conduct in a vacuum without a full appreciation of the social setting or the underlying threat of violence that a woman may perceive. . . . We adopt the perspective of a reasonable woman primarily because we believe that a sex-blind reasonable person standard tends to be male-biased and tends to systematically ignore the experiences of women.
> (*Ellison* v. *Brady*, 924 F.2d 872, 878–81(9th Cir. 1991))

Put in Gricean terms, this decision implicitly recognizes the socially-conditioned process by which communicative acts are endowed with meaning. The fact that 'women are disproportionately victims of rape and sexual assault', for example, is part of the background knowledge that informs women's interpretation of utterances within the context of male/female sexual relations. As a result, a communicative act such as sexual banter may be perceived as more threatening to women than to heterosexual men (i.e., the inferences drawn may be different for women and for heterosexual men) because a woman's stock of cultural beliefs may include the proposition that sexual banter is potentially 'a prelude to violent sexual assault'.

While feminist critics (e.g., Cornell 1995)[3] of this decision argue that 'a reasonable woman' standard runs the risk of 'unduly universaliz[ing] women's experience by obscuring other differences based on class, race, sexual orientation and so forth' (Rhode 1997: 106), there nonetheless seems to be some consensus among feminist legal scholars and critical legal scholars alike that a shift from universal standards to contextual or subjective standards exposes the masculine bias (and other biases) embedded in the 'reasonable person'. Rhode (1997: 105), for example, because of the essentializing potential of a reasonable woman standard, advocates instead a reasonable person standard that is sensitive to context; more specifically, she argues that charges of sexual harassment should be evaluated 'from the standpoint of the reasonable person in the victim's circumstances'. Whether sexual harassment is viewed from the vantage point of a 'reasonable woman' or a 'reasonable person in the victim's circumstances', for my purposes both standards recognize the same fact: that socially-structured differences among individuals influence the sort of background knowledge that interlocutors bring to bear upon the interpretation of sexual acts of communication.

Speech act theory: intentions vs. effects

Embedded in the preceding discussion is a distinction often made within speech act theory between the intentional illocutionary force of an utterance and its perlocutionary effects. The basic insight provided by speech act theory, developed by John Austin in *How to Do Things with Words* (1962), concerns the performative nature of linguistic expressions. Austin argued that certain types of verbs – performative verbs such as *promise, bet, name* – do not merely describe or report a state of affairs, but instead have the capacity to perform actions when uttered under appropriate circumstances (e.g., 'I name this ship the Queen Elizabeth' as uttered when smashing a bottle against the ship's stern). Austin eventually extended his notion of performative beyond explicitly performative verbs such as *bet* and *name* to other kinds of utterances that perform actions (Levinson 1983: 236). So, for example, the utterance 'Do you think you could open the window?' can perform a request by means of conversational implicature in the same way that the utterance 'I promise to meet you in the morning' can perform a promise. Within speech act theory, the act performed by an utterance (e.g., a request) is referred to as its *illocutionary force* whereas the effect this act has on an addressee (e.g., the addressee carries out the request) is referred to as its *perlocutionary effect*.

Departing somewhat from orthodox speech act theory, I have assumed the possibility of a disjunction between the intentional illocutionary force of an utterance and its perlocutionary effects. That a woman feels threatened by the sexual banter or sexual teasing of a male work colleague, for example, could be construed as an 'unintended' effect of that illocutionary act. That is, while the male colleague may be intending to perform the act of 'teasing' in making a sexually explicit comment, his female addressee may draw inferences or conversational implicatures from his comment based on her cultural knowledge about women's vulnerability to sexual harassment. For the woman, then, the sexually explicit remark is interpreted as threatening. Because work within the tradition of speech act theory has focused almost exclusively on the *intentional* illocutions of speakers, the contribution of perlocutionary effects to a determination of what an utterance 'means' has largely been ignored. Indeed, Duranti (1992), a linguistic anthropologist, has critiqued the speech–act view of meaning precisely because meaning is identified with speakers' intentions. For anthropologists and linguists who have investigated non-Western cultures or non-mainstream subcultures within North America, Duranti claims, this view is 'too limited and overly ethnocentric':

The work of these researchers suggests that the relevance assigned to the speaker's intentions in the interpretation of speech may vary across societies and social contexts. On many occasions what speech act theorists might call 'perlocutionary effects' and hence classify as not conventional (see Austin, 1962) can be shown to be an acceptable criterion for the assignment of responsibility to a speaker.

(Duranti 1992: 25–6)

Based on his own work in Western Samoa, Duranti argues that Samoans do not find speakers responsible for the intentions that might lie behind their speech acts; rather speakers are held responsible for the social effects of those acts. Duranti (1992: 42) provides a more concrete demonstration: 'after offending someone, an American can say "I didn't mean it." This cannot be done by Samoans, given that part of what one meant *is* what the other person understands as meant' (emphasis in text). Morgan (1991: 429) demonstrates that a similar view of meaning exists in some African-American communities: what a speaker intends to mean in producing an utterance 'is given less credence than the overall effect or interpretation' of an utterance. The idea that an utterance 'means' what its addressee understands it to mean, while seemingly at odds with a mainstream Western view of meaning, is, in fact, compatible with my emphasis on the effects that sexual acts of communication can have on unequally-positioned social actors. If interlocutors bring to bear on utterance interpretation different kinds of cultural presuppositions (arising from their unequal locations), then what an addressee understands an utterance to mean may differ from a speaker's intent. Can we, like the Samoans, ascribe responsibility to interlocutors for the social effects, 'intentional' or not, of their speech acts? This question lies at the heart of ongoing debates over the proscribing of sexual harassment within institutional and legal contexts. Feminists who have focused on the institutionalization of sexual harassment policies have generally recognized the value of considering the effects of sexual behaviour on victims. For example, Crocker (1983: 706), in an analysis of university definitions of sexual harassment conducted in the 1980s, argues that 'the victim's experience of harassment must inform the university's attitude'. Likewise, Traugott (1995: 5), who analysed the sexual harassment policies of Cornell, Harvard, MIT, Stanford, Yale and the system-wide policy of the University of California, points to 'the discursive value of pairing intent and effect' in definitions of sexual harassment. Of the sexual harassment policies considered by Traugott, MIT's policy came closest to achieving this goal. (Note that this policy deals not only with harassment on the basis of gender, but also on the basis of race, disability, religion, etc.)

19 Harassment is any conduct, verbal or physical, on or off campus, which has the *intent* or *effect* of unreasonably interfering with an individual's or group's educational or work performance at MIT or which creates an

intimidating, hostile or offensive educational, work or living environment. (emphasis mine)

As Traugott points out, a definition of sexual harassment which pairs intent with effect (like MIT's) includes under its rubric both explicitly hostile acts (e.g., sexual threats, obscene messages, insulting noises and gestures) as well as acts that are not intrinsically hostile, but under certain contexual conditions can be interpreted as hostile (e.g., sexual banter, sexual teasing). My purpose in discussing sexual harassment policies is not to engage in policy recommendations nor to speculate on how the language of such policies could increase their effectiveness (whatever 'effectiveness' means in this context). Rather, I cite a definition such as MIT's to elucidate the theory of meaning it presupposes: what it 'means' to harass depends not only on the 'intentional' illocutionary force of a speaker's words or actions, but also on the perhaps 'unintentional' implicatures/perlocutionary effects produced by this speech, or other kind of, act.

Effects: fear of escalating violence

By discursively constructing the complainants' expressions of resistance as 'deficient' and their behaviour as 'inaction', I am suggesting that the sexual assault adjudication processes analysed here failed to recognize the particularities of women's responses to the threat of sexual violence or, put another way, the effects that men's sexual behaviour − 'intentional' or not − can have on subordinately-positioned individuals with greater vulnerability to sexual coercion. Especially relevant to this discussion are the complainants' own explanations of their actions in the face of sexual violence. Consider the following representative comments from Marg during the university tribunal.

20 HL: Do you have anything more that or specific to say to the panel about the evidence that you've heard and uh that Matt has given?
    MB: The truth? I mean I don't know what else to reply to. You think, at least I do, that you know you're walking down the street and someone grabs you. I was prepared for that I thought, but you don't expect someone that you know to do that and when it's happening, I mean, you do whatever you have to to survive. ((crying)) I mean I was just thinking how to survive that second. I mean I didn't care if that meant getting back into bed with him. If he didn't hurt me I didn't care at that second. I mean I didn't want to do the things I did and looking back on them I shouldn't have gotten back into bed, I should have yelled, I should have done something, but, I was in a room full of people that weren't helping me and somebody was trying to hurt me. I did whatever I could to get by. I don't know what else to tell you.

Like other expressions of the complainants' fear illustrated throughout this book, Marg cites her fear as the driving force behind her actions. For example, here Marg refers to the need to survive (without getting hurt) as motivation for 'getting back into bed with [Matt]': 'I was just thinking how to survive that second. . . . I didn't care if that meant getting back into bed with him. If he didn't hurt me I didn't care at that second.' Connie's comments from the criminal trial are comparable (part of this example appears as 58 in Chapter 4):

21   Trial
Q: How were you feeling about this time about him and the situation?
CD: I was scared and I was disgusted and I really wanted him to leave. I was scared and I wanted it to be over and I wanted him to go away.
Q: Did you say anything to him?
CD: No. I kept trying to move away and push my head back up but he had my hair and every time – every time I tried to, he just pushed me back down.
Q: Was there any pain from that?
CD: It was more fear than pain. I mean, it was uncomfortable.
Q: What happened when you moved and tried to raise your head? What happened then?
CD: Because he had my hair and was pressing down, I mean, it pulled but, I mean, it was much more frightening than painful.
Q: Okay. And then what happened?
CD: I performed oral sex on him.
Q: Why did you do that? Did you want to do that?
CD: No.
Q: Why did you do it?
CD: Because I was scared and I really didn't feel that I was being given any choice in the matter.
Q: What did you think would happen if you didn't do what he told you?
CD: I don't know. I don't think I really gave much thought to what would happen if I didn't, except that I was afraid not to.
Q: What were you afraid of or what were you afraid would happen if you did not do the oral sex that he told you to?
CD: I was afraid that he would hurt me.
Q: When you said that you felt that you had no choice, what did you mean by that?
CD: I felt that I had to do it or get hurt.

That is, out of fear that Matt would hurt her, Connie submitted to his demands and performed oral sex on him: 'I felt that I had to do it or get hurt.' While evident in many aspects of the complainants' testimony, the idea that the complainants' behaviour was shaped and constrained by their intense fear of Matt did not generally inform the questions asked in both the university tribunal and the criminal trial. On the contrary, the complainants' behaviour was evaluated from the vantage point of a masculine subject (i.e., Matt) whose behaviour was unencumbered by the fear and paralysis illustrated so vividly in examples 20 and 21 above. After all, if Matt had been a woman subject to sexual aggression, according to his testimony, he would have reacted aggressively and forcefully: 'Yeah but if somebody takes advantage, if . . . I was a woman . . . I would get up out of bed, I would ask this person to leave, I would tell the two other people and I would deal with it then. . . . No I'm sorry I do not think it's appropriate to get back into bed with somebody who you claim was taking advantage of you.' Consistent with this interpretive standard, example 22 shows TM (Matt's representative in the university tribunal) (re)constructing Marg's attempts at resisting Matt – attempts that were developed out of fear – as consensual sex. Recall that Marg tried to avoid further aggression in the moment by telling Matt (a) that she would have sex with him on Sunday and (b) that she would have sex with him under different circumstances. These so-called lies are the subject of TM's comments below:

22 TM: Alright if uh . . . uh without going – belabouring the point in going through the record and bringing out these other instances of what we might just for the sake of a better word call lying in order to put Matt off at the time. Uh if I were just to to say that if uh those could be shown to be . . . in the record, uh would it not . . . and this is a difficult question for me to ask too uh again it goes back to hindsight. Uh but would . . . it not have been your state of mind at the time uh . . . to realize that *by telling him an untruth you were in fact giving him the impression of consenting . . . to . . . a relationship with him that evening?*

Whereas TM characterizes Marg's attempts at resistance as equivalent to consent, recall Marg's rationale (from example 57 in Chapter 4) for one of these 'untruths':

23 MB: And I thought that if I agreed at that second and said yes, that he would leave me alone, that I would be safe, that if I could just push it off. I had no intention of going there Sunday but if I could get him out of my room to leave me alone, Sunday was another day and he won't be there, so I figured I would be safe.

If viewed from the vantage point of a 'reasonable woman' or a 'reasonable person in the victim's circumstances', that is, through a lens that is clouded by cultural knowledge about women's social and physical vulnerability to sexual violence, I am suggesting that the complainants 'inaction' and 'deficient' signals of consent can be (re)contextualized as strategic acts of resistance, and not indicators of consensual sex. Weighing the relative dangers of highly restricted options – being sexually assaulted, being hit, being beaten, being killed – the complainants and their witness *acted* in ways that (they believed) would prevent more serious and prolonged instances of violence.

In an insightful critique of date rape programmes that emphasize women's direct and straightforward refusals of men's sexual advances, Kitzinger and Frith (1999) argue that attention to the way refusals are actually performed in ordinary conversational interaction shows that they are anything but direct, clear and straightforward. Rather, in the terms of conversational analysis, refusals are 'dispreferred' responses, that is, they require much more conversational work than, for example, acceptances. Included among the interactional features that characterize refusals are delays (e.g., pauses and hesitations), hedges (e.g., expressions such as *well*, *uh*), palliatives (e.g., apologies, token agreements) and accounts (e.g., explanations, justifications). Analysing young women's 'talk about doing refusals' in sexual interactions, Kitzinger and Frith conclude that the women report using normal interactional features in communicating refusals:

> That is, according to the research literature (and our own data) on young women and sexual communication, they are communicating their refusals indirectly; their refusals rarely refer to their own lack of desire for sex and more often to external circumstances which make sex impossible; their refusals are often qualified ('maybe later') and are accompanied by compliments ('I really like you, but . . .') or by appreciations of the invitation ('it's very flattering of you to ask, but . . .'); and sometimes they refuse sex with the kinds of yes's which are normatively understood as communicating refusal.
>
> (Kitzinger and Frith 1999: 309)

Significant for my purposes about Kitzinger's and Frith's research is their demonstration that women's refusals to men's sexual advances, like the performing of refusals more generally, are somewhat indirect under normal circumstances. (I say 'normal circumstances' because their data do not appear to describe women who are in situations of escalating sexual and physical violence.) My data suggest that the indirectness of refusals as they are normatively performed by women refusing men's sexual advances is exacerbated in situations of physical and sexual violence where fear inflects 'refusals' with a different character. Indeed, fear was the driving force behind Marg's agreeing to have sex with Matt in the future and Connie's performing oral sex on him. Like Kitzinger and Frith, I question the value of assertiveness training programmes and date rape prevention programmes that are not informed by empirical data – data on how women's acts of resistance are shaped by the inequities of situations of sexual violence. While Marg and Connie may not have been 'clearly and straightforwardly' refusing Matt's sexual aggression, they were attempting to resist further violence. And at times this meant submitting to coerced sex.[4] To the extent that 'no means no' date rape prevention programmes advocate clear, direct and straightforward expressions of refusals, they could conceivably characterize the complainants' refusals as deficient, in the same way that the university tribunal and criminal court did. As Kitzinger and Frith (p. 311) conclude: 'the slogan "yes means yes, and no means no" may make a good campaign slogan, but it is neither a description of actual human behaviour, nor a suitable prescription for dealing with sexual coercion.'

Conclusion

In concluding this chapter, I consider the feasibility of a 'reasonable woman's' perspective – or the perspective of a 'reasonable person in the victim's circumstances' – informing the dominant discourses that have been shown to (re)circulate in the 'talk' of sexual assault adjudication processes. Relevant to this question are the following comments from McConnell-Ginet:

> As legal scholar Kathryn Abrams has pointed out, male judges who have been educated about women's distinctive experiences are less likely to assume that they can simply look to how they themselves might be affected by an action to decide whether it is part of a pattern of sexual harassment.
>
> (McConnell-Ginet 1995: 4)

Also drawing on Gricean notions of cooperativeness and implicature, McConnell-Ginet attempts to account theoretically for the potential accessibility of a reasonable woman's perspective in the context of sexual harassment. She argues that the contextual information that interlocutors rely on in successfully interpreting utterances can also include knowledge about *others'* beliefs, experiences and perspectives, even if these are different from one's own. Indeed, McConnell-Ginet elaborates upon Rhode's *contextual* approach to a 'reasonable person standard' by defining 'reasonableness' in terms of an interlocutor's 'access to certain socially available knowledge, e.g., on recognizing and taking account of socially-structured differences among people that affect whether or not a person is substantially harmed by particular actions' (McConnell-Ginet 1995: 4). A *reasonable* man (as McConnell-Ginet conceives of reasonableness) would, for example, be able to recognize the potential harm of sexual banter for a woman even if he himself would not experience the same bad effect. (I am reminded here of men who purposely refrain from walking behind women at night, especially those walking alone, recognizing that such behaviour could be threatening to a woman.) That is, determining whether certain speech acts or actions are offensive or threatening may require looking beyond a person's own experiences and perceptions (i.e., beyond questions such as 'what effect would an action like this have on me?') to the socially-structured differences among people that may affect perceptions of harm and offensiveness.

The ability of interlocutors to look beyond their own beliefs, experiences and perspectives in interpreting and producing utterances also bears on the characterization of date rape as miscommunication. If perpetrators of sexual violence are *reasonable* in McConnell-Ginet's sense of the term and have access to the perspective of victims, then in what sense are they *misunderstanding* women's expressions of non-consent? Crucial to this question is the extent to which *culturally-dominant* background knowledge is mobilized in the service of interpretations. McConnell-Ginet, for example, points to the significance of 'readily-accessible' cultural knowledge in the authorizing of 'standard interpretations':

> The general point is that in order to mean, agents presuppose, take things for granted, and that what can be taken for granted depends on what has been (often and audibly) expressed and can be assumed to be readily accessible. Views that are little heard, that are not common currency, can reliably function as background only in linguistic exchanges between familiars. Such views will not contribute to general patterns of meaning more than what is said and thus they will not leave their mark on standard interpretations.
>
> (McConnell-Ginet 1988: 92)

That is, while 'views that are little heard' can form the background for the interpretation of utterances, for example, gay implicature, their restricted circulation limits the contexts in which 'they will . . . leave their mark on . . . interpretations'. Indeed, according to Liang, gays and lesbians use gay implicature precisely because of the restricted contexts in which it will be appropriately interpreted. By contrast, 'readily accessible' cultural knowledge will inform the interpretation of utterances in many cultural contexts. McConnell-Ginet (1989), for instance, argues that an utterance such as 'You think like a woman' functions as an insult in most contexts in our culture, not because all listeners adhere to the proposition that women have questionable intellectual abilities, but rather because listeners are aware that such a (sexist) proposition is prevalent and pervasive within the speech community; that is, it is part of a widely-held set of mutually accessible cultural beliefs. Attempting, by contrast, to make the comparable utterance 'You think like a man' function as an insult will be less successful in many cultural contexts because the proposition that men think 'illogically' is not part of that same set of dominant societal beliefs (Cameron 1998: 88). Given that dominant groups have contributed disproportionately to the background knowledge we draw upon in 'standard interpretations', then that stock of beliefs and attitudes will undoubtedly be informed by sexist (and racist and homophobic) assumptions.

I have argued that Matt explains his (re)construction of Marg's signals of non-consent in terms of a 'difference' or dual-cultures model of miscommunication: because Marg does not express her non-consent according to a 'masculine' code of behaviour (i.e., forcefully and aggressively after each of Matt's sexual advances), Matt contends that she is consenting. Put another way, Matt strategically draws upon hegemonic notions of male sexuality and of masculinity in justifying his interpretations of Marg's behaviour.[5] In keeping with McConnell-Ginet's comments above, it is precisely the pervasiveness and dominance of such notions that licences Matt's account of the events. As Lees (1996: xiii) says of rapists who invoke rape myths to explain their violence: 'rapists do not invent their rationalizations; they draw for their vocabulary on social myths reflecting ideas they have every reason to believe others will find acceptable.' Matt has likewise not 'invented' his rationalizations; on the contrary, he has the cultural weight of a sexist and androcentric belief-system informing and authorizing his (mis)interpretations. While undoubtedly having access to Marg's perspective, that is, to her fear of sexual and physical violence that shaped her communicative acts of resistance, Matt was able to strategically ignore such a perspective, given its culturally-subordinate status (i.e., it is 'little heard' as opposed to 'readily accessible'.) Indeed, what Matt and the tribunal characterized as 'miscommunication' is better understood as culturally-sanctioned ignorance.

Conclusion

This book is about the defining and delimiting force of institutional discourse. Analysing the nitty-gritty linguistic details of socially-situated interactions, I have shown how culturally-dominant notions about violence against women penetrate, and circulate within, the talk of sexual assault adjudication processes. Given the institutionally-sanctioned power accorded to questioners (i.e., adjudicators and lawyers) in these settings, such ideologies – embedded primarily in the presuppositions or (pseudo)assertions of questions – have a particular potency. That is, because witnesses are 'systematically disabled' from asking questions or initiating turns (Hutchby and Wooffitt 1998: 166), their ability to challenge or resist the assumptions encoded in questions is severely limited. To the extent, then, that this discourse is embodied in institutions and subject to institutional (discursive) constraints, it comes to build the character of the events and individuals it represents.

'Coerced' gendered identities

As discursive practices that encode powerful social discourses about female and male sexuality, the question–answer sequences of these hearings comprise part of the 'rigid regulatory frame' (Butler 1990) within which gendered identities are produced or enacted. Indeed, I have argued that the gendered identities of participants are 'coerced' performances of gender insofar as they are filtered through the cultural ideologies that circulate discursively within these institutional settings. Attending to the 'rigid regulatory frame' within which identities are produced, I have suggested, following Butler, that the accused's and complainants' linguistic practices become culturally intelligible as performances of gender to the extent that they are contextualized within normative 'rule-bound discourses' of gender formation. Matt's representation of himself as a non-agent of sexual aggression, for example, becomes culturally intelligible as a gendered identity when set against the background of the male sexual drive discourse – a discourse that absolves men of their responsibility and agency for sexual aggression, attributing it instead to their uncontrollable sexual drives. Likewise, the 'ineffectual' subject positions the complainants come to occupy (involuntarily) are culturally intelligible insofar as they reinforce and perpetuate stereotypical images of women as weak and passive. While the dominant discourse of these hearings made a range of gendered subject positions available to Matt, the same was not true for the complainants. That is, Matt's grammar of non-agency was afforded legitimacy and authority by adjudicators in both of the institutional contexts in which his case was heard; in addition, a subject position somewhat inconsistent with Matt's non-agentive positioning also received endorsement, at least in the context of the university tribunal. In Chapter 5, I argued that that complainants' signals of resistance were evaluated (by Matt and the tribunal members) against a masculine communicative code whereby signals of resistance are expressed strongly and forcefully. Here, then, forceful and aggressive behaviour becomes culturally intelligible as enactments of masculinity. Lacey comments on the contradictions that 'inform contemporary discourses of feminine and masculine sexuality':

> The rational male whose sexuality is so potent is, after all, that same poor creature who is driven to rape by the urgings of his uncontrollable sexual drives and whose cognitive capacities are so fragile that he is at times incapable of recognizing the distinction between that apparently rather straightforward dichotomy, yes and no. Similarly, the poor, passive female – the very same subject who, according to the English and Welsh law of incest, does not, like a man 'have' sexual intercourse but rather (and graciously?) 'permits' a man to have sexual intercourse with her – is also the calculating and deceptive seductress who uses her sexuality to entrap men.
>
> (Lacey 1998: 100)

Given the contradictions that inform the 'rule-bound discourses' that make performances of gender culturally intelligible, it is perhaps not surprising that Matt's variable and at times contradictory (linguistic) performances of gender are considered to make cultural sense. The same latitude and range of gendered subject positions is not, however, extended to the complainants and their witness; on the contrary, I have argued that their identities as 'ineffectual agents' are thrust upon them by a dominant discourse that constrained their possibilities for representing their strategic agency. Indeed, the gendered subject positions made available (in the case of Matt) and thwarted (in the case of the complainants and their witness) within these institutional settings all worked in service of the same goal: protecting a range of sexual prerogatives for Matt at the expense of the complainants' sexual autonomy.

The contradictory and variable (linguistic) constructions of masculinity that emerged in these settings are indicative of the indirect and non-exclusive relationship existing between linguistic forms and gendered meanings. As Ochs (1992: 340) argues, 'few features of language directly and exclusively index gender'. Indeed, the grammar of non-agency adopted by Matt (and validated by the judge in the criminal trial as a performance of hegemonic masculinity) is a strategy that may be adopted by other accuseds attempting to represent themselves as innocent in legal contexts. Komter (1998), for example, in her investigation of the interactional dilemmas of courtroom participants in the Netherlands, found at least one of her suspects to use a similar linguistic strategy to Matt while defending himself of a shooting. (See note 4 of Chapter 2.) It is probably only in the context of a sexual assault trial, however, where discourses of male and female sexuality are salient, that these kinds of non-agentive linguistic forms would take on a gendered meaning or, put another way, would become intelligible as a performance of hegemonic masculinity. Not only, then, does this analysis point to the indirect relationship between linguistic forms and gendered meanings, but also to the highly contextualized nature of this relationship. The same linguistic practices can be variably interpreted as gendered depending on context; moreover, as we have seen, very different, and even contradictory, kinds of linguistic identities (e.g., identities that are non-agentive vs. identities that are aggressive and forceful) can be interpreted as 'masculine' in the same context (i.e., the context of these sexual assault hearings).[1]

Material effects

In a variety of contemporary feminist writings, a focus on discourse or discursive practices has often been counterposed with a focus on material realities. Barrett (1992: 201), for example, points to a central issue evident in feminist scholarship that sets the valuing of 'words' against that of 'things': 'many feminists . . . have traditionally tended to see "things" – be they low pay, rape or female foeticide – as more significant than, for example, the discursive construction of marginality in a text or document.' Indeed, Comack exemplifies this dichotomizing of 'word' and 'things' in the following comments about postmodern approaches to the law:

> While postmodern analysis has the advantage of moving the focus of inquiry away from purely structural features of the position or location of law and towards a more detailed consideration of the specific manner in which law operates as a discourse, it is also the case that law is more than just discourse. As a mechanism of power, legal practice has material effects on people's lives.
>
> (Comack 1999: 67)

Rather than representing discursive realities as independent of material realities, I have pointed to ways in which the two intersect; that is, I have demonstrated how legal discursive practices can themselves have material effects. For example, insofar as the discursive constraints imposed upon the complainants and their witness severely restricted the subject positions they came to involuntarily occupy, the hearings analysed here did not allow the complainants' version of events and points of view to emerge. While I have refrained from making the strong claim that the linguistic representations of these adjudication processes directly 'caused' the adjudicators to reason and decide in the way they did, I have suggested that the absence of alternative narratives (i.e., the complainants') and the counter-hegemonic ideologies they embody did nothing to challenge prevailing notions of violence against women. More specifically, if the complainants and their witness had been able to represent themselves as 'strategic agents' in the face of Matt's sexual aggression, the adjudicators might have had greater difficulty invoking the utmost resistance standard or the male sexual drive discourse – discourses that, in part, formed the basis of the adjudicators' decisions. In other words, the subject positions that were discursively 'thrust upon' the complainants and their witness may have influenced the outcome of the hearings. Beyond the direct outcomes of these hearings, such discursive practices may also function as a form of social control (Lees 1997), for example, by discouraging rape victims from disclosing and/or reporting rape or by failing to deter perpetrators of rape.

To locate the problem of rape trials in discursive practices, embodied in institutional settings, is not to deny the power of law to enact rules and impose sanctions. Rather, it is to recognize the structuring potential of language, its capacity to constitute 'the objects of which it speaks' and the effects of this structuring on the particular way rules are enacted and sanctions are imposed. Following Marcus (1992), to understand rape trials in this way is to recognize their capacity for change.

Notes

1 The institutional coerciveness of legal discourse

1 Parts of the first half of this chapter are based on Ehrlich (1997).
2 I owe this particular formulation, '*filtered* through cultural and institutional ideologies' to Bucholtz (1999).
3 Marcus (1992: 388) also discusses the way in which women's bodies are differentially valued according to race: 'in both intra- and inter-racial rape trials, raped Afro-Americans often do not obtain convictions even in the face of overwhelming evidence of brutalization.'
4 See Lees (1996: 240–1) for discussion of statutory reform in England and Wales. She says that 'there have been significant and comprehensive reforms in other countries which are long overdue in Britain', and then points to the length of time 'it has taken to abolish the marital rape exemption, which in 1991 finally removed support for a husband's demand for the right to non-reciprocal sexual domination.'
5 A possible disadvantage of this approach (i.e., defining rape as a type of assault) is 'that it gives the impression that sexual imposition is not of much consequence unless it is accompanied by violence' (Lees 1996: 242).
6 The Supreme Court of Canada overturned the Court of Appeal ruling in *R. v. Chase*, arguing that 'the non-consensual grabbing of breasts does in fact constitute a sexual assault' (Mohr and Roberts 1994: 5).
7 In 1999, the Supreme Court of Canada unanimously overturned the Alberta Court of Appeal ruling in *R. v. Ewanchuk*. The majority decision stated that 'the complainants' fear need not be reasonable, nor must it be communicated to the accused in order for consent to be vitiated'.
8 Adler (1987), in a study of British rape trials from 1978 to 1979, found that in spite of a 1976 amendment to the Sexual Offences Act which limited the introduction of sexual history evidence, such evidence was still allowed in approximately 60 per cent of the cases she investigated. (The admissibility of such evidence was still left to the discretion of the judge.)
9 Lacey (1998: 121), for example, cites Canadian sexual assault law as coming 'considerably closer' to meeting her ideals than does the law of England and Wales.
10 Transcription conventions (adapted from Jefferson 1978) are as follows:

.	indicates sentence final falling intonation
,	indicates clause-final intonation (more to come)
?	indicates rising intonation followed by a noticeable pause
. . .	indicates pause of 1/2 second or more

= indicates no interval between adjacent utterances (second is latched to the first)

{a lot}
{I see} brackets indicate overlapping utterances

– indicates a halting, abrupt cutoff

o: colon indicates an extension of the sound or syllable it follows

bold bold indicates emphatic stress

((sniff)) double parentheses indicate details of the conversational scene or vocalizations.

11 While court transcripts may not be as accurate as those transcribed by linguists, they function as the official representation of trials and thus have an influence on outcomes at both the trial and appeal level. First, trial judges often employ transcripts in writing decisions, especially in long trials and trials that have been interrupted. Second, whenever a trial is appealed to a Court of Appeal or the Supreme Court, judges refer to the trial transcripts as the exclusive representation of what occurred in a trial.

Examples from the criminal trial are reproduced here as they appeared in the official court transcripts. The symbol . . . is used in the trial examples (as opposed to the tribunal examples) to represent intervening material. Hence, note that this symbol is used differently in the two sets of examples. (See note 10 of this chapter.)

2 'My shirt came off . . .'

1 Previous versions of this chapter were presented at the Berkeley Women and Language Conference in April 1998; at an MIT Linguistics Colloquium in May 1999; in the Margaret Laurence Women's Studies Lecture Series at University of Winnipeg in March 2000; at the Linguistics Department, University of Manitoba in March 2000 and at the Georgetown Linguistics and the Professions Conference in May 2000. I thank audiences in all of those places for useful questions, comments and discussion.

2 When men were the agents of sentences, subjects attributed greater responsibility to them as opposed to the patients of the sentences, whether or not the events were represented in passive or active voice.

3 While the female subjects in Henley *et al.*'s study were not affected by verb voice in the way male subjects were (i.e., to attribute less harm to the victim and less responsibility to the perpetrator), they were, like the males, affected by multiple exposure to stories which represented violence against women in the passive voice. After such exposure, all subjects 'became more negative about rape victims, more accepting of rape myths, and more accepting of physical abuse of women' (Henley *et al.* 1995: 80).

4 Komter (1998: 49–50), in her book analysing the interactional dilemmas of courtroom participants involved in cases of violent crime in the Netherlands, identifies a defensive strategy (among many others) that she characterizes as 'the disappearance of agency.' Her example of this strategy ('Then I suddenly remembered my gun and I reached for it and then there were shots') shows a suspect describing a shooting that he allegedly committed. As Komter says of this example, 'the shots just seem to be there, irrespective of his [the suspect's] actions'.

5 Matt's adoption of these particular grammatical forms is not necessarily a conscious one. Speakers generally possess, often inexplicit, knowledge about the functions of grammatical forms. Given his desire to construct an innocent identity, Matt undoubtedly draws upon this linguistic knowledge in producing this particular constellation of linguistic forms, all of which have similar functions.

6 In Chapter 5, I discuss other examples in which Matt portrays himself as an agent of sexual advances. However, these are represented as sexual advances to which Marg has consented.

7 Similar examples can be found in Drew (1992), where a complainant in a rape trial is cross-examined by the defence attorney in the trial. As Drew points out, in these kinds of examples the complainant disputes the version of events put forth by the attorney by providing an alternative characterization of the events, sometimes without directly and overtly rejecting the attorney's version.

8 Haegeman and Gueron (1999) distinguish between two kinds of one-argument verbs: intransitive verbs and unaccusative verbs. The subjects of intransitive verbs are base-generated in subject position, whereas the subjects of unaccusative verbs are base-generated in object position.

9 While *insertion* is a fairly neutral term for designating sexual acts of aggression, *fondling* represents the acts as loving and affectionate, thereby contributing to a depiction of the events as consensual sex.

10 The university tribunal's chair was responsible for writing the decision and reasons for judgement. Thus, the first person singular pronoun, *I*, as opposed to *we*, in the written document presumably designates the tribunal's chair.

11 Causal attributions were considered to be 'violent' if they imputed the cause of the assault to a decision or tendency of the offender 'to engage in a violent act' as opposed to some other kind of act like 'getting drunk' (Coates 1997: 285).

12 The judge made the following comments in sentencing Matt on the one conviction of sexual assault:

> In the circumstances of this case, I am of the view that with his past and his intelligence and willingness to contribute considerably to society . . . the accused has learned a lesson and is unlikely to commit this sort of offence again. He is clearly without any prior record. He has a great deal to contribute to society and I expect he will. His own rehabilitation does not, in my opinion, require a custodial term; however, for general deterrence and to reflect, as a sentence of this nature must, abhorrence of society of such conduct, and the Court's duty to extend its protection to those who are in vulnerable positions, I am content that a moderate degree of incarceration is required. I would sentence the accused then to a period of 6 months. Additionally, I would place him on probation for a period of 18 months on the statutory terms and conditions, that he must be of good behaviour and keep the peace. Additionally, that he have no contact, direct or indirect, with the complainant, and as well that he report forthwith after completion of sentence and thereafter as required by the probation officer for the purpose of counseling in respect of appropriate attitudes towards women in the sexual context.
>
> (*Reasons for Sentence in Her Majesty the Queen and M.A.*)

The conviction was appealed by the defence, but the appeal was dismissed. Thus, I assume that Matt spent six months in jail.

13 It is significant to note that the vast majority of acquaintance rape cases would not have this kind of corroborating evidence.

14 Busby (1999) argues that the foundational principles of the criminal justice system (i.e., the presumption of innocence, proof beyond a reasonable doubt, and the accused's right to silence), combined with the rape mythologies that often inform judicial reasoning, make the convictions of defendants in sexual assault cases unlikely. With respect to these two cases, the judge was only able to find guilt 'beyond a reasonable doubt' when there was corroborating evidence from witnesses present at the scene of the sexual aggression. In the other case, the

judge did not find guilt 'beyond a reasonable doubt' perhaps because the complainant had acknowledged consenting to some intimate activity, which, in turn, set in motion Matt's 'uncontrollable' sexual drive.

15 In saying that this utterance is pragmatically inappropriate, I am not saying that it is grammatically ill-formed. Rather, I am suggesting that it is somewhat odd within this particular context.

16 It is not only the accused's 'linguistic practices' that are authorized in these institutional settings, but also the version of events (and concomitant ideologies) encoded in his linguistic practices.

17 According to Connell (1987: 185), hegemonic masculinity is a dominant, cultural ideal of masculinity that does not necessarily correspond closely to the personalities of actual men: 'the public face of hegemonic masculinity is not necessarily what powerful men are, but what sustains their power and what large members of men are motivated to support.'

3 'I see an option . . . I simply want to explore that option with you'

1 This chapter is a greatly elaborated and extended version of arguments and analyses that appear in Ehrlich and King (1996) and Ehrlich (1999).

2 According to Philips (1998: 10), cultural and linguistic anthropologists, influenced by the work of Bourdieu (1977) and Foucault (1972), 'have moved in the direction of seeing culture as located in social practices . . . rather than as knowledge located in the minds of individuals.' Moreover, for some, practice is equated with language use, specifically spoken discourse.

3 In *R. v. Weaver* (1990) the Alberta Court of Appeals judge, upholding the acquittal of an accused, says the following about resistance and an accused's 'honest but mistaken belief in consent':

> The Crown further urged that the trial judge had committed error in law by imposing on the victim a requirement that she resist in order to show absence of consent. Had that occurred, we would agree that there was error in law, but a review of the trial judge's reasons does not, in our view, support the allegation. The trial judge did note that the complainant had not resisted or objected, but it seems clear that he did so in the context of determining whether Weaver's expressed belief that she was consenting. The following quotations from the reasons show what the trial judge considered to be the basic question of fact before him: . . .
>
> 'I should mention that by all accounts there was absolutely no force exerted. She was not handled roughly. She was apparently inert and her explanation of that is certainly credible and I've accepted that already. I've found that she didn't consent to this at all. And perhaps if she hadn't been so sick, or ill she might have been able to express her repugnance or her aversion to what was happening to her. I think she was helpless in the circumstance and she was being taken advantage of, obviously. But the accused still has a possible defence. Did he realize that he was doing this without consent?' . . .
>
> We must observe that, on the printed record, an honest belief in consent seems a remarkable finding. But we did not see or hear the witnesses, as did the trial judge, and we must defer to this finding.

4 McElhinny (1997: 127) argues that 'postulating ordinary and institutional interactions as separate obscures contests in institutional settings, especially those serving women, the poor and minorities, over what is legitimately institutional.

It also obscures interactional inequalities in putatively ordinary interactions (such as families), and the ways that people's interactions in work settings can shape interactional styles elsewhere.'

5 This is not the criminal trial that forms the basis of my analysis in this book.

6 Conley and O'Barr (1998: 32) argue that general cross-examining strategies, when deployed in the context of rape trials have a particular poignancy: 'a woman telling a story of physical domination by one man is subjected to linguistic domination by another.'

7 Within the context of trials, questioning of witnesses must always occur in the form of questions. While this same general regulation applies to administrative tribunals, it seems, at least in this particular tribunal, that such a regulation was not strictly enforced. Both the tribunal member, GK, and Matt's representative, TM, sometimes employed declaratives rather than interrogatives in their asking of questions.

4 'I didn't yell . . . I didn't scream'

1 I thank Lorraine Code for suggesting the term 'ineffectual agency' to me.

2 This analysis has been influenced by the insightful work of Capps and Ochs (1995) who document the grammatical forms used by an agoraphobic woman – what they term 'a grammar of panic'. To acknowledge this influence is not to suggest that the complainants and their witness necessarily bear any similarity to the agoraphobic woman whose talk is analysed by Capps and Ochs. Rather, it is to acknowledge the importance of Capps' and Ochs' work in demonstrating the powerful role of grammatical forms in building and constituting identities.

3 While I have argued that the prosecuting lawyers were not terribly successful in reframing the terms of the debate in these proceedings, it is the case that when the complainants were asked about their experience in direct testimony, they were more able to recount their *own* narratives. That is, the assumptions and presuppositions embedded in the questions I have analysed in Chapter 3 did not constrain, limit and restructure the way that the complainants were able to talk about their experiences of sexual assault. Recall that Fisher (1991) found that in interactions between nurse-practitioners and patients, by contrast to interactions between doctors and patients, the nurse-practitioner used open-ended, probing questions which maximized the patient's own 'voice' and interpretation of medical problems. Likewise, the open-ended questions of direct examination in these hearings seemed to better maximize the women's own 'voices' and experiences of sexual assault. Consider, however, the dialogic nature of the complainants' responses to open-ended questions that I observe elsewhere in this chapter.

4 In an attempt to rethink and reconceptualize (feminist) discourses about vicitims of sexual assault that she views as too victimizing, Lamb (1999: 109) provides an alternative version of victims 'that recognizes agency as well as passivity, strength as well as vulnerability, resistance as well as dissociation'. Lamb's comments resonate with my emphasis here.

5 I thank Sue Levesque for directing my attention to this particular formulation of Chancer's.

5 'The signals . . . between men and women'

1 The analysis presented in the first half of this chapter comes from Ehrlich (1998).

2 In Canada, this kind of standard has been introduced in cases involving battered women who have killed their husbands in self-defence. For example, in *R*. v. *Lavallee* (1990) the Supreme Court of Canada accepted that women's perspectives

and experiences in relation to self-defence may be different from men's and that such perspectives and experiences should inform the 'objective' standard of a reasonable person.

3 As Lacey (1998: 8) argues, the 'difficult trick' in abandoning universal standards in favour of more subjective or contextual ones 'is to do so without fixing their shape and identity within received categories of masculine and feminine'.

4 Smart (1989: 34) argues that 'there is no room for the concept of submission in the dichotomy of consent/non-consent which dominates the rape trial.' In other words, if women submit to (coerced) sex out of fear of more extreme instances of violence or out of fear of losing a job, they are 'deemed to have consented to their violation'. Smart is writing from the perspective of British law; how does the law of sexual assault in the United States and Canada deal with coerced sex? In the United States, recall that an emphasis on 'forced compulsion' as the core of sexual assault offences has often meant that only sexual assault involving physical violence or the threat of physical violence has been deemed criminally punishable. As Schulhofer (1998: 82) points out, 'many feminist critics of rape law argue that the law's concept of force should be extended from physical violence to other forms of power'. An example of this extension can be seen in Chapter 1 where I cite a New Jersey 1992 Supreme Court decision. In Canada, 1992 reforms to sexual assault statutes redefined consent such that some kinds of coercive sex, not involving physical violence or the threat of physical violence, are criminally punishable (e.g., 'if the accused induces the complainant to consent by abusing a position of trust, power or authority'). In general, the fact that women sometimes submit to sex 'because of subtle mixtures of physical intimidation, unstated threats, psychological demands, and the pressures of male status and authority' (Schulhofer 1998: 52) poses problems for most legal definitions of consent. See Schulhofer (1998) for a lengthy discussion of proposals by feminist legal theorists to rectify these definitional and conceptual problems.

5 Cameron (1998c: 451) makes a similar argument about 'miscommunication' between women and men: 'laying claim to a particular intention or interpretation can function as a strategic move in a game of power and resistance.'

Conclusion

1 Lacey (1998: 116) makes an additional point regarding the possible effects of complainants' inability to recount their own version of events in sexual assault trials. For Lacey, this 'silencing effectively denies rape victims . . . the chance to approach the court as an audience capable of acknowledging their trauma – a process which is arguably crucial to surviving the trauma and among the most important things which a public rape trial should achieve.'

Bibliography

Abrams, K. (1989) 'Gender discrimination and the transformation of workplace norms', *Vanderbilt Law Review* 1183: 1203.

Adler, Z. (1987) *Rape on Trial*, London: Routledge.

Atkinson, J. and Drew, P. (1979) *Order in Court*, Atlantic Highlands: Humanities Press.

Austin, J. L. (1962) *How to Do Things with Words*, Oxford: Clarendon.

Backhouse, C. (1991) *Petticoats and Prejudice: Women and Law in Nineteenth-Century Canada*, Toronto: Osgoode Hall Society of Law.

Bakhtin, M. (1981) *The Dialogic Imagination: Four Essays by M.M. Bakhtin*, M. Holquist (ed.), C. Emerson and M. Holquist (trans.) Austin, TX: University of Texas Press.

Barrett, M. (1992) 'Words and things: materialism and method in contemporary feminist analysis', in M. Barrett and A. Phillips (eds) *Destabilizing Theory: Contemporary Feminist Debates*, pp. 201–19. Stanford, CA: Stanford University Press.

Bartlett, K. and Kennedy, R. (1991) 'Introduction', in K. Bartlett and R. Kennedy (eds) *Feminist Legal Theory: Readings in Law and Gender*, pp. 1–11. Boulder, CO: Westview Press.

Bateson, G. (1972) *Steps to an Ecology of Mind*, New York: Ballantine Books.

Bergvall, V. (1999) 'Toward a comprehensive theory of language and gender', *Language in Society* 28: 273–93.

Blommaert, J. and Verschueren, J. (1998) *Debating Diversity: Analysing the Discourse of Tolerance*, London: Routledge.

Bordo, S. (1993) *Unbearable Weight: Feminism, Western Culture, and the Body*, Berkeley, CA: University of California Press.

Bourdieu, P. (1977) *Outline of a Theory of Practice*, Cambridge: Cambridge University Press.

Bucholtz, M. (1999) 'Bad examples: Transgression and progress in language and gender studies', in M. Bucholtz, A. Liang and L. Sutton (eds) *Reinventing Identities: The Gendered Self in Discourse*, pp. 3–24. Oxford: Oxford University Press.

Burr, V. (1995) *An Introduction to Social Constructionism*, London: Routledge.

Busby, K. (1999) '"Not a victim until a conviction is entered": Sexual violence prosecutions and legal "truth"', in E. Comack (ed.) *Locating Law: Race/Class/Gender Connections*, pp. 260–88. Halifax, NS: Fernwood Publishing.

Butler, J. (1990) *Gender Trouble: Feminism and the Subversion of Identity*, London: Routledge.

Cameron, D. (1990) 'Demythologizing sociolinguistics', in J. Joseph and T. Taylor (eds) *Ideologies of Language*, pp. 79–93. London: Routledge.

—— (1992) *Feminism and Linguistic Theory*, second edition, New York: St. Martin's Press.

—— (1995) *Verbal Hygiene*, London: Routledge.

—— (1996) 'The language–gender interface: Challenging co-optation', in V. Bergvall, J. Bing and A. Freed (eds) *Rethinking Language and Gender Research: Theory and Practice*, pp. 31–53. London: Longman.

—— (1997) 'Theoretical debates in feminist linguistics: Questions of sex and gender', in R. Wodak (ed.) *Gender and Discourse*, pp. 21–36. London: Sage.

—— (1998a) 'Gender, language, and discourse: A review essay', *Signs: Journals of Women in Culture and Society* 23: 945–73.

—— (1998b) 'Introduction: Why is language a feminist issue?', in D. Cameron (ed.) *The Feminist Critique of Language: A Reader*, Second Edition, pp. 1–28. London: Routledge.

—— (1998c) '"Is there any ketchup Vera?": Gender, power, and pragmatics', *Discourse & Society* 9: 437–55.

Cameron, D., Frazer, E., Harvey, P., Rampton B. and Richardson, K. (1992) *Researching Language: Issues of Power and Method*, London: Routledge.

Capps, L. and Ochs, E. (1995) *Constructing Panic: The Discourse of Agoraphobia*, Cambridge, MA: Harvard University Press.

Chamallas, M. (1995) Comments on papers presented at Linguistic Society of America Symposium: Linguistic Perspectives on Sexual Harassment. Linguistic Society of America's Annual Meeting (January), New Orleans, Louisiana.

Chancer L. (1997) 'The seens and unseens of popular cultural representations', in M. Fineman and M. McCluskey (eds) *Feminism, Media and the Law*, pp. 227–34. Oxford: Oxford University Press.

Chomsky, N. (1989) *Necessary Illusions: Thought Control in Democratic Societies*, Toronto: House of Anansi Press.

Clark, L. and Lewis, D. (1977) *Rape: The Price of Coercive Sexuality*, Toronto: Women's Press.

Coates, L. (1997)'Causal attributions in sexual assault trial judgments', *Journal of Language and Social Psychology* 16: 278–96.

Coates, L., Bavelas, J. and Gibson, J. (1994) 'Anomalous language in sexual assault trial judgements', *Discourse & Society* 5: 189–206.

Comack, E. (1999) 'Theoretical excursions', in E. Comack (ed.) *Locating Law: Race/Class/Gender Connections*, pp. 19–68. Halifax, NS: Fernwood Publishing.

Conley, J. M. and O'Barr, W. M. (1998) *Just Words: Law, Language and Power*, Chicago: University of Chicago Press.

Connell, R.W. (1987) *Gender and Power: Society, the Person and Sexual Politics*, Stanford, CA: Stanford University Press.

Cornell, D. (1995) *The Imaginary Domain: Abortion, Pornography and Sexual Harassment*, London: Routledge.

Crawford, M. (1995) *Talking Difference: On Gender and Language*, London: Sage.

Crenshaw, K. (1992) 'Whose story is it anyway?: Feminist and antiracist appropriations of Anita Hill', in T. Morrison (ed.) *Race-ing Justice, En-gendering Power*, pp. 402–40. New York: Pantheon Books.

Crocker, P. (1983) 'An analysis of university definitions of sexual harassment', *Signs* 8: 696–707.

Crystal, D. (1987) *The Cambridge Encyclopedia of Language*, Cambridge: Cambridge University Press.

Danet, B. (1980) ' "Baby" or "fetus"?: Language and the construction of reality in a manslaughter trial', *Semiotica* 32: 187–219.

Danet, B., Hoffman, K., Kermish, N., Rafn, H., and Stayman, D. (1980) 'An ethnography of questioning', in R. Shuy and A. Shnukal (eds) *Language Use and the Uses of Language*, pp. 222–34. Washington, DC: Georgetown University Press.

Davis, K. (1988) *Power Under the Microscope*, Dordrecht, Netherlands: Foris Publications.

Davis, K. and Fisher, S. (1993) 'Power and the female subject', in S. Fisher and K. Davis (eds) *Negotiating at the Margins: The Gendered Discourses of Power and Resistance*, pp. 3–20. New Brunswick, NJ: Rutgers University Press.

Dobash, R. E. and Dobash, R.P. (1992) *Women, Violence and Social Change*, London: Routledge.

Drew, P. (1992) 'Contested evidence in courtroom examination: the case of a trial for rape', in P. Drew and J. Heritage (eds) *Talk at Work: Interaction in Institutional Settings*, pp. 470–520. Cambridge: Cambridge University Press.

Drew, P. and Heritage, J. (1992) 'Analyzing talk at work: An introduction', in P. Drew and J. Heritage (eds) *Talk at Work: Interaction in Institutional Settings*, pp. 3–65. Cambridge: Cambridge University Press

Duranti, A. (1992) 'Intentions, self, and responsibility: An essay in Samoan ethnog-pragmatics', in J. Hill and J. Irvine (eds) *Responsibility and Evidence in Oral Discourse*, pp. 24–47. Cambridge: Cambridge University Press.

—— (1994) *From Grammar to Politics: Linguistic Anthropology in a Western Samoan Village*, Berkeley, CA: University of California Press.

—— (1997) *Linguistic Anthropology*, Cambridge: Cambridge University Press.

Duranti, A. and Goodwin, C. (eds) (1992) *Rethinking Context: Language as an Interactive Phenomenon*, Cambridge: Cambridge University Press.

Eckert, P. and McConnell-Ginet, S. (1992a) 'Think practically and look locally: Language and gender as community-based practice', *Annual Review of Anthropology* 21: 461–90.

—— (1992b) 'Communities of practice: Where language, gender, and power all live', in K. Hall, M. Bucholtz and B. Moonwoman (eds) *Locating Power: Proceedings of the Second Berkeley Women and Languages Conference*, pp. 88–9. Berkeley, CA: Women and Language Group.

—— (1999) 'New generalizations and explanations in language and gender research', *Language in Society* 28: 185–201.

Ehrlich, S. (1997) 'Gender as social practice: Implications for second language acquisition', *Studies in Second Language Acquisition* 19: 421–46.

—— (1998) 'The discursive reconstruction of sexual consent', *Discourse & Society* 9: 149–71.

—— (1999) 'Communities of practice, gender and the representation of sexual assault', *Language in Society* 28: 239–56.

Ehrlich, S. and King, R. (1992) 'Gender-based language reform and the social construction of meaning', *Discourse & Society* 3: 151–66.

—— (1994) 'Feminist meanings and the (de)politicization of the lexicon', *Language in Society* 23: 59–76.

—— (1996) 'Consensual sex or sexual harassment: Negotiating meaning', in V. Bergvall, J. Bing and A. Freed (eds) *Rethinking Language and Gender Research: Theory and Practice*, pp. 153–172. London: Longman.

Ehrlich, S. and Levesque, S. (1996) 'Discursive practices, point of view and the representation of sexual harassment', in N. Warner, J. Ahlers, L. Bilmes, M. Oliver, S. Wertheim and M. Chen (eds) *Gender and Belief Systems: Proceedings of the Fourth Berkeley Women and Language Conference*, pp. 191–200. Berkeley, CA: Berkeley Women and Language Group.

Estrich, S. (1986) 'Real rape', *Yale Law Journal* 1087: 1122.

—— (1987) *Real Rape*, Cambridge, MA: Harvard University Press.

Fairclough, N. (1992) *Discourse and Social Change*, Cambridge: Polity Press.

—— (1995) *Critical Discourse Analysis: The Critical Study of Language*, London: Longman.

Fairclough, N. and Wodak, R. (1997) 'Critical discourse analysis', in T. A. van Dijk (ed.) *Discourse as Social Interaction*, pp. 258–84. London: Sage.

Fisher, S. (1984) 'Institutional authority and the structure of discourse', *Discourse Processes* 7: 201–24.

—— (1991) 'A discourse of the social: Medical talk/power talk/oppositional talk', *Discourse & Society* 2: 157–82.

Fisher, S. and Todd, A. (eds) (1986) *Discourse and Institutional Authority: Medicine, Education, and Law*, Norwood, NJ: Ablex.

Foucault, M. (1972) *The Archeology of Knowledge and the Discourse on Language*, New York: Pantheon Books.

—— (1980) *Power/Knowledge: Selected Interviews and Other Writings*, C. Gordon (ed.), C. Gordon *et al.* (trans.), New York: Pantheon Books.

Fraser, N. (1989) *Unruly Practices: Power, Discourse and Gender in Contemporary Social Theory*, Minneapolis: University of Minnesota Press.

Freed, A. (1992) 'We understand perfectly: A critique of Tannen's view of cross-sex communication', in K. Hall, M. Bucholtz and B. Moonwoman (eds) *Locating Power: Proceedings of the Second Berkeley Woman and Language Conference*, pp. 144–52. Berkeley, CA: Berkeley Women and Language Group.

—— (1996) 'Language and gender research in an experimental setting', in V. Bergvall, J. Bing and A. Freed (eds) *Rethinking Language and Gender Research: Theory and Practice*, pp. 54–76. London: Longman.

Freed, A. and Greenwood, A. (1996) 'Women, men, and type of talk: What makes the difference?', *Language in Society* 25: 1–26.

Freeman, R. and McElhinny, B. (1996) 'Language and gender', in S. L. McKay and N. H. Hornberger (eds) *Sociolinguistics and Language Teaching*, pp. 218–80. Cambridge: Cambridge University Press.

Gal, S. (1991) 'Between speech and silence: The problematics of research on language and gender', in M. di Leonardo (ed.) *Gender at the Crossroads of Knowledge*, pp. 175–203. Berkeley, CA: University of California Press.

Garfinkel, H. and Sacks, H. (1970) 'On formal structure of practical actions', in J. McKinney and E. Tiryakian (eds) *Theoretical Sociology*, pp. 338–66. New York: Appleton-Century-Crofts.

Gavey, N. (1999) '"I wasn't raped, but . . .": Revisiting definitional problems in sexual victimization', in S. Lamb (ed.) *New Versions of Victims: Feminists Struggle with the Concept*, pp. 57–81. New York: New York University Press.

Giddens, A. (1976) *New Rules of Sociological Method: A Positive Critique of Interpretative Sociologies*, London: Hutchinson.

Goffman, E. (1974) *Frame Analysis: An Essay on the Organization of Experience*, Cambridge, MA: Harvard University Press.

—— (1981) *Forms of Talk*, Philadelphia: University of Pennsylvania Press.

Goodwin, C. (1994) 'Professional vision', *American Anthropologist* 96: 606–33.

Goodwin, C. and Goodwin, M. (1997) 'Contested vision: The discursive constitution of Rodney King', in B. Gunnarsson, P. Linell and B. Nordberg (eds) *The Construction of Professional Discourse*, pp. 292–316. London: Longman.

Goodwin, M. (1990) *He-said-she-said: Talk as Social Organization Among Black Children*, Bloomington, IN: Indiana University Press.

Graddol, D. and Swann, J. (1989) *Gender Voices*, Oxford: Blackwell.

Green, G. (1996) *Pragmatics and Natural Language Understanding*, Second Edition, Mahwah, NJ: Lawrence Erlbaum.

Grice, H. P. (1975) 'Logic and conversation', in P. Cole and J. Morgan (eds) *Syntax and Semantics 3: Speech Acts*, pp. 41–58. New York: Academic Press.

—— (1978) 'Further notes on logic and conversation', in P. Cole (ed.) *Syntax and Semantics 9: Pragmatics*, pp. 113–28. New York: Academic Press.

Gumperz, J. (ed.) (1982a) *Discourse Strategies*, Cambridge: Cambridge University Press.

—— (ed.) (1982b) *Language and Social Identity*, Cambridge: Cambridge University Press.

Gumperz, J. and Levinson, S. (eds) (1996) *Rethinking Linguistic Relativity*, Cambridge and New York: Cambridge University Press.

Haegeman, L. and Gueron, J. (1999) *English Grammar: A Generative Perspective*, Oxford: Blackwell.

Hale, S. and Gibbons, J. (1999) 'Varying realities: Patterned changes in the interpreter's representation of courtroom and external realities', *Applied Linguistics* 20: 203–20.

Hall, S., Chritcher, C., Jefferson, T., Clarke, J. and Roberts B. (1978) *Policing the Crisis: Mugging, the State, and Law and Order*, New York: Holmes and Meier.

Halliday, M. A. K. (1971) 'Linguistic function and literary style', in Seymour Chatman (ed.) *Literary Style: A Symposium*, pp. 332–3. Oxford: Oxford University Press.

Harvey, K. and Shalom, C. (1997) 'Introduction', in K. Harvey and C. Shalom (eds) *Language and Desire: Encoding Sex, Romance and Intimacy*, pp. 1–17. London: Routledge.

Henley, N. M. (1989) 'Molehill or mountain? What we know and don't know about sex bias in language', in M. Crawford and M. Gentry (eds) *Gender and Thought: Psychological Perspectives*, pp. 59–78. New York: Springer-Verlag.

Henley, N. and Kramarae, C. (1991) 'Gender, power and miscommunication', in N. Coupland, H. Giles and J. Wiemann (eds) *Miscommunication and Problematic Talk*, pp. 18–43. Newbury Park, CA: Sage.

Henley N., Miller, M. and Beazley, J. (1995) 'Syntax, semantics, and sexual violence agency and the passive voice', *Journal of Language and Social Psychology* 14: 60–84.

Heritage, J. (1985) 'Analyzing news interviews: aspects of the production of talk for an overhearing audience', in T. van Dijk (ed.) *Handbook of Discourse Analysis: Discourse and Dialogue*, pp. 95–119. New York: Academic Press.

Heritage, J. and Watson, D. (1979) 'Formulations as conversational objects', in G. Psathas (ed.) *Everyday Language: Studies in Ethnomethodology*, pp. 123–62. Hillsdale, NJ: Lawrence Erlbaum.

Herman, E. and Chomsky, N. (1988) *Manufacturing Consent: The Political Economy of the Mass Media*, New York: Pantheon Books.

Hirsch, S. (1998) *Pronouncing and Persevering: Gender and the Discourses of Disputing in an African Islamic Court*, Chicago: University of Chicago Press.

Hirsch, S. and Lazarus-Black, M. (1994) 'Performance and paradox: Exploring law's role in hegemony and resistance', in M. Lazarus-Black and S. Hirsch (eds) *Contested States: Law, Hegemony, and Resistance*, pp. 1–31. London: Routledge.

Hollway, W. (1989) *Subjectivity and Method in Psychology: Gender, Meaning and Science*, London: Sage.

Hutchby, I. and Wooffitt, R. (1998) *Conversation Analysis*, Oxford: Polity Press.

Jacoby, S. and Ochs, E. (1995) 'Co-construction: An introduction', *Research on Language and Social Interaction* (Special Issue: Co-Construction), 28: 171–83.

Jaworski, A. and Coupland, N. (1999) 'Introduction: Perspectives on discourse analysis', in A. Jaworski and N. Coupland (eds) *The Discourse Reader*, pp. 1–44. London: Routledge.

Jefferson, G. (1978) 'Sequential aspects of storytelling in conversation', in J. Schenkein (ed.) *Studies in the Organization of Conversational Interaction*, pp. 219–48. New York: Free Press.

Kiparsky, P. and Kiparsky, C. (1971) 'Fact', in D. Steinberg and L. Jakobovits (eds) *Semantics: An Interdisciplinary Reader*, pp. 345–69. Cambridge: Cambridge University Press.

Kitzinger, C. and Frith, H. (1999) 'Just say no? The use of conversation analysis in developing a feminist perspective on sexual refusal', *Discourse & Society* 10: 293–316.

Kitzinger, C. and Thomas, A. (1995) 'Sexual harassment: A discursive approach', in S. Wilkinson and C. Kitzinger (eds) *Feminism and Discourse: Psychological Perspectives*, pp. 32–48. London: Sage.

Komter, M. (1998) *Dilemmas in the Courtroom: A Study of Trials of Violent Crime in the Netherlands*, Mahwah, NJ: Lawrence Erlbaum.

Kotthoff and Wodak (eds) (1998) *Communicating Gender in Context*, Amsterdam: John Benjamins.

Lacey, N. (1998) *Unspeakable Subjects: Feminist Essays in Legal and Social Theory*, Oxford: Hart.

LaFrance, M. and Hahn, G. (1994) 'The disappearing agent: Gender stereotypes, interpersonal verbs and implicit causality', in C. Roman, S. Juhasz and C. Miller (eds) *The Women and Language Debate: A Sourcebook*, pp. 348–62. New Brunswick, NJ: Rutgers University.

Lamb, S. (1999) 'Constructing the victim: Popular images and lasting labels', in S. Lamb (ed.) *New Versions of Victims: Feminists Struggle with the Concept*, pp. 108–38. New York: New York University Press.

Lazarus-Black, M. and Hirsch, S. (eds) (1994) *Contested States: Law, Hegemony, and Resistance*, London: Routledge.

Lees, S. (1996) *Carnal Knowledge: Rape on Trial*, London: Hamish Hamilton.

—— (1997) *Ruling Passions: Sexual Violence, Reputation, and the Law*, Buckingham and Philadelphia: Open University Press.

Lempert, L. (1996) 'Women's strategies for survival: Developing agency in abusive relationships', *Journal of Family Violence* 11: 269–89.

Levinson, S. (1983) *Pragmatics*, Cambridge: Cambridge University Press.

—— (1992) 'Activity types and language', in P. Drew and J. Heritage (eds) *Talk at Work: Interaction in Institutional Settings*, pp. 66–100. Cambridge: Cambridge University Press.

Liang, A. C. (1999) 'Conversationally implicating lesbian and gay identity', in M. Bucholtz, A. Liang and L. Sutton (eds) *Reinventing Identities*, pp. 293–310. Oxford: Oxford University Press.

Lyons, J. (1977) *Semantics*, Cambridge: Cambridge University Press.

McConnell-Ginet, S. (1988) 'Language and gender', in F. Newmeyer (ed.) *Linguistics: The Cambridge Survey*, Volume IV, pp. 75–99. Cambridge: Cambridge University Press.

—— (1989) 'The sexual (re)production of meaning: A discourse-based theory', in F. Frank and P.A. Treichler (eds) *Language, Gender, and Professional Writing*, pp. 35–50. New York: Modern Language Association of America.

—— (1995) 'Can linguists help identify sexual harassment?', Paper presented at Linguistic Society of America Symposium: Linguistic Perspectives on Sexual Harassment. Linguistic Society of America's Annual Meeting (January), New Orleans, Louisiana.

McElhinny, B. (1997) 'Ideologies of public and private language in sociolinguistics', in R. Wodak (ed.) *Gender and Discourse*, pp. 106–39. London: Sage.

MacKinnon, C. (1987) *Feminism Unmodified*, Cambridge, MA: Harvard University Press.

—— (1989) *Toward a Feminist Theory of the State*, Cambridge, MA: Harvard University Press.

Maltz, D.N. and Borker, R.A. (1982) 'A cultural approach to male–female communication', in J. Gumperz (ed.) *Language and Social Identity*, pp. 196–216. Cambridge: Cambridge University Press.

Marcus, S. (1992) 'Fighting bodies, fighting words: A theory and politics of rape prevention', in J. Butler and J. Scott (eds) *Feminists Theorize the Political*, pp. 385–403. London: Routledge.

Matoesian, G. (1993) *Reproducing Rape: Domination Through Talk in the Courtroom*, Chicago: University of Chicago Press.

—— (1995) 'Language, law, and society: Policy implications of the Kennedy Smith rape trial', *Law & Society Review* 29: 669–701.

Merry, S. (1990) *Getting Justice and Getting Even: Legal Consciousness among Working-Class Americans*, Chicago: Chicago University Press.

Mertz, E. (1994) 'Legal language: Pragmatics, poetics, and social power', *Annual Review of Anthropology* 23: 435–55.

Miller, C. and Swift, K. (1976) *Words and Women*, Garden City, NY: Doubleday.

Mohr, R. and Roberts, J. (1994) 'Sexual assault in Canada: Recent developments', in J. Roberts and R. Mohr (eds) *Sexual Assault: A Decade of Legal and Social Change*, pp. 3–19. Toronto: University of Toronto Press.

Morgan, M. (1991) 'Indirectness and interpretation in African American women's discourse', *Pragmatics* 1: 421–51.

Ochs, E. (1992) 'Indexing gender', in A. Duranti and C. Goodwin (eds) *Rethinking Context: Language as an Interactive Phenomenon*, pp. 335–58. Cambridge: Cambridge University Press.

O'Connor, P. (1995) 'Speaking of crime: "I don't know what made me do it"',
  Discourse & Society 6: 429–56.
Philips, S. (1992) 'A Marx-influenced approach to ideology and language:
  Comments', *Pragmatics* 2: 377–85.
—— (1998) *Ideology in the Language of Judges*, Oxford: Oxford University Press.
Rhode, D.L. (1997) *Speaking of Sex: The Denial of Gender Inequality*, Cambridge, MA:
  Harvard University Press.
Russell, D. (1982) *Rape in Marriage*, New York: Macmillan.
—— (1984) *Sexual Exploitation: Rape, Child Sexual Abuse, and Workplace Harassment*,
  Beverly Hills: Sage.
Rymes, B. (1995) 'The construction of moral agency in the narratives of high school
  drop-outs', *Discourse & Society* 6: 495–516.
Sanday, P. R. (1996) *A Woman Scorned: Acquaintance Rape on Trial*, New York:
  Doubleday.
Schiffrin, D. (1987) *Discourse Markers*, Cambridge: Cambridge University Press.
—— (1994) *Approaches to Discourse*, Oxford: Blackwell.
—— (1996) 'Narrative as self-portrait: Sociolinguistic constructions of identity',
  Language in Society 25: 167–203.
Schulhofer, S. (1998) *Unwanted Sex: The Culture of Intimidation and the Failure of Law*,
  Cambridge, MA: Harvard University Press.
Schulz, M. (1975) 'The semantic derogation of woman', in B. Thorne and N. Henley
  (eds) *Language and Sex: Difference and Dominance*, pp. 64–75. Rowley, MA:
  Newbury House.
Smart, C. (1986) 'Feminism and the law: Some problems of analysis and strategy',
  International Journal of the Sociology of Law 14: 109–23.
—— (1989) *Feminism and the Power of Law*, London: Routledge.
Spender, D. (1980) *Man Made Language*, London: Routledge and Kegan Paul.
Steinem, G. (1983) *Outrageous Acts and Everyday Rebellions*, New York: Holt, Rinehart
  and Winston.
Sykes, M. (1988) 'From "rights" to "needs": Official discourse and the "welfariza-
  tion" of race', in G. Smitherman-Donaldson and T.A. van Dijk (eds) *Discourse
  and Discrimination*, pp. 176–205. Detroit, MI: Wayne State University Press.
Talmy, L. (1985) 'Lexicalization patterns: Semantic structure in lexical forms', in
  T. Shopen (ed.) *Language Typology and Syntactic Description: Grammatical Categories
  and the Lexicon*, pp. 57–149. Cambridge: Cambridge University Press.
Tannen, D. (1990) *You Just Don't Understand: Women and Men in Conversation*, New
  York: Morrow.
—— (1992) 'Response to Senta Troemel-Ploetz's "Selling the Apolitical"', *Discourse
  & Society* 3: 249–54.
—— (1993) 'What's in a frame? Surface evidence for underlying expectations', in
  D. Tannen (ed.) *Framing in Discourse*, New York: Oxford University Press.
Todd, A. (1989) *Intimate Adversaries: Cultural Conflicts between Doctors and Women
  Patients*, Philadelphia: University of Pennsylvania Press.
Toolan M. (1991) *Narrative: A Critical Linguistic Introduction*, London: Routledge.
Traugott, E. (1995) 'A speech act analysis of campus sexual harassment policies',
  Paper presented at Linguistic Society of America Symposium: Linguistic Perspec-
  tives on Sexual Harassment. Linguistic Society of America's Annual Meeting
  (January), New Orleans, Louisiana.

Trew, T. (1979) 'Theory and ideology at work', in R. Fowler, B. Hodge, G. Kress and T. Trew (eds) *Language and Control*, pp. 94–116. London: Routledge and Kegan Paul.

Troemel-Ploetz, S. (1991) 'Review essay: Selling the apolitical', *Discourse & Society* 2: 489–502.

Uchida, A. (1992) 'When "difference" is "dominance": A critique of the "anti-power-based" cultural approach to sex differences', *Language in Society* 21: 547–68.

van Dijk, T.A. (1988) 'How "they" hit the headlines: Ethnic minorities in the press', in G. Smitherman-Donaldson and T.A. van Dijk (eds) *Discourse and Discrimination*, pp. 221–62. Detroit, MI: Wayne State University Press.

—— (1993) 'Principles of critical discourse analysis', *Discourse & Society* 4: 489–502.

—— (1997) 'Discourse as interaction in society', in T. A. van Dijk (ed.) *Discourse as Social Interaction*, pp. 1–37. London: Sage.

Volosinov, V. N. (1973) *Marxism and the Philosophy of Language*, New York: Seminar Press.

Walker, A.G. (1987) 'Linguistic manipulation, power and the legal setting', in L. Kedar (ed.) *Power through Discourse*, pp. 57–80. Norwood, NJ: Ablex.

Weiner, B. (1979) 'A theory of motivation for some classroom experiences', *Journal of Educational Psychology* 71: 3–25.

West, C. and Zimmerman, D. (1987) 'Doing gender', *Gender and Society* 1: 25–51.

Wetherell, M. and Potter, J. (1988) 'Discourse analysis and the identification of interpretative repertoires', in C. Antaki (ed.) *Analysing Everyday Explanation: A Casebook of Methods*, pp. 168–83. London: Sage.

Whorf, B. L. (1956) *Language, Thought, and Reality: Selected Writings of Benjamin Lee Whorf*, J. B. Carroll (ed.), Cambridge, MA: Massachusetts Institute of Technology Press.

Wigmore, J. (1970) *Evidence in Trials at Common Law*, Boston: Little Brown and Company.

Wodak R. (1996) *Disorders of Discourse*, London: Longman.

—— (1997) 'Introduction: Some important issues in the research of gender and discourse', in R. Wodak (ed.) *Gender and Discourse*, pp. 1–20. London: Sage.

Woodbury, H. (1984) 'The strategic use of questions in court', *Semiotica* 48: 197–228.

Woolard, K. (1998) 'Introduction: Language ideology as a field of inquiry', in B. Schieffelin, K. Woolard and P. Kroskrity (eds) *Language Ideologies: Practice and Theory*, Oxford: Oxford University Press.

Woolard, K. and Schieffelin, B. (1994) 'Language ideology', *Annual Review of Anthropology* 23: 55–82.

Index